Slavoj Žiž

W9-DDQ-256

Modern European Thinkers
Series Editors: Anne Beech and David Castle

Over the past few decades, Anglo-American social science and humanities have experienced an unprecedented interrogation, revision and strengthening of their methodologies and theoretical underpinnings through the influence of highly innovative scholarship from continental Europe. In the fields of philosophy, post-structuralism, psychoanalysis, critical theory and beyond, the works of a succession of pioneering writers have had revolutionary effects on Anglo-American academia. However, much of this work is extremely challenging, and some is hard or impossible to obtain in English translation. This series provides clear and concise introductions to the ideas and work of key European thinkers.

As well as being comprehensive, accessible introductory texts, the titles in the 'Modern European Thinkers' series retain Pluto's characteristic radical political slant, and critically evaluate leading theorists in terms of their contribution to genuinely radical and progressive intellectual endeavour. And while the series does explore the leading lights, it also looks beyond the big names that have dominated theoretical debates to highlight the contribution of extremely important but less well-known figures.

Also available

Alain Badiou
Jason Barker

Georges Bataille
Benjamin Noys

Jean Baudrillard
Mike Gane

Walter Benjamin
Esther Leslie

Pierre Bourdieu
Jeremy F. Lane

Gilles Deleuze
John Marks

André Gorz
Conrad Lodziak and Jeremy Tatman

Guy Hocquenghem
Bill Marshall

Julia Kristeva
Anne-Marie Smith

SLAVOJ ŽIŽEK

A Critical Introduction

Ian Parker

Pluto Press

LONDON • STERLING, VIRGINIA

First published 2004 by
Pluto Press
345 Archway Road, London N6 5AA
and 22883 Quicksilver Drive, Sterling, VA 20166–2012, USA

www.plutobooks.com

British Library Cataloguing in Publication Data
A catalogue record for this book is available from the British Library

ISBN   0 7453 2072 4 hardback
ISBN   0 7453 2071 6 paperback

Library of Congress Cataloging in Publication Data
Parker, Ian, 1956-
    Slavoj Žižek : a critical introduction / Ian Parker.
        p. cm. — (Modern European thinkers)
Includes bibliographical references.
    ISBN 0–7453–2072–4 — ISBN 0–7453–2071–6 (pbk.)
    1. Žižek, Slavoj. I. Title. II. Series.

B4870.Z594P37 2004
199'.4973—dc22
                                            003022458

10   9   8   7   6   5   4   3   2   1

Designed and produced for Pluto Press by
Chase Publishing Services, Fortescue, Sidmouth, EX10 9QG, England
Typeset from disk by Stanford DTP Services, Northampton, England
Printed and bound in the European Union by
Antony Rowe Ltd, Chippenham and Eastbourne, England

To Adam

Contents

Acknowledgements

Thanks to those who read draft chapters, discussed the ideas, drew attention to additional material and saved me from some stupid mistakes, save the errors I still stubbornly cling to: Erica Burman, Daniela Caselli, David Castle, Leslie Chapman, Elliot Cohen, Alessia Contu, Paul Duckett, Christian Ingo Lenz Dunker, Babak Fozooni, Daniel Heggs, Sean Homer, Derek Hook, Matthew Jacobson, Nikolai Jeffs, Torun Kallings, Kenneth McLaughlin, Mihalis Mentinis, Ilana Mountian, Calum Neill, Ingrid Palmary, Agnes Pinteaux, Paula Reavey, Susanne Schade, Yannis Stavrakakis, John-Christopher Stirk, Jules Townshend, Christian Yavorsky, Alexandra Zavos and Slavoj Žižek.

Introduction
Something Retroactive
and Some Anticipation

Let us start with a typical Žižek joke, which is from the ex-German Democratic Republic:

> A German worker gets a job in Siberia. Aware of how all mail will be read by censors, he tells his friends 'Let's establish a code. If a letter you will get from me is written in ordinary blue ink it is true. If it is written in red ink it is false.' After a month his friends get the first letter from Siberia, written in blue ink, where they are able to read 'Everything is wonderful here in Siberia. Stores are full. Food is abundant. Apartments are large, properly heated. Movie theatres show Western movies. There are many beautiful girls ready for an affair. The only thing unavailable in stores is red ink.'

I've heard Žižek tell this joke to introduce papers several times in the last few years – this version is from a talk in London in June 2002 – and it is not surprising that this should be one of his favourite opening gambits. Why? There are at least six reasons. First, the joke is set in old supposedly-communist Eastern Europe, which is the setting for many of Žižek's anecdotes and which is also the grounding for how he understands the connection between cynicism and state power. There is a question here about how the games we play with the state fall so quickly into the games the state is playing with us. Second, the joke plays with themes from Hegel, a figure not well-known for his jokes, and works through some characteristic Hegelian dialectical reversals; two key points here being that you only get where you want to go through starting with a refusal, negativity, and that you can only speak the truth by reflexively including yourself in it. Third, it is a joke that Freud would have loved. For psychoanalysis, jokes are one of the ways that you can tell the truth, but safely wrapped up in something else, and able to deliver a charge of enjoyment at the end; and for Lacan, one of the greatest Freudian psychoanalysts, it shows us that you only get to the truth by being able to tell lies. Fourth, it draws attention to the nature of censorship in ideology that is in line with Žižek's use of Marxist theory: the guy in the joke is not at all deluded into a kind of 'false consciousness' about the delights of Stalinist fake-socialism; rather, he knows very well what he is doing but he does it anyway, and he still finds a way to resist. Fifth, this joke shows us something about the style of Žižek's writing. You think you are being told one thing, and then it changes into the opposite. Such sudden shifts from one frame to another often make the underlying structure of his argument difficult to grasp, so when you hear stories from Žižek you also need to notice how he tells them. Sixth, you need to know now that almost all of Žižek's work is written in red ink: his selective reading of Hegel is only one take on this very complex contradictory philosophical system; he picks up notions from Lacan and wilfully applies them just as he likes; and although he uses ideas from Marx he is not a Marxist at all.

This book covers what you need to know to read Žižek. The book does not repeat what he says about this or that topic, and it does not tell you exactly what his position is. This is because his interventions around different issues are inconsistent and his theoretical position is contradictory. What I can do is show you the field of conceptual and political reference points that organise his writing. Then you can at least know where he is coming from and understand better the terrain of debate he is moving around.

Žižek is a scholar and activist. He was born in Ljubljana in 1949, studied philosophy there and became one of the leading figures in the movement for the independence of Slovenia. His grounding in German philosophy was fuelled by an encounter with French psychoanalysis and ignited by political struggles in the 1980s as Yugoslavia disintegrated. This gives his writing on theories of ideology and subjectivity an urgent cutting-edge character that throws received wisdoms into question and opens up a space to think and act against contemporary capitalism. I have to tell you now that this book is not as enjoyable or funny as Žižek's writing, but perhaps after reading this you will not so easily be sidetracked or swept along by his anecdotes and jokes. And then, when you know what he is doing, you will be in a better position to make your own assessment of his arguments. Instead of being bewitched by him you can notice better how he puts together his performance for us.

Žižek burst onto the world academic stage with commentaries and interventions in politics and psychoanalysis, with powerful examples of the way an understanding of those two domains could be dialectically intertwined and powered through a close reading of German philosophy. Žižek's academic performance has also drawn attention from a wider intellectual audience, and this has given him the opportunity to elaborate some complex conceptual machinery that can be applied to music, theology, virtual reality, and, it would seem, virtually any other cultural phenomenon. His writing appeared at an opportune moment, offering a new vocabulary for thinking through how ideology grips its subjects.

ŽIŽEK'S SUBLIME OBJECTS

His first major work for an English-speaking audience was *The Sublime Object of Ideology*, published in 1989 in a book series edited by Ernesto Laclau and Chantal Mouffe. This was one of the first important reasons why people turned to Žižek, for his experience of theoretical and practical struggle in Slovenia was elaborated into richly-textured analyses of popular culture with a sharp political edge. It is clear from Laclau's preface to the book that he hoped Žižek would be recruited, if only temporarily, to a political project of post-Marxist 'radical democracy' which would solve the crisis of left politics by blending aspects of post-structuralism with pragmatism. 'Post-structuralism' is a portmanteau term, promising to go beyond the mere selection and combination of ideas from an assortment of French writers, many of whom Žižek actually takes to task. The pragmatism in the radical democratic project owes more to a typically US-style optimistic engagement with changing the world in a way that leaves any traces of history well behind than with classical Marxism, and Žižek has since distanced himself from this project. The alliance with Laclau and Mouffe, prominent figures in the turn to discourse in British politics, was eventually to come to grief, but it did launch Žižek as a key theoretical player in these debates.

Many readers then found themselves bewitched and fascinated by something inside his first book – something like the 'sublime object' itself – that they could not grasp. But they also knew it might hold the key to how subjects are held in thrall by ideology at the very same moment that they imagine that they have escaped it. *For They Know Not What They Do: Enjoyment as a Political Factor* appeared in the same series two years later (in 1991), and by this time the attraction to Žižek was already operating fairly efficiently as a political factor in the enjoyment of a growing readership of leftist cultural theorists. This second book (he then claimed) is the text of lectures serving as an introductory course on Lacan to the Slovene Society for Theoretical Psychoanalysis (in 1989–90), rooted in the political process accompanying the break-up of Yugoslavia and leading up to the first 'free' elections in Slovenia. It takes as its task the tracing of a journey from Hegel to an analysis of the transition from Tito–Stalinist rule to nationalist-populism. Alongside the political analyses in Žižek's work, then, there was another powerful reason for reading Žižek: he

provided a way of explaining how concepts from Lacanian psychoanalysis could be put to work in reading popular culture.

Much more, of course, is entailed by Žižek's analyses, which take as
examples jokes, novels and films, and the popular audience for his writing
was shortly thereafter secured with three introductions to Lacan through
readings of Hitchcock and other Hollywood productions. These three
books – *Looking Awry*, *Enjoy Your Symptom* and the edited *Everything You
Always Wanted to Know about Lacan (But Were Afraid to Ask Hitchcock)*
– appeared in quick succession, and have drawn in a readership peering into
the books a little confused, enjoying what they read, but still rather afraid
to ask what it is all about, and what Žižek is about.

The energy and enthusiasm with which he writes has itself become an
object of intense attention and discussion among admirers and detractors.
The erratic quality of his speech in interviews, seminars and conference pre-
sentations is also present to the reader in the rapid shift from theme to theme
in articles and in the pace of production of his books. The stories that
circulate about his stab at psychoanalysis with Jacques Alain-Miller for a
year without saying anything that would give him away, and his refusal to
do any administrative work connected with academic appointments are
indicative at least of what many people imagine they are reading when they
get drawn into Žižek's work. There was, we might say, a 'symptomatic'
image of Žižek, for example, in 2001 during an appearance on a BBC Radio
4 talk programme, when he was asked, by way of a link from the previous
item, whether he would visit a particular gallery exhibition. He immediately
replied that 'no' he would not, because he never goes to art exhibitions, but
that 'yes' he would in this case go because it sounded interesting, yes he
would certainly go.

Every now and again Žižek stops, reflects and attempts to tie his work
back to certain enduring theoretical resources. In *Tarrying with the
Negative*, published back in 1993, for example, there is a most convincing
elaboration of a distinctive theoretical position in a reading of Lacan
through Hegel. In *The Ticklish Subject* (in 1999) there is a review of where
he stands in relation to competing intellectual positions, including those of
Martin Heidegger, Alain Badiou and Judith Butler. And then there are
encounters in which he seems to spin out of control – in the debate with
Butler and Laclau in *Contingency, Hegemony, Universality*, for example (in
2000) – where there is something of an anticipation of his injunction to
'repeat Lenin', an injunction that very soon after looks a little too much like
the admiration of Stalin to be detected in *Did Somebody Say
Totalitarianism?* (also published in 2000). The political coordinates of his
writing are significant, and it is necessary to understand these coordinates
in order to make sense of how Marx, Hegel and Lacan are deployed by him

in his commentaries on events like the NATO bombing of Serbia or the 9/11 World Trade Center attacks.

Žižek is, it would seem so far, a Slovenian Lacanian Hegelian. How one shuffles those three descriptive terms, and how one places the final one as the theoretical anchor or final destination, is not so easy to determine though, and that final term changes depending on who he is writing for. And it depends who he is speaking for and speaking against, for there is a political urgency in his work which gives a representative function – this must be said on behalf of this or that constituency – and a stubbornly contrary aspect to his argument, which means that a theoretical position is first defined negatively, by what it is against: definitely 'no', but then of course 'yes'. To begin with a refusal serves to define the production of identity in the case of each of these three terms – 'Slovenian', 'Lacanian', 'Hegelian' – and that includes a refusal to make it subordinate to the other two.

For Žižek, the philosophical articulation of this route to truth through error is to be found first in Hegel, who defines his own position through sustained combat with Kant. Psychoanalysis is forged as a touchstone for testing the truth of the subject by way of Lacan's 'return' to Freud, which must first clear away the errors of the dominant Anglo-American clinical training organisations. And Slovene national identity also figures, as something that has emerged from the debris of the Yugoslav state in a struggle for recognition and self-definition that tangles it in broader imperialist projects. Žižek's trajectory from researcher in Ljubljana to cultural ambassador, spokesperson for a variety of political and theoretical constituencies, and visiting academic in many other countries, could just as easily be read as that of a Hegelian Lacanian Slovenian.

MAPPING THIS BOOK

The only way to grasp Žižek's peculiar combination of theoretical resources and political projects is to understand something of where he is coming from. The first chapter of this book, then, examines the political formation and disintegration of the Yugoslav state, and Žižek's place in that process. This is the setting for his ravelling and unravelling of theoretical motifs from Hegel, Lacan and Marx. And the texts we read now were woven first in the particular political context in Slovenia and France where he gathered and rehearsed his guiding philosophical, psychoanalytic and political lines of critique.

The chapter on Yugoslavia tackles two broad issues in order to arrive at a point where we can map Žižek. The first concerns the particular confluence of conceptual resources that together define the 'Slovene

Lacanian School'. There has been a wide array of interesting work across the social sciences, from criminology and law to ethics and film theory, accumulating in Ljubljana. Žižek has clearly tried to make this, as well his own, work accessible to a wider academic audience in other countries. Here, the theoretical stakes are far more than how to read Lacan, and we also need some assessment of the local uptake of other competing traditions in psychoanalysis and philosophy.

The second issue is how to capture the specific conjuncture that makes the work of the group around Žižek in Ljubljana readable, to those at home and abroad. My reading of the political-economic conjuncture which gave birth to Žižek has had to include a fairly close description of the historical formation of the Yugoslav state, and the contradictory demands experienced by its subjects as they lived out the dialectical tensions of a supposedly 'socialist' society. Here the place of Marx and Marxism is situated in relation to a state apparatus that employed Marxist rhetoric precisely in order to keep its workers and intellectuals in check.

I trace the distinctive character of Yugoslavia and the forms of ideological control the state used to deal with dissent, and then the functions that cultural and philosophical practices took in the political movement leading up to the secession of Slovenia. We can then identify better the role of Hegel, Lacan and Marx in this context, and the appeal of the peculiarly exotic Slovenian mixture of these three figures, exotic for an audience gazing in from the outside. It is no accident, perhaps, that it is exactly at the point that Yugoslavia broke up and Slovenia made its bid for free-market 'freedom' that this Hegelian Lacanian combination became such an object of fascination for post-Marxists elsewhere; Žižek's own scathing comments on how the West looked to the events in Eastern Europe so that it might there discover and enjoy 'the re-invention of democracy' implicates the process by which Žižek too has reinvented himself for the West. The forms of that re-invention and the different guises he adopts for different audiences need to be disentangled if we are not also to be trapped in the line of an admiring or dismissive gaze on his work.

We then turn to focus on Hegel, Lacan and Marx, locating them in relation to Žižek's various projects and exploring the dialectical interrelationships between them. The next chapter, on enlightenment, shows why Hegel's work is so important to Žižek, and what he does with it. I trace the argument presented in Žižek's philosophical manifesto *Tarrying with the Negative* (first published in 1993), through to his defence of Christianity in *On Belief* (from 2001). These two works anchor an account of Hegel and provide the ground for exploring certain key concepts that appear repeatedly in Žižek's writing. They also serve as the setting for examining some assumptions in Hegel's work that Žižek is happy to run with but which we should perhaps be a little more wary about.

Hegel is the founding figure for much recent French philosophy, and his work lies not only in the background of contemporary discussions of phenomenology and hermeneutics, but it is also often an implicit reference point even for arguments from within 'post-structuralism' that pretend to have nothing to do with Hegel. Žižek's retrieval of Hegel is valuable because it shows why certain theoretical notions in his writing – Truth arising through error, the production of 'substance as subject', universality in the particular – are crucial to philosophy (and then to psychoanalysis and politics). We will look at those connections between Hegel and other domains of work toward the end of the chapter.

Žižek proceeds, in true Hegelian fashion, by specifying Hegel against what he is not. This means that we also need to locate them both in relation to other philosophical traditions, the most important for our purposes here being Kant. Hegel then needs to be treated, as Žižek suggests, as a space to think, as shifting and opening up new ideas. This is more in keeping with what Hegel was trying to do than if he had been describing a positive, fully-formed system that might then pretend to solve all the problems of philosophy. Negativity is at the heart of Hegel, and it is Žižek's task to keep that negativity at work while reading him. The points at which motifs of negativity turn into formulaic injunctions in his work then need to be analysed so that the limitations of Žižek's version of Hegel can be understood.

The discussion of psychoanalysis in the following chapter focuses on two key texts to illustrate how Žižek uses ideas from psychoanalysis to read popular culture, and the way he buys into certain psychoanalytic notions about representation and the subject. The first is *Looking Awry*, which appeared in 1991. This book not only employs notions of fantasy, trauma and unconscious desire to interpret science fiction and detective novels, but it also makes of these cultural phenomena sites to illustrate key concepts in Lacanian psychoanalysis. That is the way I use Žižek's text here.

The second text is the summary and position statement in *The Metastases of Enjoyment* published in 1994, where Žižek deals, among other things, with femininity and feminist responses to psychoanalysis. That book is the setting for a review of ideas from the rival Frankfurt School tradition of psychoanalytic social theory that have been so appealing and problematic for many radicals, and it tackles the worries of those sympathetic to Lacan as a progressive alternative, and ostensibly more politically sensitive 'return', to Freud.

However, Žižek does more than this, for his description of Lacanian concepts is also an opportunity to explicate further how useful Hegel is. As we explore Lacan, then, we will also be drawing on the material in the previous chapter to explore the way Lacan is indebted to Hegel, and then to question Žižek about this. Lacanian psychoanalysis, for Žižek, is not only a reading of popular culture; it is also a way of intervening in political debate, as we will see in his discussion of the nation as 'thing' in *Looking Awry* and of 'sexuation' in *The Metastases of Enjoyment*. The way Žižek repeats standard psychoanalytic attempts to comment upon political phenomena, and the way he attempts to invent some connections of his own between psychoanalysis and culture need to be traced out and assessed.

This brings us to the chapter on politics, which turns to Žižek's relationship to Marxism, and what he says about it. After the close examination of Žižek's take on philosophy and psychoanalysis, we will be in a better position to appreciate his use of Hegelian and Lacanian ideas as political critique. His ground-breaking 1989 book *The Sublime Object of Ideology* lays out a political trajectory that is repeated and elaborated in more recent texts. It is worth spending a little time to pick apart the way his reading of Marx can give rise to a distinctive and innovative account of ideology, but also how his reading of Marx strikes some crucial political distance from Marxist politics.

I look at the place of the sublime object in the context of 'post-Marxist' political theory, as well as in Žižek's own work. This is the book that made Žižek so attractive to Marxists looking for a way out of the deadlock and failure of Western Marxism, but it is actually already quite critical of Marxism. Žižek's later writing then seems to move closer to Marxism but in such a way as to cause great anxiety among many Marxist readers. We shall take the 'Afterword: Lenin's Choice' from *Revolution at the Gates* as our second main reference point in this chapter in order to examine this paradoxical shift in Žižek's work.

Žižek's political interventions with respect to the legacy of Lenin and Stalin and what can be learnt from them, and around Kosovo and the attacks on the World Trade Center, raise questions not only about the nature of democracy and 'terror' in his work but also about what exactly is being 'repeated' when he writes about Marx. The oscillation between different political positions in his work needs to be highlighted if any accurate critical assessment of these interventions is to be made.

There is much in Žižek's work that escapes reduction to a simple mixture of Hegel, Lacan and Marx and so I look in the concluding chapter at how the different theoretical threads of work are knotted together by him. Here I also examine the existing critical responses to Žižek. If there is one good critical way into Žižek, it is actually through the claim to fidelity that he makes about each of these traditions. This is why I review briefly some main lines of argument against Žižek, within and outwith these traditions, that have appeared recently. The chapter uses the fault-lines in his readings of Hegel, Lacan and Marx that have been identified in the preceding chapters to trace some consequences for his work and its reception by academics and activists. This review cues you into the field of debate around Žižek. But then we go further. The final chapter combines what we are now able to notice, now retroactively, in his writings over the last 15 years and focuses on his writings on culture – in *Everything You Always Wanted to Know about Lacan (But Were Afraid to Ask Hitchcock)* (1992) and *The Plague of Fantasies* (1997), for example – to get a fix on how the puzzling inconsistencies in his writing are organised. What we need to be able to grasp is the specific asymmetric relationship in his writing between philosophy, psychoanalysis and politics. Then we might at least be able to get a fix on why it seems so difficult to sum up who he is and where he is going.

This book, as will have been patently obvious already by this point, lays out but one way of reading Žižek. I use slightly different theoretical coordinates within Lacanian psychoanalysis, Hegelian theory and Marxism to those he draws on. This is necessary to get a critical perspective on what he is producing. There are many problems with Hegel, even when wrapped so beautifully; the Lacanian orthodoxy carries with it at least as many problems as Freud; and Žižek's version of Marxism is not one that would be accepted by many Marxists. Marxism is the theory and practice of collective resistance to contemporary capitalism, and connections with psychoanalysis and academic philosophy have often had the effect of muddling and weakening Marxist politics. So, why should Žižek's attempt to make connections make any difference? My position in this book is that a revolutionary Marxist analysis of the corruption of socialism by the bureaucracies of Eastern Europe can now help us make sense of the disappointment and turn to the right by many ex-Leftists. Lacanian psychoanalysis is, I believe, a revolutionary way of questioning how individual subjectivity is formed, and it offers one place for speaking the truth. A Hegelian dialectical interweaving of critiques of state oppression and individual misery provides conceptual tools for making links between Marx and Lacan without reducing one to the other, or either to Hegel himself. Žižek shows us a powerful way of combining these disparate theoretical resources. It is the wrong way, but in the process he forces us to think through what might need to be done with them to get it right.

SOME INDIVISIBLE REMINDERS

You cannot be a 'Žižekian', and only Žižek can be Žižek. The concepts he works with are borrowed and distorted before they are applied and transmuted into something else, and something slightly different happens to them each time they appear. This is why there are no specific 'Žižekian' concepts that could be outlined in a glossary guide to his work. Instead, you might think of this book as being the equivalent of a subway map which connects relevant key concepts from the theorists he discusses. You will find your way around this map, but you need to bear in mind that it has no necessary correspondence with the world outside. And to find your way around this map you will need to read the chapters in order so that you are able to get a grip on what connections are possible between Žižek's own theoretical reference points.

You could say that an introductory book of this kind plugs a much-needed gap in Žižek's work. This would indeed be a problem if gaps in theoretical or ideological systems could really ever be closed over, and it seems to be the fundamental fantasy of many theorists treading the same ground as Žižek that the gap could actually be closed, and that such closure would then herald totalitarian catastrophe or mass psychosis. But this attempt to tackle Žižek is not, in any case, the final word, and he moves so fast that it can be at best a temporally-limited, partial view – subversive, contingent, awry. So, be wary.

1
Yugoslavia – To Slovenia

This chapter is about the formation, operation and decomposition of the Yugoslav state, and it is also of course about the role of the West in the reinvention of capitalism in Eastern Europe. How we make sense of this, and how we position ourselves to applaud or bemoan the rise and fall of Tito, self-management socialism, nationalist resistance and the new free-market moral majorities, will influence how we read Žižek and his attempt to make sense of the process. The chapter provides an understanding of how the amazing combinations of ideas in his writing were made possible, and so we trace the conditions of possibility for the particular combination of theoretical resources in Žižek's work. However, the theoretical resources he uses from psychoanalysis and philosophy are resources that are always distorted in some way in different geographical and historical settings. The contradictory, mutating political conditions in Yugoslavia we are about to review are not, then, merely the 'context' for how Hegel, Lacan and Marx were read and applied separately by Žižek, as if he read them incorrectly and as if we can now put them together correctly.

Theoretical resources are always already distorted, and something of them always fails to represent or capture adequately the world they take root in. The question is not merely how some ideas come to be possible in certain social conditions as if we were then explaining them away,[1] but how to develop an analysis of how certain sets of concepts are put to work to grasp conditions that have reached points of impossibility, breaking points. This is why it would be more accurate to say that we are really outlining the *conditions of impossibility* for how the theories were put together by Žižek.[2] The history of Yugoslavia is precisely a history of deadlocks and breaking points, relations of impossibility. And the sets of concepts that emerge should not then serve to solve or smooth over what they attempted to grasp; instead, they too show something of that impossibility. That is why these particular theoretical resources – Hegelian, Lacanian, Marxist – that attend to negativity, lack and dialectical fracture, are so important. We could say that the conceptual architecture of the different systems he uses was first built crookedly on the economic-political terrain of the Balkans, before being rebuilt, just as unsteadily perhaps, for an academic audience outside.

Žižek, after being refused a lecturing post upon completion of his first two degrees in the University of Ljubljana, and then working as a researcher and visitor at different places around the world, at last has a position as Professor in the Department of Philosophy. Now it would be tempting to slide too quickly over what it meant for him to have been 'politically active in the alternative movement in Slovenia during the 80s' and to have stood as 'candidate for the presidency of the republic of Slovenia in the first multi-party elections in 1990' (as his little biography on the departmental website puts it).[3] The years of intellectual and political compromise and challenge in and against Yugoslavia were part of a dialectical process of the making and unmaking of Stalinism. So what we need to grasp, then, are what the conditions of impossibility of Yugoslavia were that made it possible for the Republic of Slovenia to appear, and so what the conceptual conditions were for Žižek to appear as he did both here and there.

How Žižek appears here and there is precisely the issue, for conditions of impossibility also mark the relationship between what we think we see when he appears to us and what has actually been going on in Eastern Europe. This chapter traces the theoretical resources that organised philosophical and political work in Yugoslavia and the way these were lived and reworked in Slovenia. If we want to understand what Žižek is up to we need a good historical account, not to sum him up or explain him away but to cut our way through the circuits of lies that have structured how Yugoslavia has often appeared to the West. Then something different that includes Žižek can appear to us, something we can mark our own theoretical positions against.

THE PERFECTION OF THE STATE

How can we begin to make sense of these conditions? Maybe like this: Tito steered the Yugoslav revolution towards a more open, democratic form of self-management socialism, during which it was necessary to break with Stalinist bureaucratic traditions and adopt a third-way non-aligned position between capitalism and communism. The problem is that this characterisation is wrong in almost every respect, but different versions of this representation of the Yugoslav state for its own populations, and such images of Yugoslavia for the West, have served to spin a mythology that was potent enough to stifle opposition for many years, and to discredit Marxism fairly efficiently along the way.[4]

Actually, the respect in which this characterisation is right lies not in any of the particular elements of the description but in the space that the mythology opened up. This paradox, a space in which dissident academics were able to take the bureaucracy at its word and enact the very freedoms it claimed to endorse, struck at the heart of one of the impossible points where the hypocrisy of the regime could then be made to implode. In Slovenia, the northernmost republic in the Yugoslav Federation, Žižek was one of those who noticed that the regime required its population to take a cynical distance from the claims it made about democracy in order for it to function. This requirement meant that an enthusiastic embrace of democratic claims – in practices of 'overidentification' – might be able to open up and detonate the ideological apparatus from the inside. We will look at strategies of resistance like this in more detail later, but for the moment we need to dismantle the different aspects of the structurally-necessary symbolic deception that enabled the bureaucracy to seize and hold power until it started to disintegrate in the 1980s.

What the Yugoslav resistance was already locked into

The personality cult constructed around the figure of Josip Broz Tito, a Croatian locksmith drawn to Marxism and then swiftly into the Comintern – the Communist Third International – during his time in Moscow, itself testifies to the Stalinist cast of the Tito regime in Yugoslavia. Tito worked as a Comintern agent with responsibility for the Balkans, and became secretary of the Communist Party in Yugoslavia in 1937. Tito was even groomed at one point to be the leader of the Comintern to succeed Stalin, and it is worth recalling that there was a good deal of grotesque adoration of this single individual from before the break with Stalin in 1948 through to his death in 1980. The bizarre doubling of the image of the leader – modelled on Stalin yet with the pretence that he was in some sense the more progressive reverse image – already introduces into the symbolic texture of Yugoslav politics a particular kind of duplicity.

Up to the point of the expulsion of the Yugoslav Party from the Cominform, Tito was quite explicitly a good Stalinist. The Cominform, or 'Communist Information Bureau', was set up in 1947 as replacement and successor to the Comintern, which had been dissolved in 1943. That dissolution was partly as a goodwill gesture to the capitalist world, and a message to the West that the Soviet Union was willing to embark on a period of 'peaceful coexistence' during which it could get on with the task of building 'socialism in one country', and thus demanding that the local communist parties subordinate their activities to the needs and diplomatic manoeuvres of the Soviet bureaucracy. For Tito, what being a good Stalinist meant until 1948 was to respect the compromises made with the imperialist powers, including agreement between Stalin and Churchill as to how

Europe would be apportioned between the Western and the Soviet spheres of influence.[5]

Yugoslavia would then be neutralised as a threat to both sides, and function as part of the buffer zone. The Communist Party in Italy, which was clearly assigned to the West, and bordering on Slovenia as a component of the new Federative People's Republic of Yugoslavia, dutifully handed over its arms to its government. In Greece, which was also assigned to the West, bordering on Tito's southernmost republic (now Macedonia), a bitter civil war broke out between the Western-backed government and partisans. The Stalinists were then torn between instructions from Moscow to stifle revolutionary activity and communists on the ground who refused to hand over their weapons, particularly in the north of the country (Greek Macedonia).

The West had already assumed that Yugoslavia would adhere to the diplomatic agreements made between Moscow and London in 1944, which was when the Allies and the Yugoslav government in exile stopped their military aid to the Chetniks – the Serb 'Royal Army in the Homeland' dedicated to the elimination or expulsion of traitors and implicated in massacres of Croats and Muslims, as well as Gypsies and Jews.[6] Support from London then went to Tito's Partisans in the Anti-Fascist Council for the National Liberation of Yugoslavia, with collaboration continuing well after the war was over, to the extent that captured Chetnik and Croatian fascist Ustashe[7] would be handed over to Tito to be executed. What we need to keep focused on here is the way that despite Tito's refusal to close down the 'proletarian brigades' in the Partisan forces, there was no intention of breaking from the Stalinist conception of historical stages of development, in which there was the notion that proletarian revolution should be delayed until there had been a sustained period of bourgeois rule.[8]

This is not to say that there was no conflict between Tito's partisans and Stalin as early as 1941, when the Soviet Union was still negotiating directly with the Royal Yugoslav Government in exile. Every local Stalinist apparatchik at that time had to manage the extremely difficult task of balancing orders from Stalin with what was actually possible, what activists on the ground would accept.[9] The Tito–Subasich Agreement for a coalition regime that would keep Yugoslavia on track for its capitalist stage of development at the end of the war would conform to the cynical conceptual distortions of Marxism emanating from Moscow, but this meant that any mention of 'socialism' by the partisans, and then by the new government, had to be carefully guarded. The eventual re-designation of the Socialist Federal Republic of Yugoslavia in 1963 was then designed to mark symbolically the 'socialist' character of the regime as, we might say, drawing on a favourite phrase from Žižek, 'precisely the reverse' of what it actually was. There had been no revolutionary overthrow of capitalist property relations, rather a neutralising of the 'proletarian brigades' and stabilising of the economy, initially as capitalist and then as a bureaucratically-regulated market system.

What we are unravelling here, then, are the conditions of impossibility in which things are in many key respects precisely the reverse of what they seem to be. Because there had been no socialist revolution, there was no process of degeneration from the conditions of thriving democracy that flourished all too briefly during the October 1917 revolution in Russia.[10] Instead, the state that was instituted in Yugoslavia first stabilised capitalism and then assimilated it to the needs of the bureaucracy. As was the case with other countries in Eastern Europe (those that had less space for market mechanisms to operate) this process of 'structural assimilation'[11] of Yugoslavia to the mould of the Stalinist command economies meant that it occupied some kind of temporal space between capitalism and socialism, as a state that was a parody of both.

Staging the myth of the Yugoslav state

One of the structurally-necessary founding myths of the Yugoslav state, part of the symbolic apparatus of Stalinist rule after the break with Stalin in 1948, was that Tito had led a revolutionary movement that defied Moscow by carrying through a socialist transformation of society. The Tito–Stalin split actually arose over trade and military relations between Yugoslavia and the USSR at a time when Stalin was attempting to consolidate his grip over the buffer zone between his sphere of influence and the West. In Yugoslavia the seizure of power by the Communist Party already made its status as a fully-fledged capitalist power untenable. It is instructive to note that while Greece had by this time been engulfed in civil war, with Stalin's agents attempting to stifle all-out opposition to capitalist rule, there was a significant exception to the rule of different spheres of influence on the borders of both Greece and Yugoslavia. This significant exception was Albania. Stalin wanted Albania absorbed into Yugoslavia after the war, but the Tito–Stalin split saw Enver Hoxha's incredibly repressive Tirana-based regime ally with Stalin. It was only when there was some rapprochement between the USSR and Yugoslavia in the early 1960s that Hoxha constructed a new destiny for himself as the only Leninist in the region, and sided with China during the Sino–Soviet split.[12]

The material, economic-political status of Albania in relation to Yugoslavia can easily be re-described in terms of Serbia's fantasmatic points of traumatic origin in Kosovo, and we will consider these later. These are issues that have been fairly crucial to Žižek's account of what drove Serbia under Slobodan Milošević. What it is important to emphasise for the time being is that 'Albania' already figures here as some kind of sticking point – even as a symptom we might say – of the historical foundation of the Yugoslav state. A symptom is a point of symbolic condensation of conflict that causes anguish but which has a function, and so it is difficult, perhaps impossible without the disintegration of the identity founded upon it, to give up. What is being symbolically condensed in 'Albania' and 'Kosovo' for the Serbs in Yugoslavia is crucial, but already we can see how these places were functioning for the Yugoslav state, ostensibly integrated but operating as points of conflict. The partisans took power in Albania without any military support from the Red Army, but no one would try to pretend that Hoxha's was not a quintessentially Stalinist regime.[13] Tito's regime, which was formed with the help of the Red Army, then had to spin much rhetoric and spill some blood to persuade its supporters that it had really distanced itself from Stalinism.

It is easy to confuse the nationalisation of enterprises as part of the reconstruction of the economy in Yugoslavia after the Second World War with socialism, but we need to keep in mind the early attempts by Tito to remain faithful to a Stalinist stage conception of history, in which the primary task of the regime was the stabilisation of capitalism, if we are to understand how 'self-management' of the economy was to flourish later on. The stabilisation of capitalism turned out to be but a precursor to the instal-lation of the bureaucracy as the only way that Tito could maintain power after the break with Stalin. This 'workers' state' was forced to carry out the task of subjugating capitalism as the overtly dominant mode of production, but only so it could also keep control of the workers or any dangerous aspirations to socialist democracy. The main theoretician of 'self-management', the Slovenian Edvard Kardelj, had been one of Tito's comrades during the partisan struggle, and his history with Tito as an economic policy advisor was to prove useful. He had a good track record in political spin, making the management of dissent and the steering of a pragmatic political course appear to be in line with anti-capitalist struggle.

To advertise the success of the Yugoslav model as 'democracy and socialism', as Kardelj later did,[14] requires some breathtaking facility with signifiers. On the one hand, of course, the absence of democracy and the presence of a corrupt and secretive police apparatus[15] meant that signifiers like 'democracy' could be juggled around by the regime without much opposition – with the exception, as we have already noted, that the opponents of the regime might take the rhetoric of democracy too seriously and actually hold the regime to its word. One thing the opposition, in Belgrade and Zagreb as well as Ljubljana, was able to notice from the 1960s was that words are dangerous things, dangerous to the regime. On the other hand, the presence of 'socialism' in this description of 'self-management' was predicated on the denationalisation of economic enterprises.[16] That is, the use of the signifier 'socialism' rested on practices that required the absence of anything actually approaching socialism. The signifier was thus evacuated of the content that Western leftists usually summon up when they appeal to socialism. Self-management, as we shall see, was to have some fairly disastrous effects, with incitement to competition between enterprises accelerating into a wider centrifugal force that central state repression was eventually unable to contain.

The break from Moscow did give the Tito regime some measure of free play in its handling of internal dissent, and this included a little less pressure from the West over the policing of political opposition in return for a little more obedience to the West over its own policing of spheres of influence in other parts of the world. Yugoslavia was admitted to the UN Security Council, and in 1950 backed imperialist intervention in Korea. What we should notice here is that Yugoslavia's status as a 'non-aligned' country meant that it could play itself against the Soviet Union and the West, with the proviso that it kept its own populations in check so as not to disturb that delicate balancing act. The sixth party congress in 1952 changed the name of the Communist Party to the 'League of Communists of Yugoslavia', and there was some open discussion at the seventh congress in 1958 as to whether it would be possible to introduce a multi-party system in the federation. The answer was no, multi-party democracy would not be appropriate, and it was this congress that opted formally for 'self-management' as an economic-political system.

Yugoslavia operating in this buffer zone between the USSR and the West perfectly displays the characteristics of 'civilisation' described by Freud in *Civilization and Its Discontents*. Civilisation is able to manage an individual's desire for aggression by 'weakening and disarming it and by setting up an agency within him to watch over it, like a garrison in a conquered city'.[17] One of the problems is that outsiders need to be constantly reassured that diplomatic relations with them will be maintained, and so any internal dissent, perceived as aggression, must be strictly contained. And this kind of state apparatus, which monitors its own population for fear that hostile messages and impulses might be sent into the outside world, requires a strict separation between the observing apparatus and its inhabitants. At the very least, it means that any 'self-management' can only operate as a form of self-discipline, where the agency of the super-ego (which is what Freud is talking about here) is relayed into the interior of each particular subject so that they will each take responsibility for managing themselves.

This then is exactly the setting for the management of disciplined, self-regulating individuals described by Michel Foucault.[18] Perhaps it is not surprising that Foucault would be one of the theoretical reference points for the opposition movement in Yugoslavia in the 1980s, in Slovenia at least. Foucault's account of discipline and confession would, however, need to speak to the particularity of conditions at this edge of Europe. What is for sure is that this process of formation of the Yugoslav state is far from any dismantling of the state machine proposed by Marx in the course of proletarian revolution. Tito was able to dismantle the 'proletarian brigades', and so to accomplish, instead of the overthrow of capitalism, the taking over and *perfection of the state*.[19]

In and against the state

The conceptual reference points picked up and elaborated by Žižek during the 1980s were already embedded in the fabric of the ideological apparatus of the Yugoslav regime. And Žižek himself was at times embedded in this apparatus. After completing his first degree in philosophy and sociology at the University of Ljubljana in 1971 he completed his MA thesis on 'The theoretical and practical relevance of French structuralism' in 1975, only to find that he was deemed ideologically unsuitable for a lecturing appointment by the authorities. He was supported for a while by his parents, who were apparently hard-line communists.[20] He made some money translating philosophy from German, until he found some more secure work in 1977, a job with the Central Committee of the Slovenian League of Communists which included writing speeches for the bureaucracy. This work, which included taking minutes for committee meetings and assisting with the odd speech, producing the very forms of symbolic apparatus that he was then to critique, not only gave him some inside working knowledge of the party apparatus at the level of the republic, but he was also able to obtain financial support for attendance at academic conferences abroad.[21]

This history of Yugoslavia is not designed simply to explain in some way why Žižek writes what he writes, as if we could drain it of its broader relevance. Rather, this reading of how the symbolic space that was Yugoslavia was fabricated around certain kinds of lies and points of impossibility is a reading that also includes those from the West who gaze in at what is happening now in the new republics. The West had a key stake in the alienation of Tito from Stalin, and it was then to have a fairly important role in the separation of Slovenia from the Federation. We need to keep our eye on that process if we are not to fall into one of the simplest and most seductive explanations of the break-up of Yugoslavia, which is that deep ethnic rivalries always lay under the surface ready to explode into life when the socialist system broke apart. The image of the break-up of Yugoslavia as driven by atavistic rivalries also keys into one of the most powerful ideological explanations for conflict under capitalism. The films of Emir Kusturica set in the warring communities of Bosnia-Herzegovina, such as *Underground*, function ideologically in exactly this way,[22] and the hopeless plaint that all sides are to blame made by some radicals in the West is just as problematic. The question that would take Freud's account of the garrison in the conquered city further, and bring it into contact with later psychoanalytic theory – specifically Lacan's – would be how the very aggression that the observing agency fears is brought to life in the first place.

The protection of the nation in these circumstances always also requires the intensification of control and violence directed against women as signifiers of the nation – through motherhood and the reproduction of future generations.[23] The semi-autonomous women's organisations of the partisan struggle that evolved into the Union of Women's Associations were abolished in 1961, and 'The Conference for the Social Activities of Women' was set up by the Party. Abortion, which had been made freely available after 1974 but used as a form of contraception, came under attack towards the end of the 1980s. By the early 1990s the independent women's networks ceased functioning across the different republics. Military violence was reflected and reproduced by increasing violence against women, and anti-war groups in Belgrade like 'Women in Black' were often physically attacked.[24]

Antagonism between communities was thus intimately interwoven with antagonism between men and women, a phenomenon that Lacanian theory was to describe in terms of the deadlocks of 'sexuation'.[25] The role of 'sexuation' and feminist responses to the violence provoked and unleashed by the state pose problems for Marxists making sense of the break-up of Yugoslavia, and for those using Žižek's work. How is the libidinal economy of the state constituted such that there is an impossible relationship between its component parts, which then becomes filled with malevolent fantasies of rivalry and revenge? To answer that question we need to narrow our focus now from the formation of Yugoslavia to the particular problem of Serbia.

BROTHERHOOD AND UNITY

There was a further serious complication in the case of the Socialist Federal Republic of Yugoslavia, which was that the perfection of the state also entailed the reproduction of the imperfection of relationships between each separate state in the Federation. The care taken in selecting signifiers to designate the different state components of the Federation indicates something of the problem. There were five 'nations' with their own Republic as home reference point – Croatia, Macedonia, Montenegro, Serbia and Slovenia – and nine different recognised ethnic categories by the early 1980s, which include some that do not easily correspond to a geographical area: as well as Croat, Macedonian, Montenegrin, Serbian and Slovenian, the other ethnic groups were Hungarians mainly in the province of Vojvodina, Albanians mainly in Kosovo,[26] and Muslims ('a national category which refers to the South Slav population converted to Islam during Ottoman rule')[27] to be found mainly in Bosnia.[28] There was also the ethnic self-designation 'Yugoslav', which more than doubled in size between 1971 and 1981, as some indication that new identities could be forged.[29]

Identity traps and the language of ethnic domination

Tito's well-worn phrase 'brotherhood and unity'[30] – which was to be taken up later by Milošević and injected with more sinister content – simultaneously expressed something of the project of Yugoslavia as a federation, and 'repressed', we might say, the dominance of Serbia. Although the Communist Party had formally abandoned its early position, from 1919 to 1923, which was then in favour of a centralised state that would dissolve national particularities into a new Yugoslav nation,[31] traces of old Great Serb chauvinism remained embedded in the workings of the state when the Party took power. The nature of this 'repression' needs to be carefully spelled out if we are not to lapse into some kind of collectivised conspiratorial image of the Serbian psyche. On the one hand, the iron grip of Tito, a Croat, meant that there was occasion enough for Serbian nationalists to complain that the Communist Party and then the League of Communists were plotting against the interests of the nation. For example, the shift from the project for a centralised state to a federation followed, in part, from a similar shift of policy in the Soviet Union, and the Comintern had to exert some pressure during the 1920s to bring the Yugoslav party into line.[32]

In this sense, a certain degree of 'repression' of the ambitions of the Serb nationalist current did take place, and the later triumphant emergence of this current around Milošević could be understood in a very loose (and not a very psychoanalytic) way, as the 'return of the repressed'. The subjugation of Albanian activists in Kosovo after the Second World War was also a concession to Serb sensitivities that linked repression with an incitement to resistance, to the 'return' of what had been shut out. On the other hand, the structural dominance of Serbia within the different forms of state apparatus was organised in such a way that complaints against it would seem to be unreasonable if not traitorous; the stage was set for those with most privilege to interpret opposition as a provocation, and for interpretation of responses to that provocation as the justifiable exercise of what might be seen as 'defence mechanisms'.

There are quite evident issues of language here. While Slovenian had been viewed as but a dialect of Serbo-Croat by the party in the 1920s, the complex patchwork of 'nations', 'nationalities' and 'national minorities' recognised by the League of Communists did include recognition of different languages. However, while the writing of Serbo-Croat in Serbia was in Cyrillic script – that is, the notation adopted in the Soviet Union as well as Bulgaria – in Croatia the Roman alphabet was used. And the different material inscription of signifiers which marked the presence of either of the two different main ethnic groups was quite explicitly at work in the military apparatus. The military command structure used Cyrillic script, and the argument that there would be less confusion if only this single alphabet was used also served to privilege Serbs within the military. The different republics had their own Territorial Defence Forces but did not have their own armies (and the Federal army was controlled from Belgrade). We do not, then, even have to bring into play claims that Serbs in the different parts of the Federation were preponderant because they were more attracted to military life[33] in order to understand how this privilege was repetitively inscribed in the relations between the different nations. One of the key trials in the 1980s in Slovenia was conducted in Serbo-Croat, on the basis that it was a military trial; but by this time the manoeuvre simply served to make more visible domination by Belgrade.

Self-management in practice

There was a fatal paradox in the economic functioning of the Yugoslav state which meant that a loosening of control by Belgrade served to intensify competition between the different republics. The ostensible shift from a 'planned economy' and control over the private sector before the break with Stalin, to the implementation of self-management, required an abandonment of state ownership and collectivisation of agriculture, a 'reliance on market mechanisms', the 'increased use of financial instruments' and decentralisation of budgeting, the free distribution of income locally and the 'rehabilitation of consumer sovereignty'.[34] Central economic control was eventually relaxed to the point where banks and economic enterprises in the different republics had to take responsibility for budgeting and financial management. The allocation of responsibility to a local level, where the republics were expected to be self-supporting, meant that a prerequisite for this form of 'socialism' was intense competition.

By the 1980s there were marked regional differences in levels of unemployment and indices of economic growth between the different republics. Kosovo was quite badly off, as were parts of Serbia (the exception being Belgrade), and Slovenia was way ahead of the other republics.[35] This made political attempts to exercise economic control from Belgrade even more transparent as the opposition movements gained strength during the 1980s. There was much unnecessary duplication of industrial production for local, pragmatic political reasons, and decisions made at the centre exacerbated the situation. Steel production, for example, had been shifted by the bureaucrats from Slovenia to Bosnia, and this meant that it then became cheaper to import steel than produce it within the country.[36]

Self-management also contained within it a centrifugal dynamic, in which the articulation of dissent would come to be necessarily linked to dissatisfaction with Serbian control. The absence of any arena for open democratic discussion across the Federation – that is, the prohibition on organising on a party-political basis across the borders of the republics – meant that opposition could only be aired locally, within the republics and against the centre. Any demand for universal democratic rights then tended to be distorted, 'particularized, "nationalized"', as it entered the political stage.[37] Belgrade was faced with local resistance not only from the more economically advanced republics, Slovenia being the most outstanding example. There were more pressing problems facing Belgrade by the 1980s, which included holding onto Kosovo, a poor and backward part of Yugoslavia but operating as a much more potent indicator of Serb integrity than Slovenia. We will turn in a moment to examine in greater detail the emergence of the resistance movement in Slovenia – that, after all, is where we will get a better sense of the economic-political coordinates from which Žižek views the world. But we do first need to look a little closer at the issue of Kosovo.

Žižek's first writings for the Left in the English-speaking world provided some Lacanian coordinates for making sense of 'the re-emergence of national chauvinism in Eastern Europe as a kind of "shock absorber" against the sudden exposure to capitalist openness and imbalance',[38] but before we translate what was happening into Žižek's particular dialect of Lacanese (something we will only be able to do in sufficient detail in Chapter 3) we need to know how the particular nationalist obsession Milošević had with Kosovo could have been turned into something susceptible to a psychoanalytic reading in the first place.

The Italian occupation of parts of Yugoslavia during the Second World War – a division between Italy and Germany that also put Ljubljana under Italian jurisdiction – had brought together on common land the Albanian population in Kosovo and what was to become Enver Hoxha's Stalinist fiefdom next door. Tito's envoy to Kosovo and Macedonia in 1943 reported that the conditions for partisan military struggle against fascism were more difficult in Kosovo because the local population feared a return to Serbian rule. The state had used systematic terror before the Second World War to make Albanians emigrate from Kosovo to Turkey or to Albanian territory.[39] Serb and Montenegrin settlers also continued to dominate the local Communist Party apparatus inside Kosovo, and there was a clearly expressed wish on the part of the Albanian partisans that Kosovo should be integrated into a new unified Albanian republic after the war. However, Tito chose to placate the Serb population, as part of the project of stabilising Yugoslavia in line with Stalin's demand that the country should fall within the Western sphere of influence, and promises made to the Albanian resistance movement were reneged on in 1945.[40] An uprising against the new Yugoslav military occupation was crushed. Kosovo was given limited regional autonomy in 1946, but there was further repression in 1956, which saw about one hundred killed by the security forces, and display of the Albanian national flag was punishable by imprisonment until 1966.[41]

Stains purged by the pure

We have already noted how Albania became a Stalinist reverse image of the Yugoslav regime, itself a doppelganger of the Soviet regime. Albania was thus a remainder and reminder of the Tito–Stalin split, itself split between Stalin's loyal ally Hoxha and a seething population inside Yugoslav borders subject to Serb government. It was then, in the context of the revival of Serb nationalism, that charges of 'ethnic cleansing' first started to be raised against Albanians in Kosovo. A petition by Belgrade intellectuals and church representatives in 1986 demanded 'the right to spiritual identity, to defence of the foundations of Serb national culture and to the physical survival of our nation on its land'.[42]

Charges of 'ethnic cleansing' and accusations of rape made against Albanians also draw attention, of course, to the explicit and implicit agendas of the burgeoning 'moral majorities' in the republics. Struggles over the control of land and anxieties about diminishing populations of the different ethnic groups did also quickly mobilise motifs of the 'community' and the 'family', and so of the position, role and responsibility of women. In these conditions of national threat, 'women are pronounced both culprits and victims'; the tragedy of the Croatian nation, for example, was blamed on 'women, pornography and abortion' by the 'Croatian Democratic Community', which came to power in the republic's multi-party elections in 1990.[43] While the actual position of women in Eastern Europe did not in practice correspond much to the claims about equality between the sexes made by the Stalinist bureaucrats,[44] the nationalist movements that swept to power as the bureaucracy disintegrated revelled in images of the woman as bearer of children for the homeland.[45] Here too, however, we need to take care not to see these reactionary images as bubbling up as if they were instinctual natural desires that were only then quelled by the state. In fact, during those 'socialist' times, 'the state-control process of socialization and the mistrust of the family as the agent of socialization paradoxically coincided with elements of traditional patriarchal ideology'.[46] What the new nationalist movements were able to do was to bring to fruition the desire for authentic motherhood – itself an ideological fantasy – that had been both incited and frustrated by the bureaucracy.

There is another potent ideological motif that was able to mobilise and divide the ethnic communities in the republics, that of anti-semitism. But the image of the 'Jew' during the times of disintegration of Yugoslavia had a particular quality that will be worth bearing in mind when we turn to Žižek's theoretical account of the role of anti-semitism under capitalism. Massacres of Jews were carried out both by the Croatian Ustashe and by the Serb Chetniks during the periods of fascist occupation, and the image of rootless cosmopolitanism figured powerfully enough in the purges conducted by Stalin and in the anti-semitic pogrom planned by him just before he died in 1953. The 'Jew' operated as a specific identifiable cosmopolitan category that cannot be completely assimilated to any of the republics and cannot be counted on to be loyal to the host community.

There is a further complex, contradictory series of significations given to the figure of the Jew in the conflict between the Yugoslav republics, providing a convenient displacement and reinforcement of anti-semitism. One aspect of this can be found in the condensed images in Serb discourse about Albanians as 'dirty, fornicating, rapacious, violent, primitive' and Slovenians as 'non-productive merchants', condensed images which amount to something worse, like the stereotypical image of the Jew.[47] In the Croat imagination there is another set of condensations, in which the Serbs are conspiring with the Jews to cheat them. Yet another bizarre facet of this ideological process, a mirror-image of these attributions, which serves to refract and repeat particular forms of anti-semitism, is that the Serbs sometimes position themselves as 'Jews', as the 'chosen people' of Yugoslavia. In this self-positioning (a positioning that also serves to confirm the conspiracy theories of the Croats) the Albanians are Muslim 'terrorists' who want to drive the Serbs from Kosovo in much the same way as the Arabs are supposed to be trying to drive the Jews out of Israel.[48] The collusion of the different sections of the bureaucratic apparatus in these fantasies of ethnic purity and gender in the name of 'communism' made the task of those critics on the left who saw Stalinism as a distortion of Marxism very difficult. (We will examine Žižek's relation to Marxism in more detail in Chapter 4.)

If, in the eyes of many, Marxism was already efficiently discredited by the Yugoslav regime (which implemented free-market competition between different enterprises and republics in the name of 'self-management socialism'), the Left had still more shocks to come. In 1987, editors of *Praxis International* publicly defended their decision to sign the appeal for Serbian rights in Kosovo a year earlier. The *Praxis* group, based in Belgrade, had been the critical conscience of the Left inside Yugoslavia, and it brought together Marxist intellectuals who refused to allow the regime to co-opt completely the word 'Marxism' as part of its ideological legitimation strategies.[49] Their appeal for Serbian rights marked a shift from Marxism to nationalism, and played on the idea that Serbs were being 'cleansed' from Kosovan villages. In fact, as of 1987, when Milošević came to power, even the evidence for such a campaign of 'ethnic cleansing' directed by Albanians against Serbs was very flimsy.[50] Kosovo was rapidly becoming a touchstone for the integrity of the Serbian nation. An 'Appeal for Protection of the Serb population and its Holy Places in Kosovo' issued by the Serbian Orthodox Church in 1982 had already ratcheted up the pressure in terms that are hauntingly similar to the theoretical elaborations of Žižek on the role that Kosovo plays as object cause of desire for the Serbs. The appeal referred to Serbia's fight for the 'remembrance of its being' in Kosovo since 1389, and rehearsed again the Milošević line that there is 'no more precious object for the Serb nation, no dearer reality, no more sacred object, past, present or future, than the existence and holiness of Kosovo'.[51]

It has been suggested that Milošević's visit to Kosovo in April 1987 for a party delegate meeting was a turning point in the development of Serb nationalism and the 'reactivation of the Serb's chosen trauma'.[52] This psychoanalytic account, which is far from a Lacanian or Žižekian reading, does usefully draw attention to some key motifs and problems. It was after 13 hours listening to tales of victimisation at the hands of Albanians that Milošević became converted to the mythical anchoring point of Serb identity in the battle with the Turks at the battle of Kosovo in 1389. Milošević 'emerged from this experience a transformed person, wearing the armor of Serb nationalism',[53] and then, with the decision to bring the body of Lazar, the hero of the 1389 battle, on a tour of Serb villages and towns, the 'chosen trauma' that had 'been kept alive throughout the centuries' was brought to life. This is how events in the 1980s served to reactivate 'affects' (intense bodily states that we experience as distinct emotions) connected with 'traumatized self-images'.[54]

Our concern here is not with the historical accuracy of the story of the battle of Kosovo, but with how the story came to be transmitted through the generations as a binding force of identity for the Serbs. The key issue is how this 'affect' could be transmitted and reactivated 500 years later. The only way to answer this question without resorting to some kind of genetic or telepathic account is to treat the 'reactivation' as a process that comes to fix something unbearable and incomprehensible, to make it real *retroactively*. That retroactive production of the event in the past so that it will then be felt to have 'caused' the traumatic affect in the present is exactly how Freud accounts for the appearance of a symptom. This retroactive production of trauma is something that was discovered by Lacan in his return to Freud, and has been used to good effect in Žižek's work. There is still, however, another precipitating cause that is necessary for a figure like Milošević to be drawn to an event like this as a traumatic moment and for the Serb population to circle around it lamenting what has been done to them, so that they could feel driven to wreak revenge on all those who remind them of their abject condition. In this way 'trauma' comes to function as a point of origin for collective history and individual experience.

Theoretical resistance and political practice

As Žižek points out with respect to the civil war,[55] we need a 'theoretical framework' if we are not to get facts wrong. A simple recitation of 'what happened when' is likely to lead us into factual errors as well as conceptual ones. If we are using a theoretical framework like psychoanalysis, however, we also need to be able to account for how the conceptual assumptions within it can actually come to be operative. If psychoanalytic explanation of any kind is to be put to work, we need to know how the different elements of it come to be so potent. The structuring of the political field has come to be articulated in such a way that psychoanalytic explanation works. Psychoanalytic subjectivity – an experience of something shut out from everyday discourse – appears when populations have been wrenched from the land and their labour power alienated from them in the course of capitalist development. These irrevocably divided subjects then witness the return of the repressed from what has been constituted in these new conditions of impossibility as something 'unconscious' to them. It is in these conditions that the nostalgic yearning for some organic sense of connection with community through the motif of the nation comes to function not only at an ideological level but also, and as a condition for its ideological appeal, at the level of affect.[56]

The same point about the role of theory applies to readings of Hegel, for which the distinction between three main classes would appear to provide an almost perfect ideological image and a good deal of solace to bureaucrats administering the buffer states in Eastern Europe. For Hegel, the 'agricultural class' comprised nobles and peasants, the 'business class' capitalists and workers, and the 'universal class' was composed of civil servants.[57] We know how seductive it is to portray society as bringing together workers and employers as if they had common interests,[58] and it was exactly this shared interest between the two components of the 'business class' that was contested by Marx.

We may also imagine how attractive an image of shared interests between the business class and the 'universal class' of administrators, charged with shepherding the business class and agricultural classes, would be to Stalinist apparatchiks. It would, perhaps, be all the more appealing to those in Yugoslavia seeking intellectual comfort from the idea that they occupied the position of the enlightened 'universal class', that of the bureaucracy. The development of 'self-management' accomplished the blurring of class distinctions between employers and workers, and the subordination of the workers' organisations to the imperative of business.[59] The attempt to provide some reflexive self-critique of what was happening in Yugoslavia by describing the emergence of the bureaucracy as a 'new class' would then simply serve to legitimate this displacement from Marxist to Hegelian categories.[60]

The conceptual architecture of Yugoslav society was able to sustain these various ideological trends, but as the state started to disintegrate the fault lines in the texture of life under the bureaucracy started to become lines of battle. And it is then that we see the conditions of impossibility for the Yugoslav state also start to operate as conditions of possibility for Žižek's combination of Hegel, Lacan and Marx to become effective, not only as legitimation but also as critique.

Žižek's account of the break-up of Yugoslavia in 1990, first published in *New Left Review*,[61] uses a Lacanian frame first to describe the 'theft of enjoyment',[62] in which what was never possessed in the first place is felt to be stolen by others. For psychoanalysis, the object of desire after which we unconsciously strive is always already a 'lost object', never having had an empirical reality but functioning as a fantasmatic lure, as if it were something we did once enjoy. The way Žižek develops the Lacanian take on this idea to render it into something compatible with Marxism requires a separate discussion, something we will return to in Chapter 3. But for now, what we can see in Žižek's account is a description of national antagonism that has already been structured into the Yugoslav state apparatus and its forms of ideological legitimation.

On the one hand, Žižek insists that the notion 'theft of enjoyment' does not only apply to the 'backward' Balkans but is also applicable to political processes exemplified by patterns of US ideology in the 1980s. In this respect, the clustering of ideological fantasy around our own special national 'Thing' that is felt to be under threat is portrayed as something that will explode into life – life as deathly hatred of others – whenever capitalism goes into crisis. One of the key features of capitalism, of course, is that it is always in 'crisis'. Its 'innermost antagonistic character' makes it function as an economic system that provokes ever newer needs that cannot be completely satisfied.[63] On the other hand, Žižek offers a thumbnail sketch of Yugoslavia as a 'case-study' of this process in which each nationality has 'built its own mythology narrating how other nations deprive it of the vital part of enjoyment the possession of which would allow it to live fully'.[64]

The 'reinvention of democracy' in Eastern Europe that the West enjoyed so much at the end of the 1980s was thus a reintroduction of the forms of antagonism necessary to capitalist economic organisation. When the lid of 'totalitarianism' was lifted, instead of the 'spontaneous' eruption of democratic desire that the West keenly looked for, what we saw were 'more ethnic conflicts, based on the constructions of different "thieves of enjoyment": as if, beneath the Communist surface, there glimmered a wealth of "pathological" fantasies, waiting for their moment to arrive'.[65]

What we need to focus on here are the crucial little caveats in Žižek's account. It is 'as if' there were pathological fantasies below the surface, and it is the *construction* of the different enemies that gives rise to certain kinds of enmity when an imbalance is introduced into the system. There is always a danger when a psychoanalytic account of ethnic hatred is being employed that it will be read as the discovery of biologically wired-in instinctual processes, and the same danger applies to readings of Žižek.[66] What we have seen so far, of course, is that the Yugoslav state was constituted around certain forms of structural imbalance, and that the difference between the republics already constructed certain distinctive forms of ethnic rivalry.

Žižek's paper concludes with a call for '*more alienation*', for some distance from the suffocating fantasy of the new capitalist regime as an organic community, and from the corresponding 'nationalist populism' that configures every other community outside it as responsible for the 'theft of enjoyment'; 'the establishment of an "alienated" state that would maintain its distance from civil society, that would be "formal", empty, embodying no particular ethnic community's dream' would then be a way of 'keeping the space open for them all'.[67] One thing to notice about this proposal is that the call for a 'distance' between the state and civil society repeats what Žižek had been calling for well before capitalism had been reintroduced. The strategies of resistance he had been advocating during the 1980s were already being used to contest the local bureaucracy and the grip of the Slovenian League of Communists. So, we shift our attention now from Serbia to Slovenia, to see how that resistance played itself out.

THE SLOVENE SPRINGS

The various points of impossibility in the economic and political relationships between the different components of the Yugoslav Federation were brought to breaking point by events well beyond its control: economic crisis in the West, and the political decomposition of the Soviet Union. The International Monetary Fund started to call in the massive debts that the Yugoslav economy had been accumulating when crisis hit the capitalist world in the 1980s, a time when several large countries with IMF loans were heading for bankruptcy. The national antagonisms within Yugoslavia were compounded by economic intervention from capitalist economies in Western Europe, particularly Germany. Here, though, we need to bear in mind that one of the effects of economic crisis in capitalism is precisely to exacerbate national rivalries as the different economic systems compete for diminishing resources. Europe and the US had different stakes in the fate of Yugoslavia.

Slovenia prized out by the West

Slovenia in particular was a key economic prize to be seized by the West and incorporated into capitalism. In 1991 it comprised about 8 per cent of the population of Yugoslavia, but was responsible for near on 18 per cent of its gross domestic product. It was the most economically developed and efficient republic. And there were already strong trading links between Slovenia and the West, for it had contributed 30 per cent of exports from Yugoslavia. The ambitions of imperialism to break into Yugoslavia and to absorb the most profitable sectors into its own circuits of production coincided with particular national interests and amenability to free competition inside Slovenia.[68] As has already been noted, Slovenia was one of the wealthiest republics and had clearly benefited from the 'market' aspect of the Yugoslav 'socialist' economy. A consultant with the World Bank and vice-prime minister with the Slovenian government after the secession in 1991 indicated how the different periods of Yugoslav economic policy were viewed from Slovenia. Note that 'socialism' figures rather negatively in his account of the different periods of the 'formal allocation of decision-making in the economy': 'administrative socialism' (from 1945 to 1952), 'administrative market socialism' (from 1953 to 1962), 'market socialism' (from 1963 to 1973) and 'contractual socialism' (from 1974 to 1988).[69] The democratisation process during the 1980s in Slovenia can also be connected with its more flexible patterns of economic development, for unlike the other small republics in Yugoslavia, industry is located in a number of provincial centres rather than in the capital Ljubljana, which makes a downturn or closures in one sector more easily absorbable.[70]

Žižek's view was that at least until 1991 the West tried to keep Yugoslavia together.[71] However it does not seem so clear that the publicly avowed wishes of Washington were necessarily the same as Western European interests. The ten-day conflict between Serbia and Slovenia in 1991, when Belgrade made a last bid to clamp down on opposition forces inside Ljubljana, was resolved fairly easily. Slovenia agreed to delay its secession for three months,[72] and Belgrade withdrew. It would seem that while the United States may well have wanted to forestall the fragmentation of

Yugoslavia – and the evidence that Žižek gives is that he saw US Secretary of State James Baker on television supporting the Yugoslav army[73] – this was as much to keep German ambitions in check as anything else. Other Western European countries suspicious about German designs would then also have had all the more reason to be more cautious about Yugoslavia disintegrating, with the UK, France and Greece for different economic and political reasons lining up with Serbia quite explicitly at different times during the 1980s and early 1990s.[74] By 1991 even Milošević seemed to want to be rid of Slovenia.[75] At that point Kosovo was a much more pressing problem for Belgrade, and the ideological imperative to maintain Serb integrity by holding onto its 1389 battlefield and point of traumatic foundation became more important than holding onto Slovenia.

Slovenia is not a big country, with a population of about 1.7 million people at the time it broke from Yugoslavia in 1991. This has consequences for the texture of political life, throwing some light on Žižek's comments in various interviews about his personal enmities with this or that figure in competing political groups. One estimate of the composition of the different opposition movements in the 1980s, for example, was that the peace movement might have comprised about 20 people and the feminist movement consisted of about a dozen.[76] This must also be borne in mind when we read of the activity of campaigns like the Committee for the Protection of Human Rights, which collected 100,000 signatures for the release of editors and journalists from the radical youth magazine *Mladina* in 1988, during the 'Slovene spring', for it indicates something of the scale of mobilisation of people around political issues at that time.[77]

The birth of theoretical culture

The growth of this opposition movement was very rapid, and there are two distinctive features of the movement that we now find reflected in Žižek's work. The first is the role of French theoretical resources, and the second is the importance of popular culture. According to one account from within the opposition movement, the 1970s were characterised by, on the one hand, 'a total depoliticization of society' and, on the other, widespread involvement in study. One political theoretical current which emerged was concerned with mainly Marxist political economy, and another current – around the journal *Problemi* – was influenced by Althusser, Foucault and Lacan.[78] Žižek and the so-called 'Slovene Lacanian School'[79] were involved with this second theoretical current, and to some extent the political opposition to the bureaucracy in Slovenia was theoretically driven by resources that academics in the West often group together as 'post-structuralism'.

Although Žižek has become the most visible figure from that emerging group of political and theoretical activists in Ljubljana, some of the others have clearly played a key role in his writing, and we will have cause to refer to their work in later chapters to explicate further where he comes from and what he is up to. We have already drawn on some of the reflections on gender and feminism in the break-up of Yugoslavia by Renata Salecl, and her discussion of Lacan's notion of 'sexuation' will be important later.[80] Alenka Zupančič's work on Kant includes a sustained discussion of ethics, which provides crucial background to the place of phenomenology in Ljubljana.[81] The rubric 'post-structuralism' is actually quite misleading to characterise the work of Žižek, Salecl or Zupančič, or that of Mladen Dolar or Miran Božovič, whose interests lie mainly in seventeenth-century philosophy.[82]

Three 'imperatives' emerged from theoretical work carried out during the 1970s.[83] First, that there should be a critical examination of the claims made about political economy and self-management that would include study of Marxism and of distortions of Marxist ideas by the 'socialist' state. The second concerned the historical formation of the Slovene nation so as to lay bare the ideological effects of claims that it was something 'natural' that simply needed to be restored. And the third was a critique of 'dissidence' as a phenomenon that simply served to keep the bureaucracy in place. The argument here was that 'dissidents in East European (and other socialist) societies played a state-constitutive role: that their way of thinking was essentially similar to that of the bureaucratic elite, though with an inverted meaning attached to things'.[84] The specific forms of cultural resistance that emerged at the beginning of the 1980s turned opposition to the regime into something that went well beyond the limits of 'dissidence'.

The resistance movement in Slovenia was characterised by a specific set of cultural reference points, and by an articulation of popular culture as a form of resistance. This resistance took some distinctive and surprising forms. 'At the beginning was punk',[85] and the appearance of punk in 1977 was later to be seen as the birth of the first new social movement in the country that would challenge the bureaucracy. The appearance of punk culture triggered a new phase in Slovenian politics, and there was a massive politicisation of youth media – *Mladina* and 'Radio Student' – which then hit the Slovene Socialist Youth Alliance (the youth wing of the Slovenian League of Communists).[86] By 1986 the Youth Alliance was coming into direct conflict with the League of Communists, and it adopted a 22-point programme for changing Yugoslavia at its congress in 1986.[87]

One striking example was the formation in the early 1980s of the Neue Slowenische Kunst (NSK), which was a grouping of music, theatre and visual arts projects. The band *Laibach* – the German name for Ljubljana – had already been in trouble with the authorities for wearing Nazi insignia as a direct refusal and provocation of the state (the ripping of political images from their context was also one of the characteristics of punk in the West at that time); the *Laibach Kunst* manifesto pitted itself against the rest of the Slovenian 'alternative culture' scene, and against the realm of 'dissidence' as a personal free space in which individuals imagine that they are able to be distant from the party apparatus and so free of its effects. The manifesto called for 'the principle of conscious rejection of personal tastes, judgements, convictions', and for 'free depersonalisation, voluntary acceptance of the role of ideology'.[88] A key strategy introduced by *Laibach* – and one taken up by the different arts projects as part of the 'retro-avant-garde' deconstruction of the claims of the state to be socialist, progressive and unassailable – was that of 'overidentification'.

Overidentification here meant refusal of any distance, the taking of dominant symbolic forms at face value and, through repetition and reflexive considerations of their tactical impact, taking the response of the state to breaking point. Overidentification offered a way of breaking from the deadlock between apologists for the regime and the unwittingly loyal opposition, shattering the strategies of 'dissidence' that seemed simply to serve as another alibi for the regime. Through the 1980s the main focus was on state rituals, and in the 1990s the NSK set up its own embassies and consulates. In retrospect, it is now possible to see the phenomenon of the NSK as 'a kind of theatricalization of a few Žižek theses',[89] but in the 1980s this was 'the language of the alternative society'. Activists from the NSK did attend Žižek's lectures, but later insisted that it was *Laibach* that first used the 'method' of overidentification, and that Žižek then theorised what they did.[90] There is a twist though, which is that for Žižek overidentification is but a tactic; it refuses the covertly state-sanctioned position of 'dissidence', but only in order to buy time for some more dramatic refusal of power. As we shall see in later chapters, such dramatic refusal is at the level of an individual 'act', not really envisaged by him as taking place in the domain of collective political action.

The strategy of overidentification also keys into the way that 'civil society' is often understood by Hegelians and Marxists in the 'Eurocommunist' tradition, after Antonio Gramsci,[91] as operating in opposition to the state. Some trends in the Slovenian opposition did see the constitution of a sphere of civil society as 'the necessary condition for democracy'.[92] This would not only have to be forged in distinction to the way the state tried to articulate all activities within its scope, but also be 'opposed to any idea of harmonious community' that would represent nationalist and xenophobic interests. The first of these options – the assimilation of all activity in civil society to the state so that opposition would be effectively stifled – was a powerful strategy employed by the state during the first half of the 1980s. In fact the Slovenian League of Communists did itself desperately resort to Gramscian rhetoric to try and co-opt the left opposition towards the end of the 1980s.[93] Perhaps this is why Žižek holds onto the Hegelian distinction between the state and civil society but refuses the Gramscian attempt to claim civil society as the site for progressive politics. For Žižek, it is civil society that often seems to be the problem, and the mobilisation of civil society against the opposition movement in Slovenia is a warning to those who would idealise it against the state.

This kind of 'totalitarianism from below' (at that time mobilised by the state) entailed the often unplanned but efficient suffocation of alternative spaces, 'initiated, put into practice and executed by the people themselves', so that the people 'were the socialist consciousness and the nation's conscience synthesised'.[94] The development of a republic-wide movement for democratic rights, following the formation of the Committee for the Defence of Human Rights campaign to defend those framed in a military show-trial of journalists connected with *Mladina* and a Slovenian sergeant-major in the Yugoslav army, led to the formation of different political parties in 1988.

The first 'free' elections in 1990 saw Demos – an alliance of five different opposition groups – obtain about 55 per cent of the vote, and a Christian Democrat became Prime Minister. The programme of economic 'shock therapy' implemented by the new government delighted the IMF and the World Bank, but actually did little more than accelerate the programme already set out by the 'Socialist Federal Republic of Yugoslavia' in July 1990. According to this programme the measures of economic shock policy – convertibility of the dinar, changes in fiscal policy and restrictive monetary policy – were to be complemented by 'heterodox shock' policy which would 'blow out psychological inflation' and prepare the population for massive privatisation.[95]

The triumph of parties set on the goal of turning Slovenia into a thriving capitalist country allied with the West brought into play a different notion of civil society, and Slovenia saw the flourishing of the new 'moral majorities'.[96] The programme of these movements included not only cultural chauvinism, but also the promotion of family life and the celebration of child-bearing mothers who would contribute to the growth of the nation, with consequent restriction of abortion rights and attacks on homosexual 'degenerates'.[97] In this respect the rise of the moral majority in Slovenia paralleled the rise of the right in the other Yugoslav republics. There was also, of course, the not-so-little element of differentiation from

Serbia as morally governed by the Orthodox Church, for 82 per cent of the population in Slovenia were Catholic. Christianity was also a force ready to be mobilised as part of the project of building the nation. Already in 1991 one commentator writing from Ljubljana noted that women had almost disappeared from politics, with the new mission given to them to produce as many new Slovenes as possible, concluding that 'the new democracy is male, phallocratic democracy'.[98] In the run-up to war with Iraq in 2003, Slovenia was one of the 'gang of ten' new capitalist states from Eastern Europe eager to sign a statement of support for US action.

New order

So where was Žižek in the birth of the new order in Slovenia? As we noted earlier, Žižek had been one of the candidates for the collective presidency in the 1990 elections, and had stood on the ticket of the Liberal Party (for which he came within a hair's breadth of being elected). After the elections he did something that, in his own words, 'no good leftist ever does' – he 'supported the ruling party' – and by 1995 he was claiming that 'it was our party that saved Slovenia from the fate of the other former Yugoslav republics'. He had clearly made a choice in this new capitalist context that was informed by a Hegelian view of the difference between the state and civil society. Hegel was suspicious of civil society, and Žižek repeats Hegel in this respect. If it was indeed the case that civil society was then functioning as 'a network of moral majority, conservatives and nationalist pressure groups, against abortion', then this 'real pressure from below' would need to be countered by the state; as Žižek put it, 'in Slovenia I am for the state and against civil society!'.[99] Here Žižek abandons the tactic of 'overidentification' with the state, and opts instead for a straight-forward identification with it; it is as if 'the establishment of an "alienated" state that would maintain its distance from civil society'[100] was a dream come true.

The reinvention of capitalism in Yugoslavia was also, as Žižek pointed out in his 1990 article for *New Left Review*, a reinvention of 'democracy' which the West has enjoyed immensely, and when the Left gazes with such avid desire it is, of course, implicated in the scene. He is understandably touchy about the Left in the West delivering its verdict about strategies that have been adopted by the various movements opposing the Yugoslav state.[101] The fascinated gaze of Western liberals on 'victims' in Sarajevo during the civil war in Bosnia-Herzegovina was, as he pointed out, a gaze that could not contemplate supporting the victims if they started to fight back. He is most contemptuous about the 'apparent multi-cultural, neutral, liberal attitude' which 'posits itself in a witness role' and which fails to see that the war after the break-up of Yugoslavia was 'strictly the result of European cultural dynamics'.[102]

It should be pointed out, however, that Žižek himself plays to those audiences. His response to the 1999 bombing of Serbia, 'Against the Double Blackmail', which was published in *New Left Review*, for example, complained that the NATO bombing 'signals the end of any serious role for the UN and Security Council', and he called for the building of '*transnational* political movements' that would refuse the option of siding with Washington or Belgrade.[103] This was music to the ears of the Left campaigning against imperialist intervention, perhaps, and it did seem at the time that Žižek was lending his support to the anti-war movement. There is a significant difference, however, between the two versions; an omission from the original version that circulated on email just before the publication of these articles was the phrase 'So, precisely as a Leftist, my answer to the dilemma "Bomb or not?" is: not yet ENOUGH bombs, and they are TOO LATE.'[104] And in other interviews he is quite happy to say that he has 'always been in favour of military intervention'.[105]

When we read Žižek telling a journalist from the West, 'Do not forget that with me everything is the opposite of what it seems',[106] we should take him at his word. Žižek is contradictory, and my analysis of the contradictoriness of life at the edge of Yugoslavia is a way of mapping that. Tactical collusion with the Stalinist bureaucracy in order to make a living in the 1970s, and open support for the Slovenian state after the restoration of capitalism in the 1990s, do not at all serve to discredit what Žižek writes; but when he claims to be a Marxist we can respond with some comradely Marxist assessment of the political strategies he has adopted. When he claims to use psychoanalytic theory, we need to examine those claims to see whether they make sense and what the limits might be. Lacanian theory is particularly useful for returning a message to a subject in its reverse form, as truth, returning the message here to Žižek – who says that for him everything is the opposite of what it seems – so that we can treat the claim seriously, as something true rather than a mere joke designed to disarm critics. And the Hegelian rhetoric needs to be assessed in order to determine whether it really is being used for critique or legitimation of the state. We turn to that question in the next chapter.

2
Enlightenment – With Hegel

The Western European Enlightenment was an intellectual and cultural movement driven by the power of reason and set on the defeat of medieval obscurantism. It is not only a way to understand the world and our place in it, an accumulating series of philosophical exercises for improving the mind, but a system of moral improvement institutionally embedded in forms of government, and has even come to operate as a programme for mental health. This Enlightenment is only nominally restricted to the eighteenth century, for the foundation point of a thinking-reasoning core of the individual human subject was set in place much earlier, in the seventeenth century, by Descartes, and put to work much later, in the twentieth century, by Freud.

Freud once defined the aim of psychoanalysis as being to 'strengthen the ego', to 'widen its field of perception and enlarge its organization', and he concluded his account then[1] with a phrase that neatly combines this image of self-illumination with one of progress and the expansion of civilised dry land: 'Where id was, there ego shall be. It is the work of culture – not unlike the draining of the Zuider Zee.'[2] This prescription will have to be rigorously reinterpreted to make it Lacanian, to make psychoanalysis into something that is at one and the same moment part of the Enlightenment and a reflexively negative critique of it. This is a matter for the next chapter. But first, well before Freud, there is another proto-psychoanalytic figure lying at the heart of the Enlightenment who Žižek uses as a compass to orient himself. For Žižek it is Hegel who shows us, after the event, what the project of enlightenment was about and what it could become.

There are three main components in Hegel's work that interest Žižek – universality, reflexivity and negativity – and we will be focusing on these components in this chapter. Hegel can be seen to lie in a tradition of philosophical reflection that Žižek borrows from and intervenes in, and we can only make sense of what Žižek is doing with other theoretical, cultural and political debates if we bear these key Hegelian reference points in mind. This is a Hegel who is very different from the usual received image of him as celebrant of the World Spirit unfolding and revealing itself as fully-formed in the Prussian state.[3] Žižek's Hegel is a revolutionary spirit who opens up theoretical systems, and for whom the moments of fracture that make critical thought possible are enduring dialectical points of impossibility. It would be misleading to say that this is the 'positive' aspect of Hegel in Žižek's work, because this is the Hegel of perpetual refusal, the 'no' of Žižek that is the running sore of his sustained critique of ideology through a critique of philosophy in *Tarrying with the Negative*. That book opens up Descartes' claim to have identified a point of which and at which he could be certain – '*Cogito ergo sum*', 'I am thinking, therefore I am'[4] – and it locates that illusory mastery of reason in a history of philosophical reflection in order to show how it will not work conceptually, at the same time as it does work so well ideologically.

Tarrying with the Negative is, we might say, Žižek's big book of enlightenment as bleaching illumination; his description of the eruption of nationalist rivalries in Eastern Europe towards the end of the book is designed to dismantle 'the tale of ethnic roots' as a 'myth of Origins'. What we have learnt from Hegel here is that 'national heritage' is 'a kind of ideological fossil created retroactively by the ruling ideology in order to blur its *present* antagonism'.[5] And right from the beginning there is an injunction to the 'critical intellectual' to occupy the position of whatever keeps open the present antagonism, to refuse any lure of harmonic resolution of contradictions. The book opens with the example of the demonstrators in Bucharest celebrating the overthrow of Ceauçescu and ripping out the red star from the Romanian flag; the hole itself was a point of mobilisation. This is the open point to be occupied by a critical intellectual and kept open, as an attempt to keep open something 'not yet hegemonized by any positive ideological project'.[6] This is Žižek's reflexively negative Hegel in action.

But there is also some implicit invitation to say 'yes' in Hegelian philosophy, and it is this 'positive' aspect that we will turn to presently as the marker of something that is a little more problematic in Žižek's writing. Žižek's enthusiasm for Christ in *On Belief* is not really accidental or surprising in the light of his comments on Christianity in his earlier books. *On Belief* traces its way from pagan belief systems through the lures of Buddhism and cyberspace to the theme of Christian rebirth. Here we arrive at a moment when the open wound that is the human subject looks like it could be healed.[7] This book is, perhaps, Žižek's little book of enlightenment as illuminated manuscript. Some positive historical moment is posed by the Christian notion of being 'reborn in faith'; according to Žižek it is the first time in human history we have formulated for ourselves 'an unconditional subjective engagement on account of which we are ready to suspend the very ethical substance of our being'.[8] The problem is that this promise of a new 'absolute beginning' cannot relieve us of the historical weight of Christian notions of progress in European culture that have been relayed so powerfully by Western philosophy, and used as arguments against lesser religions, relayed by figures like Hegel. So, this chapter tarries with Hegel enough to show how revolutionary he can be, and it also refuses to take on board the ideological baggage that still makes him sometimes reactionary beyond belief.

WHAT IS THE THING WITH HEGEL?

Žižek's Hegel is quite different from the versions of Hegel that usually circulate in Western philosophy.[9] There are good reasons for this difference, which are to be found in local patterns of recuperation; that is, the absorption and distortion that make him readable to certain kinds of audience, particularly to conservatives who find an account of the development of 'Spirit' that confirms their sense of how things have come to be the way they are, quite independently of material conditions. These local patterns have made Hegel into an acceptable figure to be admired or reviled in academic philosophy. The difference also lies in culturally specific strategies of resistance – the reading of him negatively, against the grain; strategies that are necessary to retrieve what is radical about his work. Žižek has had to combat what he sees as certain errors in the mainstream readings of Hegel so that he can make a case for the retroactive construction of the Truth of his work that we might then always already find in his writing. But the ground of combat is quite specific: it is France.

No, no, no, no

Hegel was a founding point of German idealism and then phenomenology, but he is also a pivotal figure for much late twentieth-century French philosophy. Žižek's early work was in German philosophy – his first book was on Heidegger and language[10] – but his reading of the German idealists was radically reorganised by his encounter with the French intellectual debates. The so-called 'post-structuralist' philosophers are as much 'post-phenomenologists'; the elaboration of hermeneutics and the relation to the 'Other' in the writings of Derrida and Foucault, for example, are at least as much the continuation of an argument with Hegel as an attempt to make sense of the structure of language in the historical production of subjectivity. What Žižek does, then, is to retrieve what is most radical in Hegel in and against this tradition, pitting Hegel against deconstruction, say, in such a way as to reveal what is lacking in it, and the way it elaborates itself as if it were a 'metalanguage' (speaking as if it were completely outside the language it comments upon). In this light, Derrida's deconstruction is not as radical as it seems, for it repeats the moves of mainstream philosophy, and respect for the otherness of the other seems condemned to repeat quite traditional forms of religious argument. We will see how Žižek uses old Hegel to open up a space between these two positions, between Derrida and Hegel.

Hegel was transformed into a key French philosopher of history and subjectivity in the 1930s, in lectures by the Russian émigré philosopher Alexandre Kojève.[11] Kojève's lectures in Paris between 1933 and 1939 were regularly attended by many of the French intellectuals who shaped debates around structuralism and phenomenology after the Second World War, with the list including Maurice Merleau-Ponty, Georges Bataille and Jacques Lacan.[12] The puzzle for some as to why Kojève referred to himself as a 'Stalinist of the strictest obedience'[13] was only to be cleared up many years later, after his death, when it transpired that he had actually been working then as a Soviet agent. Even if we do not now reduce Kojève's reading of Hegel to this specific political position, we do need to be aware that intellectual debate in France from the 1930s was heavily politicised, with short-circuits repeatedly made and remade between philosophical positions and their consequences – as to whether one should support the French Communist Party or not, and then whether one should support Mao in the Sino–Soviet split.[14]

However, when Žižek comments that his leanings are 'almost Maoist'[15] we need to bear in mind that it is the index to philosophical debate that may be more important here than direct political allegiance. Of course, the way the short-circuit between positions in philosophy and politics operates is itself a political question (and we will come to that in Chapter 4). It does at any rate seem that the Hegel that reappeared in Paris in the 1930s was a bit of an ultra-leftist, and we can find a motif of total rejection of any taken-for-granted assumptions about the world in his work on at least four counts.

First, this French Hegel draws attention to the irremediable separation between what we know about the world and the world itself. The very process of naming is emblematic of a certain kind of violence that human beings do to the world, and the idea that representation itself is a form of subjugation of the objects and subjects held in it was to be an important theme in later French philosophy.[16] What has been captured in language has also been necessarily misrepresented, and so the motif of 'misrecognition' that plagues relations between human subjects is already at work in the relation between human beings and the world around them. A softer take on Hegel's argument would be to say that he aimed 'to undermine *all* representationalist models':[17] for Hegel the process of representation – the attempt to fix something outside of our perception of the world – cannot actually succeed in reflecting fully any thing outside of itself.[18] Either

way, for Žižek it is crucial that we read Hegel in such a way as to refuse
the lure of 'dialectical synthesis', and so avoid any evolutionary notion of
how things as such become reflexively aware of what they really are, a
'progressive development of in-itself into for-itself'.[19] We are not arriving
at some point of realisation of what we were, or reconciliation with what
we have eventually been fortunate to have accurately named.

The second way the motif of rejection – Hegel terms it 'negativity' – is
manifested is in relations between human subjects, and it is the account of
the struggle for recognition from another that Kojève made the centrepiece
of his argument. For Hegel, the 'fight for recognition is a life and death
struggle';[20] a battle between the victorious subject who will gain
recognition from the other to be the master, and the loser reduced to the
status of an object giving recognition as the slave.[21] This master–slave
dialectic contains within itself the fateful logic of its own reversal, for the
master is already also locked into a relation of dependence on the slave, and
when the slave comes to realise this the tables will be turned. As we will
see, Žižek takes up the Kojèvean structure of this struggle for recognition
in order to foreground the failure of attempts to form 'intersubjective'
bonds in which there is genuine and open communication. The collapse of
relationships between individuals and communities into ethnic feuds or
nationalist wars is not a function of irrational instinctual forces, but is
built upon the very nature of human beings' representation of and
dependence on the other.

The third way Hegel's rejection of taken-for-granted assumptions works
is through the occasional glimpses in his writing of what the ground zero
of human subjectivity might be when it is stripped of the relation to the
other. Here, in his motif of the 'night of the world', one arrives at something
that already looks like the 'murder of the thing' without the words to patch
it over.[22] When Hegel is inveighing against the position of those who
declare that everything is wrong in the world but that they have no part in
it – the position of the 'beautiful soul' – he warns that 'The extravagance
of subjectivity often becomes madness; it abides in thoughts, so it is caught
in a vortex of the reflecting understanding, which is always negative against
itself.'[22] However, what Žižek draws attention to is that this is a fate that
afflicts all human beings engaged in creative imaginative activity when they
break with comfortable commonsensical images of the world. It is here, at
this ground zero when one refuses the taken-for-granted everyday world,
that some madness in the subject appears: 'This night, the interior of
nature, that exists here – pure self – in phantasmagorical representations,
is night all around it, in which here shoots a bloody head – there another
white ghastly apparition, suddenly here before it, and just so disappears.'

For Hegel this night is ever-present: 'One catches sight of this night when one looks human beings in the eye – into a night that becomes awful.'[23]

Fourth and finally, Hegel's total rejection of given truths is the way to something more important. To 'tarry with the negative' is also to find a way to Truth. It is a necessarily circuitous route, and it is only by tracing our way through a certain kind of misrecognition, and grasping something of the nature of that misrecognition, that we can grasp what it is about Truth that makes it Truth for us, and makes it structurally unavailable to be simply and immediately recognised and grasped. Žižek emphasises that the gap between misrecognition and what may be grasped as Truth is a function of the internal structure of representation, not of something outside us hindering our ability to see things as they are. The dialectic of the obstacle that is also the condition for something to be possible reappears again and again in his writing: 'For Hegel, external circumstances are not an impediment to realizing inner potentials, but on the contrary *the very arena in which the true nature of these inner potentials is to be tested.*'[24] To give a rather prosaic example, Žižek describes his time of unemployment after failing to get a lecturing post in Ljubljana as something that seemed at the time to be a terrible impediment, but actually turned out to have been the arena in which he was able to develop intellectually and intervene politically.

Reflexive ways to say yes

In Kojève's reading of Hegel then, the gap that is opened up between our representation of the world and the thing itself cannot be closed over, the battle for recognition that was necessary for the formation of self-consciousness is unending, the point of absolute self-destruction has to be risked repeatedly if anything is to be achieved, and the truth that emerges through error is only fleeting. Žižek's writing is marked by that accent on negativity in Hegel, but he also insists on a reflexive element in Hegel that is just as important. We do already have more than some intimation of reflexivity in our account. It has been unavoidable. Let us return for a moment to the problem of the separation between our representation of the things in the world and the way those things actually are, for example. It would be tempting to imagine a third point from which we could view the two sides of that gap; and if we could occupy that third independent position it would be possible to perceive things accurately the way they are, and to perceive the way our forms of representation distort those things. This is the temptation of the 'metalanguage' as a place outside or beyond the messy separation. The necessarily reflexive quality of Hegel's writing is bound up with his argument that any position is always already part of the mess. So, as a counterpoint to the four aspects of negativity, let us turn to four aspects of reflexivity in Hegel.

First, perception is always 'dialectically mediated by the observing subject'.[25] Once this elementary phenomenological position is taken seriously it is impossible to conceive of any judgement that does not also already carry with it the peculiar subjective stance of the observer. The gaze of the outsider on a scene of horror is always, then, a particular kind of horror for them, and the fantasmatic mediation of what they see carries with it what they want or do not want to see there. One of Žižek's favourite uses of this notion is around the gaze that finds evil: 'as Hegel puts it, what is effectively evil is ultimately the gaze itself which perceives a state of things as evil'.[26] The gaze of the West on the destruction of Sarajevo, for example, was itself 'evil' insofar as it anxiously searched for images of victims, victims whose fate was sealed at least in part by imperialist design.

There is a way of fairly systematically shutting out one's own place in what one sees. This second reflexive aspect in Hegel is where he noticed something more seductive than the simple 'bad faith' of French existentialism. For Hegel, the strategic attempt to absolve oneself of responsibility is itself a position, a position he characterises as the 'beautiful soul'. His description of the beautiful soul – which has significant resonance with Rousseau's *belle âme* in the French Romantic tradition[27] – usefully draws attention to various strategies of anti-political hand-wringing among liberal academics; the one 'who is forever above actually doing anything and who is forever intoning against the corrupt world' or the one who refers to 'fine intentions and the complexities of the situation' to justify what they do.[28] Hegel's characterisation of the subjectivity of the beautiful soul, however, is one that has implications for all those subject to the desire of others, to the necessary interdependence of self-consciousness on others: 'Subjectivity exists in a lack but is driven towards something solid and thus remains a *longing*.'[29] It would indeed be a beautiful soul who could imagine that it is only other people who are afflicted in this way. The question is how one will own up to this position.

The third reflexive aspect is that one's position is always given by certain cultural, historical circumstances, and for Hegel this constitution of particular kinds of human experience, and the embedding of life conditions in forms of subjectivity, was what he termed the production of 'substance as subject'. In his discussion of Greek culture, for example, he described how the emerging forms of communal self-reflection produced a certain teleological shape to social life, and then to individual consciousness of what it was to be alive: 'this necessarily led to these agents coming to understand the basic determining ground of their practices as lying within the structure of those practices themselves'.[30] This example of Greek culture is not at all incidental to Hegel's argument; for Hegel and the German idealists, and then for many of those writing in France after the Second World War, what happened in Greece when substance became subject inaugurated something progressive and irreversible in European culture.[31] Žižek's reworking of this notion is then applied to the way the split between the subject and the mysterious, unattainable substance which seems to lie beyond it then becomes embedded in the very subject itself – the subject as split. At the same time as he describes this process as if it were timeless, and in relation to the Absolute subject as God,[32] he still holds to the production of subject as substance as a repetition of a founding cultural historical moment of enlightenment.

Fourthly, as we have already noted, for Hegel the journey to Truth is through error, and that journey is characterised not only by forms of recognition that turn out to be only more misrecognition, but also by the retroactive constitution of what it is we will find. This retroactive effect entails the presupposition of the very foundations that will then make it possible for us to approach it. The retroactive effect of positing the very pre-suppositions of our interpretation and action is also at work in the cluster of Hegelian concepts concerning the 'reflexive determination' of the things we appeal to as things that seem to be independent of our judgement. The motif of 'speculative identity' in Hegel also sometimes functions to draw attention to the complicity between a system and what pretends to stand outside it. Lacan's rediscovery of the importance of this retroactive effect in Freud's analysis of trauma also turns Hegel, retroactively, into a philo-sophical resource for psychoanalysis.

This positing of the very foundations upon which we act is crucial to Žižek's descriptions of the retroactive constitution of 'heritage' in nationalist imagery, for example. The powerful ideological notion that our 'nation', 'community' or 'ethnic group' was always already there needs to be tackled and laid bare, so that we can see that the life we live is one that we have come to create for ourselves. Žižek also brings this idea to bear on the way in which revolutionary movements eventually succeed through their very ability to assume, as part of their historical memory, the failures of the past. In a link with the German idealist tradition and its later incarnation in the work of Walter Benjamin, we see again that, for Žižek, what was mere error becomes the precursor for the emergence of truth – here in Benjamin's 'notion of a revolutionary gaze which perceives the actual revolutionary act as the redemptive repetition of past failed emancipatory attempts'.[33]

From particularity to agonistic universality

To work with the reflexive process – to recognise one's position in the gaze through which one constructs the world, to own up to one's part in the imperfections of the world, to assume consciously one's position out of the circumstances that form the substantive setting of subjectivity in given cultural conditions and to know that one is retroactively constituting the very grounds on which one acts – is also to shift from the sphere of the self-enclosed individual to the realm of the 'universal'. That link with universality is a crucial theme in Hegel's writing that Žižek worries away at. There are different, competing versions of universality in readings of Hegel: two simple reductions – to the development of the individual or to the onward march of history; an attempt to combine these two elements in some kind of 'third way'; and a genuinely dialectical agonistic combination. It is in that fourth version that negativity and reflexivity are put to work to link individuality, the particular and the universal.

In the first version, which homes in on the individual, we find the lures of traditional humanism, a reading which revels in Hegel's comment that 'universal self-consciousness is the affirmative awareness of self in an other self'.[34] To reach the 'universal' here is to flower as a human consciousness alike and alongside the others, a beneficent self-actualisation of what it is to be truly and everywhere fully human. A good deal of reflexivity would help in this developmental process of self-formation – what was termed by the German idealists and the chattering classes of the time *Bildung*[35] – but it actually ends up in the smug self-satisfaction of the bourgeois subject when it erases all the traces of negativity that constitute the subject and structure it at its heart.

The second version is Kojève's way, and here it is seen as an ineluctable historical struggle for recognition in which the masters will come to learn that they cannot hold power when their slaves realise that the masters are utterly dependent on them. This is a bloody historical process which did not reach its end in the Prussian state when Hegel was writing, and Kojève did not tempt his audience with the idea that the battle had reached a happy, harmonious conclusion in the Soviet Union. There was, however, a little bait for those hoping for an eventual resolution; and in this misreading of Hegel Kojève evokes the movement of History much as the early moderns evoked Nature, as 'a self-correcting enterprise that ensured that the right outcome would be ordained even if we limited humans could not see how it was working out'.[36]

One way of combining these two perspectives is to take a 'third way' reading of Hegel that resolves the conflict between the individual and the social into the enlightened activities of the 'universal class'. This is an option that is particularly attractive to academics of course, and all the more so when they imagine that the role of a critical intellectual is to contribute to the good management of society. As we saw in the last chapter, this would be an especially attractive option to soft Stalinists at the helm of the bureaucratic apparatus in Yugoslavia. In this way 'the *unconscious identity* of individual and universal interests promoted by class divisions and conflicts of bourgeois society is forged into an active, self-conscious principle within what he [Hegel] terms the "rational" or "social" state'.[37]

In contrast, Žižek's reading of Hegel retrieves the two dialectically inter-related aspects of human activity and experience. As we have already noted, for Žižek the role of the 'critical intellectual' is to keep things open, not to close up gaps. The master–slave dialectic could be read as an anthro-pological fairy-tale and reduced to the story of self-consciousness in each individual subject, and the dialectical unfolding of spirit in history could be read as an account of the development of civilisation and of the progressive achievement of human community. But each of these narratives, separated into the individual and social sides of an equation, tear out what is most radical in Hegel. We can see how the two sides of the equation are dialectically interrelated through the way belief in the belief of others is constituted, and in the way that what appears to be a limit is the very condition of possibility for something to be thought.

The intertwining of one's own belief and the belief of others is something that Žižek often addresses, and it is productively worked up in his account of the way an appeal to the existence of a community of believers can sanction cynicism and a peculiar form of passivity, 'interpassivity'.[38] When the two sides are dialectically interrelated we can see how the 'universal' does not appear either as an add-on to a particular event or as a qualitative-ly different transformation of an accretion of quantitative changes or instances. What is specific may at the very same time speak to what is universal about the human condition, a condition that will itself be understood as historically grounded. This fourth version of universality can only be realised through radical breaks with the past and an opening to the dialectical interdependence of each human subject with the history that bears us all. Now we have a problem, neatly summarised by Žižek as if it were simply a solution: 'In a revolution proper, such a display of what Hegel would have called "abstract negativity" merely, as it were, wipes the slate clean for the second act, the imposition of a new order.'[39] Negativity is an opening, a revolutionary fracture, but it also may portend a more terrible redemptive closure.

REVOLUTIONARY FRACTURE

Of the impact of Kojève on French intellectual debate, Vincent Descombes remarks in his influential survey of philosophy there from the 1930s to the 1970s that 'Nothing could be more characteristic than the change in connotation undergone by the word *dialectic*.'[40] The transformation –

from dialectic viewed by neo-Kantians as a mere 'logic of appearances' to the claim that it 'could never be the object of concepts, since its movement engenders and dissolves them all'[41] – could be seen as a shift of attention from surface to depth, to something underneath that would explain why things appear as they do. That formulation of the dialectic, which was offered by Jean-Paul Sartre in 1960, draws attention to the way recent French philosophy repeats the very history it attempts to escape. Note, for example, that Sartre's formulation cited here about the dialectic engendering and dissolving all other concepts still supposes it to function as an underlying, numinous, dynamic force. That formulation anticipates some of the later appeals to *différance* much beloved by the followers of Derrida and deconstruction, and it is not clear that *différance* as 'originary delay' is not itself 'reducible to Hegel's dialectic of identity'.[42] This is the tradition Žižek is borrowing from and pitting himself against.

What Žižek is able to open up is the way that this transformation itself demands a dialectical reading. Then the Hegelian dialectic resuscitated by Kojève can be put to work backwards, as it were, to read Kant so as to retrieve something disturbingly dialectical in his work, and forward to read Heidegger to stop the dialectic from being shut down. When Žižek seizes an understanding of the dialectic from Kojève he is thus taking it well beyond that rather partial presentation of Hegel in the 1930s lectures, and bringing it out of the limited frame of the French disputes. By tarrying with the Kantian moment for a while, then, we will be able to see why Hegel spends so much time battling with Kant, and why Žižek is so keen on Hegel. Žižek's Hegel keeps the enlightenment open as a revolutionary force, but this openness is more ambiguous and less revolutionary than it seems.

Backward: A Hegelian angle on Kant

In his essay 'An Answer to the Question: What is Enlightenment?', written in 1784, Kant raises the slogan of enlightenment as 'have the courage to use your own understanding'. For Kant, 'the freedom to use reason publicly on all matters' is the only requirement for the development of an 'age of enlightenment' in which we have emerged from our 'self-imposed immaturity', immaturity which he defines as 'the inability to use one's own understanding without guidance from another'.[43] Metaphors of development jostle alongside images of independence of thought and rational appraisal to make it seem as if the Kantian subject is an uncomplicated, clear-thinking, autonomous individual, but things are actually a little more complex than this.

What Kant opens up is a rigorous examination of the 'conditions of possibility'[44] of our experience of objects, in such a way that it also requires an examination of how it is that those objects are constituted by us. When

Kant likens his shift of focus to the Copernican revolution in astronomy it is clear to Žižek that what this shift requires is a radical transformation of how we think about the place of the spectator. Kant comments that Copernicus discovered that he could not make any progress when he still assumed that the heavenly bodies revolved around the spectator, and so 'he reversed the process, and tried the experiment of assuming that the spectator revolved, while the stars remained at rest'.[45] Now what this entailed, according to Žižek, was that 'the subject loses its substantial stability/identity and is reduced to the pure substanceless void of the self-rotating abyssal vortex called "transcendental apperception"'.[46] Note here the resonance between this image of the 'abyssal vortex' in Kant and Hegel's 'night of the world' as a reduction to degree zero of experience that is chaotic, void of reason.

This means that consciousness itself is cracked open, and the question now shifts from one of 'conditions of possibility' to 'conditions of impossibility'.[47] For Žižek, 'self-consciousness is positively founded upon the non-transparency of the subject to itself',[48] and this non-transparency not only causes havoc with traditional readings of Kant but also opens up a fracture in Kant's own image of the subject so that it becomes other to itself: 'the Kantian transcendental apperception (i.e., the self-consciousness of pure I) is possible only insofar as I am unattainable to myself in my noumenal dimension, qua "Thing which thinks"'.[49] After Hegel, then, we can see how the Kantian subject of reason is split so that reflexive consciousness is inhabited by a disturbing negativity.

The Kantian reasoning subject is also a moral subject, and the ability to reason with others for the good of oneself, as a good that one might also imagine as applicable to them, also holds within it an impossible, irresolvable tension. The problem is that conscience does not complement consciousness to make it more beneficent to others, but rather plagues it, so that the will to do good will feel diseased and hateful; there is only one thing of which moral conscience can be certain, and that is that it will be aware of infractions of the moral law. Kant argues that 'there is no man so depraved but that he feels upon transgressing the internal law a resistance within himself and an abhorrence of himself'.[50] So here Kant is not posing two separate phenomena, the moral law and transgressions of it; rather 'he is arguing that our only consciousness of the law is our consciousness of our transgression of it'.[51] As Gilles Deleuze puts it, the law for Kant 'defines a realm of transgression where one is already guilty, and where one oversteps the bounds without knowing what they are'.[52] This comment by Deleuze is symptomatic of the way Kant has returned to the scene in recent French philosophy, as a figure who is read through Hegel and turned into someone who then seems to anticipate psychoanalytic specifications of the role of the super-ego. Against that symptomatic background, Žižek's own work does in many respects seem less startlingly original.

Joan Copjec – a key and not fully acknowledged resource for many of Žižek's linking arguments around Kant and psychoanalytic social theory[53] – points out that if we do 'freely choose to obey our sensible inclinations', as Kant says, 'then some evidence of our freedom or of our capacity to resist these inclinations must betray itself in our actions'.[54] This brings us up against the limits of moral reasoning in Kant, to a necessary irrational underside to the apparently so reasonable Kantian subject. If it is the case that 'Our guilt is all we know of the law',[55] then the leap from the level of a particular individual to the universal will pose more problems than it solves. To follow the law may not only bring us into line with things that are good for us or others, it may take us somewhere less pleasant.

Alenka Zupančič, one of 'the Slovene Lacanian inner party circle',[56] elaborates the argument – which is a well-known one to Lacanians[57] – that the Kantian moral subject is not at all cleansed of pathology. Precisely the reverse, for Kant supposes a slavish obedience to the law that smacks of perversity: 'we could say that the pathological takes revenge and imposes its law by planting a certain kind of pleasure along the path of the categorical imperative'.[58] Note here that once the Hegelian reflexive question about the subject's constitutive role in phenomena it relates to is brought into play we have to ask what the subject gets out of obeying the law. There is no place of innocence, no place for a 'beautiful soul' who is able to sidestep responsibility for their own part in obedience to the demand posed by the categorical imperative. What is at stake is obedience as such, rather than any particular good effect the individual can point to as a reason for having taken this or that course of action.

For Kant, the moral law does not define exactly what should or should not be done. It is 'an enigmatic law which only commands us to do our duty, without ever naming it'.[59] The worst that could happen, perhaps, is that Kantian subjects could turn themselves into instruments of the law, enjoying their relationship to law as the logical ultimate end-point of the desire to do good. And this worst outcome, which lies hidden inside the system supposed by Kant, is realised by those who make their enjoyment conform to a law. The Marquis de Sade, for example, is not the obvious candidate for being considered a good moral subject, but he does subordinate himself to the principle that full enjoyment is in line with the laws of nature, and the ultimate Sadeian fantasy is one of perpetual enjoyment in which the victim wants more and will never actually die.[60] Zupančič's reading of this logic – endorsed by Žižek in his foreword to her book[61] – is that 'Kant's immortality of the soul promises us, then, quite a peculiar heaven; for what awaits ethical subjects is a heavenly future that bears an uncanny resemblance to the Sadeian boudoir.'[62]

In a Hegelian reading of the historical emergence of the Kantian moral subject from times of 'revolutionary Terror', Žižek opens up once more the dependence of the individual on others and the way this dependence is relayed even into the apparent freedom of the individual: 'the passage to moral subjectivity occurs when this external terror is internalised by the subject as the terror of the moral law, of the voice of conscience'.[63] The 'age of enlightenment', then, does not come out of nowhere – there are certain historical conditions in European history that are the necessary background for it – and it does not issue in wholesome, free-thinking individuals. Hegel suspected as much, and Žižek drives home that lesson.

There is a paradox in Žižek's reading of Kant, which is that at the very same moment that Kant seems to be positing a subject who follows universal maxims in order to act ethically there is also, Žižek argues, 'a crack in universality'. That is, the fracture that is opened up in the Kantian conception of the subject, conscience and the relation to the law – opened up with the aid of Hegel, something that we are now able to see in Kant after the event – is, perhaps, primary. For Žižek, then, 'Kant was revolutionary because he was antiuniversalist',[64] and the relation to the universal is precisely something that has to be struggled with and assumed by the subject. It cannot be taken for granted as an unproblematic ground for action, with deviations from it being consigned to the realm of pathology. At moments Žižek too is toying with the idea of what Kant at one moment in his later writing[65] called 'radical evil' as an 'ethical' position that precedes adopting the course of the good in line with the categorical imperative (in which one treats as ethical only those actions that would be applicable to all others). However, 'radical evil' is also for Žižek but another way of opening up the split in the subject. It is a way of forcing a split between the 'thinking' and 'being' of the Cartesian subject and keeping open the split between the individual subject and the subject called upon by a community – the poison chalice of Heidegger's humanism.

Forward: A Hegelian angle on Heidegger

For Žižek earlier on in his career – well before the interest in his work outside Slovenia – Heidegger was quite an attractive theoretical option, and Žižek was not much dissuaded by the official academic party line that Heidegger was suspect because of his support for the Nazis.[66] Heidegger notoriously gave a speech upon assuming the position of Rector of Freiburg University in 1934 praising Hitler, and never fully recanted this crime. The claim that a philosopher should not be taken seriously because of some act of stupidity or mendacity is a spurious reason for excluding them from the canon if it fails to attend to the intimate connection between that act and the philosopher's theoretical framework. That intimate connection, obscured by purely personal attacks, did become clear to Žižek (as it did also to Derrida and other writers in France).

One of the peculiarities of philosophy in Yugoslavia, and a marker of the distinct path the bureaucracy took away from Moscow, was that there was hardly any Soviet-style dialectical materialism taught. In Slovenia from the 1970s forms of 'Western Marxism', mainly around the axis of Frankfurt School Critical Theory, were dominant – and this would mean that some of the positions of the *Praxis* philosophers based in Belgrade would be acceptable[67] – and Heideggerians working alongside other forms of phenomenology occupied the position of dissidence. To be sceptical about critical theory and Heidegger was a third position that Žižek eventually adopted, and this would entail a turn to French theoretical debates. This situation was made still more complicated by the way Heideggerianism operated as the orthodoxy and Western Marxism as dissidence in other parts of Yugoslavia; in Croatia one could be dismissed from an academic post with the reasons articulated in Heideggerian terms, such as (in Žižek's own sarcastic caricature of such academic formulations at the time) 'the essence of self-defence was the self-defence of the essence of our society'.[68] 'All of a sudden', Žižek claims, he became aware that 'the Yugoslav Heideggerians were doing exactly the same thing with respect to the Yugoslav ideology of self-management as Heidegger himself did with respect to Nazism'.[69]

While Heideggerians might sometimes be sniffy enough about any particular existing community, Žižek's argument is that they will eventually be seduced by one that seems powerful and all-embracing enough, for they operate on the assumption that beneath, behind or before technologically-distorted forms of Being-in-the-world there is some way of Being in which we are genuinely at one with others. The merely empirical 'ontic' things of the world are insufficient for Heideggerians because they yearn for the real thing, the real things with deep 'ontological' weight, things that inhere in our very Being. There is, then, a paradoxical substantialisation of Truth as Truth, something that would one day wipe away error. A community that would promise to retrieve the Truth of Being would thus be truly great. Heideggerians are 'eternally in search of a positive, ontic political system that would come closest to the epochal ontological truth'.[70] This is 'a strategy which inevitably leads to error',[71] but the Heideggerians will never learn the lesson that the fact of error does not necessarily portend the disclosure of deep Truth. Heidegger's 'mistake' in hailing the 'greatness' of Nazism, then, was deeper and more dangerous than it seemed. Bad enough as an endorsement of Hitler, Heidegger's mistake revealed how the lure of a substantive coherent community would always be operative for a philosophical system that was waiting for some authentic *Volkish* rebellion against inauthentic modern life.

A Hegelian attention to the 'reflexive determination' of phenomena – that we constitute as objects for us those others we relate to – is useful here. Heidegger was looking for the Nazis, for something like them. To understand this fatal flaw in Heidegger, then, we need 'to grasp the complicity (in Hegelese 'speculative identity') between the elevation above ontic concerns and the passionate "ontic" Nazi political engagement'.[72] Heideggerians in Yugoslavia, and particularly in Slovenia, could see that the fascination with the German *Volk* was an 'error', but they could not resist the lure of another apparently more genuine community – one with an essence worthy of self-defence – and so their identification with that community led to defence of it against those seemingly inauthentic elements that disrupted it. The Hegelian attention to reflexivity, then, needs to be augmented with an emphasis on negativity, something Heidegger had attempted to seal over, for what he lacked was 'insight into the radically *antagonistic* nature of every hitherto communal way of life'.[73]

The dialectical leap from particular, internally differentiated communities and the universal then entails some suspicion of the idea that any community is deep down authentic. This is why Žižek pours scorn, for example, on the claim that with the breakdown of Stalinist bureaucratic rule in Eastern Europe the 'original' cultures were able once again to reassert themselves. In a comment that connects nicely with Marxist historical studies of the 'invention of tradition',[74] he points out that in the case of Slovenia the 'national costumes were copied from Austrian costumes, they were invented towards the end of the last century'.[75]

What Žižek does in *Tarrying with the Negative*, then, is to use Hegel to trace a line through the development of Western philosophy and to show how the analysis can be put to work to understand the disintegration of the Eastern European bureaucracies and the concomitant explosion of nationalist movements. The analysis has implications for how we read recent phenomenological and 'post-structuralist' theories, and for how we locate theory in history. The claim in phenomenology, for example, that it is possible to strip away all presuppositions and so to return to the things themselves has rendered itself subject to the temptation of the metalanguage, but it also produces an illusory, disengaged form of subjectivity which does not own up to its own contribution to what it sees around it. In the case of the 'post-structuralists' – pretenders to the throne after the apparent displacement of Hegel – the elaborate rhetorical hedging in deconstruction of philosophical argument so that one will not be caught advocating any particular position also falls prey to the temptation of the metalanguage.[76] Žižek uncovers the various ways in which the image of an individual, rational, thinking subject, the return to the things themselves free of any mediation, or a theoretical system or community that will serve as a self-sufficient homogeneous guarantee of the truth, all operate as lures to entice us into positions that are dodgy theoretically and dangerous politically.

REDEMPTIVE CLOSURE

Tarrying with the Negative also takes the much riskier step of stringing together the arguments in and against the different philosophical systems into a narrative, in which later writers accumulate earlier theoretical resources and improve upon them. So, 'Plato accepts from the sophists their logic of discursive argumentation, but uses it to affirm his commitment to Truth', and then 'Kant accepts the breakdown of the traditional metaphysics, but uses it to perform his transcendental turn.'[77] Hegel is not the Absolute master at the end of the story for Žižek, but he does come to stand at the highest point of the Žižekian conceptual universe. So far we have seen that the conceptual struggle between Kant and Hegel serves to define Hegel's own position, and how this is crucial to an understanding of where Hegel and then Žižek are coming from, in terms of the rhetorical structure of their arguments as well as the theoretical grounds from which they argue. One finds buried in this rhetorical structure many of the theoretical motifs in Hegel's work, and Žižek then mines that work as a revolutionary resource to critique later philosophical frameworks that only apparently supersede Hegel.

Absolutely European

Where Hegel does not seem so easily assimilated to revolution is where he develops an historical analysis of the relationship between Judaism and Christianity that is very much in line with German idealism's mixture of casual and deliberate anti-semitism.[78] (This is an analysis that will also have repercussions for the way Freud will be placed and read by Žižek, as we shall see in later chapters.) The argument in *On Belief* – eight years on from *Tarrying with the Negative* – takes up already oft-rehearsed positions on these issues in Žižek's earlier writing, and it connects with current theological motifs in French intellectual work. One question here is whether Žižek's attempt to retrieve Christianity speaks to something genuinely present in Hegel, to which the answer seems yes. A further question is whether it also speaks of something worse in the role Christianity plays in contemporary Eurocentrism. Perhaps it is possible to disentangle

Christianity from European thought, but it does not appear that Žižek wants to do that; what we end up with then are some bad premises and an evasion of where they lead through the adoption of some strange contradictory positions. For Žižek, the universalism he finds in Hegel and champions against petty rival particularities – of individual subjects seeking to dominate others so that they may be the master among slaves, or of ethnic communities establishing their superiority over lesser peoples – is rooted in Europe: 'universalism is a Eurocentrist notion'.[79] He is upfront about it, and insists there is no way of avoiding it. The appeal to 'freedom and democracy' in Third World countries against European imperialism is itself endorsing European premises.[80]

These premises then encompass the history of philosophical development in Europe, so that the kind of pluralism in which it is possible to argue against Eurocentrism is something that is 'only possible against the notion that tradition is ultimately something contingent, against the background of an abstract, empty Cartesian subject'.[81] The legacy of Descartes is precisely that he opened up a space in which the purely formal quality of thinking was the only thing of which we could be certain. The peculiar ethnic content of what it is to be a subject is something that may be mobilised against Western European enlightenment notions as its hideous reverse; but claims to universality, even when used to seek independence from Europe, are set in and against, embedded in that tradition.

This 'radically Eurocentric' stance has been an enduring theme in Žižek's work. Back in 1992 he gave the example of the Congress Party in India being founded by Indians educated at Eton, Cambridge and Oxford so that 'the very idea "let's get rid of English colonialism, let's return to our autonomous India" was strictly a product of English colonialism'.[82] In a recent interview, Žižek asks his interviewer to remember 'that in the struggle against apartheid in South Africa, the ANC always appealed to universal Enlightenment values, and it was Buthelezi, the regime's black supporter in the pay of the CIA, who appealed to special African values'.[83] The trick here, of course (as with his claim that the West really wanted to keep Yugoslavia together), is that it overlooks the way rivalries between Europe and America are played out through different, competing forms of intervention.

The trajectory of Western philosophical thought – from Plato to Descartes to Kant to Hegel to Heidegger – thus includes within it retroactive determination aplenty, but it is still presented as a trajectory that is proceeding to greater enlightenment. One of the striking things about *On Belief* is the way that Heidegger is used to warrant arguments about the value of Western thought. There is something of a cyclical movement of fascination and frustration with Heidegger in Žižek's work, and in *On Belief* nearly all the references to Heidegger are positive. For a start, despite his own interest in 'Oriental thought' – a preoccupation that Žižek is keen now to consign to the world of the 'pagans' – we are told that Heidegger saw 'the main task of Western thought today' as 'to defend the Greek breakthrough, the founding gesture of the "West"', something which also requires 'the overcoming of the pre-philosophical mythical "Asiatic" universe'.[84] And perhaps the worst of Heidegger is still alive in Žižek when his discussion of the 'catastrophe that is man himself' leads him, in *The Puppet and the Dwarf*, to pose the question 'Is it possible to claim, in a nonobscene way, that the Holocaust is nothing in comparison with the catastrophe of the forgetting of being?'[85] Surely this reveals the necessary and inescapable perverse core of this strand of German idealism.

What are the consequences of defending the 'Greek breakthrough' today, after Hegel? The aim does not seem to be to seal things over directly with the promise that we would at last realise some greatness in the European Community. It does, however, still seem to search for some event of the kind that happened in Greece when substance became subject and there was a reflexive assumption of what it is to think as a human being linking the individual with the universal. And, worse, it seems to hold out the hope of a search for something that would offer an image of openness, the production of a subject as split – reflexive, negative, universal – but which performs that openness as redemptive closure nonetheless.

Already Žižek has embedded his account of this new, ostensibly more open subject in relation to the god of Judeo-Christian thought – and the running together of these two terms 'Judeo' and 'Christian' is problematic enough, as we will see shortly. Further, in the context of a relationship to God as the Absolute, he argues that 'to conceive Substance as Subject means precisely that split, phenomenalisation, and so forth, are inherent to the life of the Absolute itself'.[86] In *Tarrying with the Negative*, he claims that the 'truly subversive gesture' is to 'grasp Christianity itself "in its becoming", before its horizon of meaning was established'.[87] Now in *On Belief*, the reference point is more concrete, for that moment of 'becoming' is the moment when Christ died to redeem us all.

Why is the Christian legacy worth fighting?

Although much of Žižek's writing about Christianity – both in *The Fragile Absolute* and *On Belief* – does have the flavour of an evangelical pamphlet bringing the 'good news' to the reader, he also takes pains to emphasise that the 'good news' is a mixed blessing; that Christianity offers a 'religiously mystified version' of 'a radical opening' to universality. He is actually, he claims, still a 'fighting atheist', and cheerfully proposes that churches should be 'turned into grain silos or palaces of culture'. It is what Christianity opens up as 'direct access to universality' that is important, and he insists that 'What interests me is only this dimension.'[88] However, Žižek's account of what is 'opened up' in the course of European history places it in a linear succession of belief systems, so that it is only possible to think of 'substance becoming subject' in Greece and then of a 'new beginning' in such a way as to privilege Christianity. What is 'opened up' is then the possibility of redemption, but this move also closes down other religions that were mere precursors to the arrival of the really good news.

Significantly, the relation of the community of believers to the figure of the Jew as outsider comes into focus in a different way in Žižek's recent writing, and it is reconfigured as Christianity in relation to Judaism. The logic of the argument here is still strictly Hegelian, and all of the problems with Hegel in relation to Judaism also start to flood into the picture. The 'history of the West', then, is put by Žižek into a series of different kinds of 'unplugging'.[89]

First, 'the Greek philosophical wondering "unplugs" from the immersion [of the subject] into the mythical universe'.[90] Here we have an appeal to a fairly orthodox Hegelian conception of the way the 'substance' of a particular form of community life – the 'mythical universe' Žižek is referring to here – became 'subject', so that a new self-reflexive form of human experience could open up. This is pretty much of a piece with Heidegger's account of the 'founding gesture' of the West in Greece. After that gesture, that opening, nothing will be the same again. Really this is not so very different from the standard self-image of enlightened Western philosophy. Žižek's position here echoes that of colleagues and friends in Slovenia and France in the 1980s.

In this conception, the universalising moment which saw the birth of European civilisation is neither to be taken lightly nor to be lost and forgotten. This is a question with deep import, for it stands in 'relation to the general history of humanity', according to Cornelius Castoriadis in a commentary on the question of universality quoted and endorsed by Renata Salecl: 'this history, this tradition, philosophy itself, the struggle for democracy, equality, and freedom are as completely improbable as the existence of life on Earth is in relation to the existence of solar systems in the Universe'.[91] Castoriadis, an exile from Greece writing as an ex-Trotskyist who practised as a Lacanian psychoanalyst, is now recruited into a narrative about the birth of the European enlightenment elaborated by one of the leading lights of the 'Slovene Lacanian School'. And again, this is in a well-worn tradition of Eurocentrism in French thought, adopted and adapted from German idealism.

The second moment is where 'Judaism "unplugs" from the polytheistic *jouissance*'.[92] The multiplicity of gods and their obscene excessive enjoyment that is always too much for the mere humans, who are often only their playthings – which is what the Lacanian term 'jouissance' is indicating here – is replaced with one god. This is a step forward, Žižek claims, for 'the Jewish–Christian openness to the Other' is 'thoroughly different from the pagan tribal hospitality'.[93] For pagans, there is still a clear separation between their community and the Other outside it,[94] whereas, in another use of 'Hegelese', 'Jewish–Christian openness involves the logic of "positing its presuppositions": it instigates us to remain open towards the Otherness which is experienced as such only within its own horizon.'[95] For those still immersed in Judaism, however, the news is still not as good as it gets, for Jews 'enact the necessity of a mediatory figure', either in God or in external laws; 'Jews focus on the rules to be followed, questions of "inner belief" are simply not raised.'[96]

On the one hand, Žižek does make some acute comments about the gentile fantasy of Jews as rootless cosmopolitans who stand for 'universality', sometimes to be admired if not idealised, but who are also suspected as having no intrinsic loyalty to any other national community, which is where more potent forms of anti-semitism usually kick in. But he is drawn into these fantasies himself when he seems to want to divine what it really means to be a Jew in relation to God so he can evangelise about what it means to be a Christian. Jews, he says, are still faced with a God who is omnipotent and wrathful,[97] which is why Žižek borrows from Saint Augustine to characterise Judaism as a 'religion of Anxiety' as opposed to the next new 'religion of Love'.[98]

The third moment – and for Žižek this is the big one – is where 'Christianity "unplugs" from one's substantial community'.[99] It is here that *On Belief* really gushes on the glory of Christ on the Cross. This is not a simple linear succession, but the 'sublation' – erasure, incorporation and improvement – of what went before. Hegel is once again summoned to bear witness, and we are told that he was 'right to emphasize' that 'Judaism is the religion of the Sublime: it tries to render the suprasensible dimension … but in a purely negative way, by renouncing images altogether'; 'Christianity, however, renounces this God of Beyond, this Real behind the curtain of the phenomena' so that there is nothing there except 'an imperceptible X that changes Christ, this ordinary man, into God'.[100] Thus 'Christianity inverses the Jewish sublimation into a radical desublimation: not desublimation in the sense of the simple reduction of God to man, but desublimation in the sense of the descendence of the sublime beyond to the everyday level'.[101] Now with direct and explicit reference to Christianity, it is 'the impotent God who failed in his creation'[102] who is the split

Absolute subject in relation to which the Christians become split subjects: 'the traumatic experience *of* God is also the enigma *for* God himself – our failure to comprehend God is what Hegel called a "reflexive determination" of the divine self-limitation'.[103]

The unplugging is not total, of course, because we cannot unplug ourselves from notions of unplugging. In fact, Žižek wants us to hold onto what we have unplugged ourselves from so that the 'Judeo' part of the 'Judeo-Christian' tradition is conceptually and experientially assimilated. So, he argues that the 'position to adopt between Judaism and Christianity is thus not simply to give preference to one of them, even less to opt for a kind of pseudo-dialectical "synthesis"'. The sting in the tail – the bad news about the difference between the realm of words and deeper truth – is that 'as to the content of the belief, one should be a Jew, while retaining the Christian position of enunciation'.[104] Remember that for this Hegelian the word is the murder of the thing, and truth arises through error. For Žižek it is fine to keep the reference to the Jewish God at the level of statements about God, but in the way of personally speaking as testimony to one's relation to God – at the level of the position of enunciation – one should be Christian. That is the definitive 'unplugging' that will clear the way for a 'new Beginning' for each particular subject.

At the end of *Tarrying with the Negative* the eponymous Hegelian motif of 'tarrying with the negative' is rendered by Žižek into 'our ability to consummate the act of assuming fully the "non-existence of the Other"'.[105] To consummate this act we will simultaneously be arriving at the purest end-point of philosophical inquiry.[106] As a crucial part of this process we will also come to know that these questions have not been resolved, and this is also something to be approached at the end of Lacanian psychoanalysis for each individual subject. For Žižek, the philosophical and the psychoanalytic are intertwined, and his narrative switches back and forth between points of rupture in the history of philosophy and how individual subjects might clear their way through personal trauma. We will turn to psychoanalysis in more detail in the next chapter. There we will see how Lacan retrieves a commitment to *Truth* as contingent and particular, and is also able to reinstate Truth at a higher conceptual level as something universal in us as speaking subjects.

3
Psychoanalysis – From Lacan

In *The Interpretation of Dreams* Freud points out that it is 'in the nature of every censorship that of forbidden things it allows those which are *untrue* to be said rather than those which are *true*'.[1] The project of psychoanalysis – in the realms of culture and for the individual subject – is to allow the truth to be said. This project immediately raises a question as to how 'interpretation' might be given by an other who is in the position of the analyst, and in this reflexive question we are already tangled in the history of psychoanalysis, which has also allowed the 'untrue' to be said; the adaptation of psychoanalysis to the imperatives of bourgeois culture and the adaptation of the individual to what we take to be civilisation made it convenient to play along with censorship. Even to say that we should be concerned with 'The Interpretation' of Dreams is to mistranslate the endeavour of pointing to something as explaining the dream away.[2] And the practice of psychoanalysis as a 'cure through love'[3] requires close attention to how subjects allow themselves to say things that are untrue in their own distinctive and self-defeating ways.

Jacques Lacan's 'return to Freud' was an attempt to open up these questions, and to retrieve the truth about psychoanalysis as something revolutionary, that enables us to see the real stakes of censorship. This is Žižek's Freud: psychoanalysis read through Lacan as one of the most advanced points of the history of human enlightenment. For Lacan, psychoanalysis embeds its clinical work in a view of the subject as necessarily and irremediably divided between the forbidden things – the censorship and what is said; this means that it is not so easy to speak the truth, nor even to say what the truth is that is to be spoken. It is in this respect that, according to Žižek,[4] Lacan repeats the move undertaken by earlier Western philosophers – from Plato through to Kant – in which questions about the nature of truth are used to improve and supersede[5] old conceptions, rather than leading to the abandonment of truth. So, just as Plato takes seriously the rhetorical grounds of truth that are championed by the sophists but refuses to dissolve truth in rhetoric, and as Kant tackles the claims of the empiricists all the better to affirm his commitment to truth, so Lacan absorbs and transcends arguments from deconstruction[6] to rework and refound a psychoanalytic project for truth. In the process the position of the subject is transformed so that they undergo what might be termed a radical *Destruktion*.[7] There are wide-ranging consequences of this argument for how we think about culture and the place of individual subjects in it, and Žižek addresses both issues – Lacan in culture and Lacanian psychoanalysis – head on.

The Metastases of Enjoyment takes us from a discussion of 'culture' to the place of the individual subject in culture through a reading of the Frankfurt School tradition of critical theory, with a particular focus on psychoanalysis, sexuality and what Lacan terms 'sexuation'[8] as the production of sexual difference as a key site of the real; that is, as resistant to cultural coding (at the level of the symbolic) or one-to-one resolution (at the level of the imaginary). Žižek's sustained critique of the Frankfurt School's recourse to psychoanalysis – the first Hegelian reading of Freud in social theory – is from the vantage point of Lacan; for Žižek, Lacan's Freud is also thoroughly Hegelian, but now this is Hegel reconfigured at the level of the individual subject.[9] This raises a question about the degree to which Lacan must actually be read like this, and how far the practice of psychoanalysis in his teaching must correspond to cultural critique.

Looking Awry traces a trajectory through Lacan's work that snakes around the distinction between 'reality' – the fantasy world fatally infected by the censorship (as something indicated with the definite article here to emphasise its role as a distinct psychic agency) so that the forbidden things are said in ways that are untrue but satisfying enough – and the 'real', which reappears, as a traumatic kernel of our being and as the limit of our representation of the world, when we least expect it. While 'looking awry' at phenomena might be thought to be merely a way of sidestepping the ideological work of the censorship – and it sometimes functions like that in Žižek's writing – it also characterises the way our 'reality' is structured so that we must see that little special aspect in it that fascinates us and holds us in place only from a particular position. This is where Lacan's[10] discussion of 'anamorphosis' in Holbein's painting 'The Ambassadors'[11] – in which the smear across the bottom of the canvas can only be seen as a skull when looked at sidelong – is emblematic. This motif also raises a question for Žižek's reading of popular culture, which presumes that each of our own particular positions coincides so that tell-tale smears and enigmatic objects function for us all in the same way.

What both readings of Freud – Frankfurt School and Lacanian – take for granted is a displacement from the level of politics as such to something that we might suspect is the 'untrue' that can be said to be coded as 'culture', and then read by those traditions. We will turn to Žižek's politics in more detail in Chapter 4, but for the moment suffice it to note that his own claims about the subversive role of psychoanalysis raise more questions than they answer. When Žižek argues that 'the strictly dogmatic Lacanian approach combined precisely with a not-post-Marxist approach is what is needed today',[12] this should cue us in to examine carefully what happens at the level of the individual in Lacanian psychoanalysis, where we arrive at the end of analysis and what the consequences of Žižek's 'strictly dogmatic' reading of this process might be.

THE DISAPPEARING SUBJECT

A 'dogmatic' reading of psychoanalysis needs to elaborate any radical innovation in clinical practice with reference to Freud, and it is only from that dogmatic starting point that we can recover what is subversive about psychoanalysis and what can be subversive about the emphasis on language in Lacanian returns to Freud. However, there is a sticking point – an obstacle to the extent of subversion in Lacanian analysis – that Žižek himself sticks to with grim satisfaction. That sticking point is sexual difference. But first, Freud.

Rooting for Freud

Lacanian psychoanalysts are Freudians, and the kind of questions to be asked of analysis, and in analysis, are rooted in the theoretical frameworks we find in Freud's writing; 'frameworks' in the plural because although there have been many attempts to tie down what Freud really said,[13] he said a good number of different things. Psychoanalysis changed while Freud was alive, and it is still changing. The field of clinical psychoanalysis, organised in the English-speaking world mainly around the International Psychoanalytical Association (IPA), founded in 1910, is now divided into many different, mutually incompatible traditions, and this division has provided opportunities for recent dialogue initiated by Lacanians.[14] The main strand of critical social theory founded in the Institute of Social Research in Frankfurt in 1923 has, like the IPA, tended to be hostile to Lacanian ideas, with the main burden of their argument directed against the 'anti-humanism' of the Lacanian position.[15] Frankfurt School theorists have often wanted to rescue the individual subject from the alienation wrought by capitalist society, rather than put it into question. Psychoanalysis does, of course, provide a clinical space for rigorous dialectical self-questioning, and to work psychoanalytically we must take seriously two things.

The first is the unconscious. Psychoanalytic treatment rests on the assumption that there is more to human experience than what we are immediately aware of, or what we can easily retrieve from our memory. Something in our lives escapes conscious control, and that means one of the tasks of analysis is to bring to awareness at least the sense that when we speak we say more than we mean. Slips of the tongue, dreams and jokes are the signs of something other to us, something other that determines how we respond to things and who we think we are. So, in analysis the analyst is looking for signs of the work of the unconscious in the speech of the 'analysand'. The 'analysand' is Lacan's term for the 'patient' or 'client', because they are the ones who are doing the analysing.[16]

The second thing we need to take seriously is sexuality. Not so much sexuality as it appears in adult life – something that often seems to have a fixed point of origin and stable object, though that idea about sexuality is quite important insofar as it structures the induction of the subject into sex – but sexuality as something that drives us into sensuous desirous relations with other people, and something that presents us with puzzles about what sexual difference is and what to do with it. In Lacanian psychoanalysis there is a rejection of appeals to notions of wired-in 'instincts'[17] and there is an emphasis on the way that the component parts of the drive are put together as a kind of 'montage', rather than having biologically determined coherence. This means that in analysis the analyst is looking at the organisation of desire, how it emerges in relation to others out of the drives, and how the analysand is trying to deal with those relations and the points where things go too far, where pleasure turns into pain, as an unbearable excessive pleasure. This unbearable excessive pleasure, 'beyond the pleasure principle', is what Lacan terms 'jouissance'.

For any reading of Lacan we need to start with Freud, then, but this starting point is already a little uncertain for Žižek, and he is happier tracing a lineage from earlier German idealist philosophers[18] to Lacan when it suits his argument. This then has consequences for the kind of Lacan who emerges in his writing. On the one hand, Žižek does often refer to Freud.[19] On the other hand, Freud is often sidestepped, and Hegel appears in his place as predecessor of Lacan. Žižek will, for example, turn to Hegel's description of the plant as an animal with its intestines outside itself in the form of roots, and then reverse the formula so that we may view the human being as a plant with its roots outside, getting nutrition from the symbolic: 'is not the *symbolic order* a kind of spiritual intestines of the human animal outside its Self'.[20] This startling image may tell us something more about the unconscious, which for Lacanians is implicated in the symbolic order, but it also serves as another way to bypass Freud altogether. Although Žižek does root his reading of Lacan more closely in clinical practice than much recent social theory claiming to be Lacanian, he has his eye firmly on how it might be turned into something interesting philosophically and subversive politically.

This is where Lacan really starts to become important, because what his reading of psychoanalysis does is to bring to the fore that radical unravelling of human experience Freud initiated. Žižek's discussion of the limitations of the Frankfurt School take on Freud is pursued in comradely fashion,[21] a settling of accounts with a rival Hegelian tradition at the same time as it is a linking with older radical Freudian political debates. Lacanian psychoanalysis has been marginalised in the English-speaking clinical world partly because it refuses the commonsensical self-enclosed model of the bourgeois individual, and of the ego as the captain of the soul, that the mainstream analytic tradition governed by the IPA demands. What we are starting to see now is the re-emergence of Lacan's work, and growing awareness that around half of practising psychoanalysts in the world, if we include those working in France, Spain and Latin America, are Lacanian.

Articulating oneself for a change

There is clearly a political aspect to this subversive role of psychoanalysis. There is a connection with radical politics – which the early psychoanalytic movement in Freud's day had often made – and with a radical political understanding of the way contemporary institutions try to tame psychoanalysis. There is also a connection with what we could see as a radical personal politics of self-understanding and transformation that the analysand embarks upon. Lacanian psychoanalysis is the practice of that self-understanding and transformation, and that is why it avoids quick fixes, suggestion or the attempt to bring about identification between analysand and analyst.

This is why, although Lacanian psychoanalysis includes therapeutic moments, it goes far beyond the usual psychotherapeutic aims of developing coping strategies or recasting problems into opportunities by way of more positive thinking. Psychoanalysis is the space for 'deconstructing' how someone copes and how their problems are bound up with the way they think. For Žižek, another homologous space is that of cultural critique and political action. When Freudian concepts are embedded in language, psychoanalytic understanding of the relationship between what is forbidden, the truth and enjoyment can become a tool to tackle ideology. For Lacan in his later writing, for example, and for Žižek, the super-ego operates not only through prohibition but also through an obscene injunction to 'enjoy'. It incites and contains jouissance, and it then functions as an incitement to 'ironic distance' that actually confirms the hold of the system upon individuals; thus the strategy of 'overidentification' elaborated by groups like Laibach in Slovenia is driven by a psychoanalytic under-standing of the way desire is structured in the service of ideology: 'by bringing to light the obscene superego underside of the system, overiden-tification suspends its efficiency'.[22]

The translation of strategies of individual self-questioning in the clinic into political strategies in public collective space also draws attention to a two-fold political problem. First, political agency requires some degree of self-discipline and coordination with others that is anathema to the attempt to follow the rule of 'free association' when one is alone on the couch. Second, psychoanalysis is not *only* subversive, of course. Psychoanalytic theory has often been used to pathologise people who do not fit in, or those who refuse to accept dominant definitions of how their desire should be organised.[23] To take psychoanalytic rhetorical procedures as the guide to politics, then, is to advertise a practice to all those who resist power that can all too easily come to operate as an alternative system of power.[24] This is something Žižek is all too aware of, but he is nonetheless still content to endorse the 'spirit' or 'structuring principle' that found distorted expression in the Stalinised communist parties in 'the Lacanian community of analysts', and he waxes lyrical about the 'Stalinist' choice of accounting for one's own analysis – a procedure known as the *passe* – 'as an act of total externalization through which I irrevocably renounce the ineffable precious kernel in me that makes me a unique being, and leave myself unreserved-ly to the analytic community'.[25] What we are being asked to swallow here, of course, is the claim that the 'analytic community' under the steady guidance of the Lacanians is politically progressive and worth giving oneself to 'unreservedly'.[26] To account for oneself, as Foucault noted, is always to speak oneself into a certain kind of language and a certain organ-isation of power.[27]

Lacan's work is best known for its concern with language as the phenomenon that marks off human beings, as speaking beings, from other animals, and this is one of the aspects of his work that seems to mark him off as a Hegelian rather than a Freudian.[28] It is the acquisition of language – the attainment of a position within the symbolic domain of human culture – that is the necessary condition for communication with others. At the same time, language is the medium that frustrates and sabotages the possibility of direct contact with others and with our objects of desire.[29] As we speak we are also brought into relation with what we cannot say, realms of discourse that are 'other', that are 'unconscious' to us; this is one meaning of Lacan's dictum, 'the unconscious is the discourse of the Other'.[30]

The entry into the symbolic is Lacan's Oedipal myth, and it brings with it a relation to power – an impossible paradoxical relation to power that Lacan characterises, in a transformation of Freudian theory, as a relation to the 'phallus'. As we enter language to strike up a relation with others we are struck out, and lose the possibility of that relation; and as we enter the symbolic to get access to the phallus we are rendered powerless, there is a symbolic 'castration' and division of the subject under the rule of the signifier. The powerlessness – the lack of a child in the face of language and the fantasy that language will be access to power – is a matter that is suffused with questions of gender, and specific issues of sexual difference may be the key issues for an analysands from the beginning of the analysis. It is the speech of the analysand that reveals to them as they speak how they have become a conscious sexed being in the world through a certain artic-ulation of language. This speech in the attempt and failure of 'free association' renders more explicit and open to reflection how they have been articulated in the symbolic order that determines how they speak for themselves, and how they speak to others, including to the analyst. The articulation of elements of the symbolic, their defining 'signifiers' as the irreducible elements of language, also defines for the analysand what objects of desire their lives and symptoms revolve around, including a key desired lost 'object'.[31]

This means that the analysis does not search below the surface of language for the meaning of things, though fantasies about what lies below the surface will be very important; the analyst keeps their attention on what is said, on the chains of signifiers. This also means that the questions to be asked always attend to what was actually said and not said rather than 'feelings' conjured into place below or behind the symbolic, that seem to explain what is happening. Here, Lacan refuses notions of 'depth' to char-acterise what is happening beneath the symbolic, and instead describes the mutually implicative registers of the symbolic, the imaginary – one-to-one communication with the illusory pretence of transparency, another arena for the struggle for recognition between master and slave that Hegel describes so well – and the real.

Real sex

When we touch the real we come up against a limit to what can be said. It is then more comforting to turn that limit into something that can be symbolised, as if it really were one of the operations of the censorship, or a traumatic event that needs to be brought to mind clearly in order to dissolve its force, or into something that could be imaginarised as the intentional constraints placed by another person, perhaps as the machina-tions of a group that wants to prevent us realising our desires. The Lacanian notion of the real as the structurally necessary limit to representation that is resistant to a simple recoding – whether as something symbolic or imaginary – raises a key question about the status of psychoanalysis as a form of knowledge, a question that Žižek continually fudges and displaces. Is psychoanalysis a function of particular kinds of discourse[32] – to which Žižek sometimes answers in the affirmative[33] – or are there underlying truths about the human condition that only psychoanalysis has been able to detect? It is this second side to the question that Žižek evades, and instead of answering he displaces the problem onto the question of sexual difference, where the ambiguity in his position returns once again.

His discussion of enjoyment, sublimation and femininity in *Metastases of Enjoyment* is precisely a way of elaborating that displacement. There he rehearses the Lacanian account of 'sexuation' as a deadlock of positions between men and women that constitutes man and woman in non-relation to each other in such a way as to ensure that 'there's no such thing as a sexual relationship'.[34] For Žižek, then, 'sexual difference is a Real that resists symbolization',[35] and the book traces the ways in which woman figures variously as traumatic Thing for the man in the olden times of European 'courtly love',[36] as access to jouissance beyond the forms of satisfaction attainable by man in sadism and religious imagery,[37] or as the 'shadowy double' of the man that appears to him to hold power but is cast into that place only by his position as the master.[38]

So, on the one hand there is in Lacan some radically different way of thinking about the problematic of 'sex differences' or 'gender roles' than as biologically governed, or as sets of learned behaviours. Sexuation is a way of specifying the different forms in which the categories of 'man' and 'woman' – as 'nothing but signifiers'[39] – operate in relation to one another by virtue of the particular way that men and women enter language. For man, absolute submission to symbolic castration – that he cannot enter language without subordinating himself to the law of the signifier – still keeps in reserve a significant escape clause, which is the fantasy that although everyone is subordinate to law, there is an exception. In classical Freudian iconography this exception would be the father of the primal horde who was the one who enjoyed all the women while denying that enjoyment to all the other men. And we could say that in the structure of psychoanalytic institutions that first 'father-of-enjoyment', the one who did not subordinate himself to analysis by another, was Freud himself.

On the side of 'woman' in Lacan's formulae of sexuation, there is a different kind of relation to language and the law, in which there is always something in her that escapes. In Freudian accounts of her trajectory through the Oedipus complex, she does not arrive at castration as a point of humiliating defeat, as the boy does, but the sense of lacking something is what initiates and opens up the Oedipal process, the culmination of which includes a position outside and against the male figure who she will,

[handwritten annotations: UC embodies the male exception / C embodies parallel Woman who is not there / tension interplay forces of sexual difference]

in the normative narrative of heterosexual development, come to take as her object. Each particular woman will find a way of dealing with this lack, but no overall category or identity of 'Woman' can sum up everything that she is. It is in this sense that 'Woman' is barred from existence, 'cannot be said'.[40] This means that while she is not wholly included in the symbolic order she is, like all women, still speaking within it. We can see the traces of Kojève's Hegel once again in Lacan's formulation that 'The word strives to reduce the woman to subjection.'[41] In the history of psychoanalysis, for example, we observe a process of rebellion by women repeated in each generation, in which the refusal of Freud as the commanding figure is replaced by an appeal to the experience of all women who can as women take a distance from him.

This rethinking of castration and relation to the law, in terms of 'exception' on the part of man and 'not all' on the part of woman, has been used by Renata Salecl to throw light on the contradictory way that stereo-typically masculine and feminine perspectives on 'human rights' operate.[42] Dominant 'patriarchal' notions of human rights are organised by a 'male' logic in which 'all people have rights, with the exception of those who are excluded from this universality (for example, women, children, foreigners, etc.)', and against this there is a 'feminine' logic in which 'there is no one who does not have rights, but precisely because of this we cannot say that people as such have rights'.[43] There is an ambiguity at the very heart of the inclusion of 'people as such', then, and this kind of inclusion without exception is characterised by the Lacanian term 'not all'. For Salecl, this 'difference' is the marker of a deeper antagonism necessary to political activity, and we should thus avoid closing it up either around a humanist image of all mankind, or by way of an appeal to a standard Western feminist reworking of that humanist image around the nature of womankind. It is not at all certain, though, that this theoretical framework actually avoids romanticising 'woman' as the bearer of what it is to be 'not all'.

Žižek is also attentive to culturally stereotypical images of 'woman'. His discussion of Otto Weininger's misogynist and anti-semitic tirade against femininity, for example, written just before that writer's suicide in Vienna in 1903, homes in on Weininger's discovery that 'Woman' 'does not exist'.[44] Weininger's *Sex and Character* is quite a potent index of images of femininity and sexuality, and of race: it was favourite reading for the young Wittgenstein, who often recommended the book to friends in later life;[45] and it drew some comment from Freud, who wanted to distance himself from the oft-repeated claim at the time that theories of human bisexuality – crucial to psychoanalysis – were first elaborated by Weininger.[46] Woman is something that appears to have substance but which is actually not much more than a lure for men, and her seduction of men is her 'infinite craving of Nothing for Something'.[47] This non-existence of woman drew Weininger to a horror of what lies inside the kind of human subject that has no substance, a horror that Žižek identifies as the kind of 'fantasy formations that emerge where the Word fails', as 'absolute negativity' described so graphically by Hegel as the 'night of the world'.[48] When Lacan comments that 'the sexual relationship doesn't stop not being written',[49] we can then take this as an invitation to examine how woman is always written out of history. This calls for analysis of the specific discourses that simultaneously define and exclude women, and for attention to psychoanalytic discourses that constitute woman and man as irreconcilable positions. So, for Žižek, Lacan opens something up, and what we think of as sex and sexual difference is located in and in relation to discourse.

On the other hand, sexuation functions as something resistant to symbolisation precisely because it always exists and will always return to haunt men and women. It is, in Salecl's words, 'the articulation of a certain deadlock that pertains to the most elementary relationship between the human animal and the symbolic order',[50] and, as Joan Copjec points out, it refuses the lure of recent takes on feminist theory which make it seem as if 'sex is incomplete and in flux because the terms of sexual difference are unstable'.[51] The risk, of course, is that this insistence on the nature of impossibility around sex in the human condition will then entail specifications about what women want and what they will not be willing to give up because of it; and Žižek, not surprisingly, is quick to leap in with such specifications.

With respect to the 'deadlock in contemporary feminism', for example, he argues that this fantasy of access to some mysterious jouissance beyond the symbolic is as important to the women who are idealised by men as to men themselves. While it is indeed the case that the position of women in the times of 'courtly love', when they were so elevated in male fantasy, was actually more miserable – something that Lacan points out in his discussion of images of man serving his Lady[52] – the prospect of giving up 'femininity' provokes panic on all sides: 'By opposing "patriarchal domination", women simultaneously undermine the fantasy-support of their own "feminine" identity.'[53] Furthermore, Žižek maps the deadlock between the sexes onto Kantian 'antinomies' – irresolvable oppositional terms – that lock them into something that can never be transcended.[54] This account appeals not so much to an analysis of and distance from the historical constitution of man, and of woman as other, and with some mysterious access to the Other, but to a tragic repetition of the failure of both men and women to measure up to the figure of man in their own

distinctive ways. This is also a repetition of themes in 1950s French existentialism, but stripped of its feminist rhetoric.[55]

The position of 'woman' as traumatic and alluring cause for the 'man'
poses a further question for what is happening in psychoanalysis when the
subject is 'hystericised', when the subjects of whatever biological sex come
to position themselves against what it is to be a man (of whatever biological
sex). That process, which is still organised around the binary opposition
man–woman set out by Lacan in the diagram and formulae of sexuation,[56]
may serve to subvert stereotypical positions and shift us from culturally
dominant images of femininity, but it still mobilises potent cultural images
of women as objects of fascination when viewed from within the coordinates
of male fantasy. Psychoanalysis can be a space to examine things that have
been turned into trauma, and then to turn them into something other. As
Žižek has it, 'the trauma has no existence of its own prior to symbolization;
it remains an anamorphic entity that gains its consistency only in retrospect,
viewed from within a symbolic horizon',[57] and psychoanalysis is a way of
looking awry at this object, coming face to face with it in the analysis, and
being able to shift positions in relation to it.

THE OBJECT OF ANALYSIS

Lacanian psychoanalysis has a distinctive view of symptoms, diagnosis and
'clinical structure' that opens up the domain of clinical practice to social
space, and it can locate personal pathology in a broader historical process
of exploitation and alienation. However, these analytic specifications of
order and disorder also place certain limits on the extent to which there can
ever be full demystification of the ideological forms that hold us in check.
When Žižek draws upon descriptions of the psychoanalysis of individual
subjects as his model for social critique, these limits become ever more
apparent.

The fun is over!

The problematic paradoxical relation to language we all experience is
exactly what may bring someone to an analyst one day. The particular way
we entered any language structures how we will experience distress, and
psychoanalysis as a 'talking cure' also takes place as a problematic
paradoxical relation to an other, the analyst, within our own language.
This means that the formulation of what the 'problem' might be is, from
the beginning, framed by a particular kind of relation to an other. What we
call an analytic 'symptom', then, is something that appears under transference. The peculiarity of the analytic relationship is reason enough, then, for

many Lacanians to be suspicious of the wider 'application' of the theory to those not actually in analysis.[58]

The analyst wants to know not only what the focus of the analysis might be but also why the problem has emerged now as a 'symptom' that is called into question. This symptom is not viewed as if it were an expression of an organic disease to be treated as such, or to be traced to an underlying condition that can be cleared up so that the discomfort will disappear. The question early in the analysis is not so much what work the symptom does and how it causes so much suffering to the subject, this human subject, as why it is *failing* to work. The injunction to 'enjoy your symptom'[59] is something that has broken down when the subject appears as analysand in the consulting room, and Žižek's formulation of this enjoyment opens a question about the aim of analysis in Lacan's later work, in which 'identification with the symptom' as the end of analysis might be thought of in the political domain through procedures of 'overidentification'. We all love our symptoms so much that something must be going wrong for us to be brought to the point where we might be tempted to take them in for repair, and we may want them repaired so they can carry on performing their function for us. The presentation of the symptom to an analyst opens up the possibility for analysis, but the demand for analysis then has to be powerful enough to take analysands to the point where they are willing to ask what this symptom means to them, and willing to risk giving it up.

This brings us face-to-face both with how we differ from others – how others intrude on our enjoyment – and with those fantasies we may cling to, fantasies in which certain categories of people have stolen our enjoyment from us. Jacques-Alain Miller's discussion of the 'theft of enjoyment' that Žižek takes up and runs with to account for ethnic rivalries in Yugoslavia, for example, is situated first in the clinic.[60] The problematic of 'difference' that is posed here raises questions about new forms of 'segregation' Lacan drew attention to,[61] and about the rise of racism and its grip on subjects in the West. These are questions that have not been elaborated in as much detail in Lacanian clinical practice as that of 'sexuation', and what is striking about Žižek's use of the notion of 'theft of enjoyment' is that the way it is formulated does not serve to disturb standard Lacanian clinical categories. Here is a first indication that while he is keen to draw Lacanian concepts from the realm of individual analysis into the social sphere, he is not willing to work through the impact of social changes on the project of psychoanalysis as a clinical practice. Clinical practice is concerned with how analysands appear and disappear one-by-one, each marked by their own entry point and trajectory through the symbolic.

The first stages of an analysis – in the 'preliminary meetings'[62] – revolve around the question of clinical structure. One of the most important decisions a Lacanian psychoanalyst must make is whether this person who turns up for help is in a state to unravel who they are, or whether it is wiser to assist them in weaving more closely together their sense of self as a place in the symbolic. Lacanians make a categorical distinction for analytic purposes between neurotic structure, which is characterised by repression as the main mode of defence, and two other structures – 'perverse' and 'psychotic' – much less common in psychoanalysis. Žižek elaborates 'perversion' – a structure characterised by 'disavowal' of the marks of difference between men and women – in quite orthodox Lacanian terms as *père-version*, a 'version of the father', but he then uses this motif to point to the presence of 'the perverse figure of the Father-of-Enjoyment' as always operative as an underside of the subjective effect of the Oedipal father, and this is where the super-egoic imperative to 'enjoy' binds us to the law.[63] The pervert 'simply takes for granted that his activity serves the enjoyment of the Other. The psychotic, on the other hand, is himself the object of the Other's enjoyment.'[64] While perverse structure is underpinned by the defence of disavowal and the formation of a fetish to stand in the place of what has been disavowed, psychotic structure is initiated by the most extreme early defence of 'foreclosure', in which what has been foreclosed becomes unthinkable and experienced as returning in the real – in hallucinations for example.

Because the extreme early defence of foreclosure is a dramatic refusal to be of the symbolic order, certain fundamental signifiers that operate to mediate between self and others are not present, and there are thus no 'quilting points' – *points de capiton* – to hold words to concepts, signifiers to signifieds. These *points de capiton* are the anchoring points that then permit relatively free movement through the symbolic, and then make 'free association' in analysis such a useful way of revealing repression.[65] In the absence of such anchoring points a delusory system may be developed, quite successfully perhaps, in order for the subject to function in the absence of those fundamental signifiers that usually anchor the subject in the symbolic.[66] The analyst attends to those aspects of the speech of the analysand where things seem a little too sure-set, a little too certain, and to those parts of speech that seem marked by imaginary phenomena of narcissistic mirroring and rivalry; where it seems the imaginary is the register organising the world of the subject rather than the symbolic. If the system they have constructed fails to function, the analytic work with someone with psychotic structure is to help them elaborate and develop that system. To undermine or unravel the way they hold their everyday reality in place would be disastrous. The decision as to how to proceed with someone characterised by psychotic structure is not made quickly or completely, and Lacanians will spend the first months, maybe many months, talking face-to-face with an analysand.[67] The analyst does not invite someone to move onto the couch, to move into that rather disturbing position of speaking to someone who you cannot see, and who does not respond according to the rules of everyday conversation, without being fairly sure that this disturbance will be productive.

Big knows

The analyst behind the couch is, as Žižek points out, a kind of detective, but this detective does not catch the murderer out and solve a case by clearing away deceit to arrive at the truth. Rather, she or he is conjured into place by the murderer as a 'subject supposed to know' – the Lacanian characterisation of transference – and it is the murderer who produces the truth for this supposed subject by virtue of their very attempts to cover it up. So, the analysand is speaking to the analyst under transference, with assumptions and expectations that are based on past relationships which organise what they say. The analysand has little else to go on, for they do not know who the analyst really is, and so the transference relationship reveals something of their relation to others. In psychoanalysis transference is a love relationship, and for Lacanians that relationship is to knowledge, as a love of knowledge. The signs of transference, then, are those points when the analysand speaks to the other, the analyst, as someone who knows something; the analysand supposes a subject who knows. It is important that the analyst keeps that space open and indeterminate, because the analyst is concerned with what the analysand *supposes*.

This is why interpretations should not seem to offer knowledge, and so close down the relationship so that it is defined by what the analyst actually knows. Lacanians do not, as a rule, make interpretations of the transference. The analyst does make comments and allusions about the transference relationship, but these are usually ambiguous in order to open up possibilities for different positions to emerge. The ending of a session at a point that has not been determined in advance is one way of making an interpretation that marks something in a way that is enigmatic.

The seemingly trivial details scattered into the speech of the analysand in their 'free association' to the analyst will function as clues, but it is only when they function in this way as clues for the analysand as well that they will be an occasion for them to speak the truth; '*the detective* [Žižek's exemplar of the Lacanian psychoanalyst here], *solely by means of his presence, guarantees that all these details will retroactively acquire meaning*. In other words, his "omniscience" is an effect of *transference*'.[68] And the 'trauma' will come to be seen by the analysand 'anamorphically'

– only from their own particular position as subject – and 'retroactively', when they can make sense of it as appearing at the scene of the crime.

Although Lacanians expect to find neurotic, perverse and psychotic traits in everyone, there is not the same notion of a continuum of psychotic experience that there is in some other traditions of psychoanalysis.[69] But neither is there a notion of 'normal' structure, for the entry into the symbolic is always problematic, and it always calls for some measure of defence.[70] These different modes of defence are crucial for Lacanians precisely because it is the entry into the symbolic order that constitutes the unconscious as a kind of underside of language, as the system of gaps in our speech.[71] When we are articulated by language as subjects with neurotic structure, our existence is also organised by questions about what our place in language is. The diagnosis homes in on those questions and the way they are articulated in analysis so that the analyst can make some finer-grain distinctions that will help them gauge how the analysis may progress.

Lacan uses the classical Freudian distinction between obsessional neurosis and hysteria.[72] Obsessional neurosis, which is more stereotypically masculine, revolves around questions of existence and death, and guilt. The questions 'Why am I here, and by what right?' can be worried away at, with possible answers and doubts set up that can sometimes make the analysis difficult because they are so closed in together on themselves, like a labyrinth in which analysand and analyst lose themselves. It is here that the 'hard-boiled detective gets mixed up in a course of events that he is unable to dominate',[73] and this type of detective is the one who will fail as an analyst. Žižek points out that this type of detective novel is written in the first person, and it often begins when the narrator recounts how he was first hooked by a series of deceptive lures. It is this hard-boiled detective who comes to grief in what French critics were to categorise as *film noir* at the hands of the *femme fatale*.

Hysteria, which is more stereotypically feminine, is organised around the question of sex and gender, and accusation. 'What is a woman, and what does a woman want?', for example, are questions about the nature of desire, sexual identity and what the other wants; and these are questions that bring us closer to the kinds of questions the analysand asks of the self and other in analysis. It is here that the analyst as 'detective' risks an entanglement in the complaints and claims of the analysand. Žižek argues that, in contrast to the figure of the 'hard-boiled' detective, the psychoanalyst is more like a 'classical detective', and in this genre that detective–analyst figure is not the narrator. Rather, there is an external vantage point from which the story is told, either as if it were by someone omniscient or as if it were by a companion – like Dr Watson in the Sherlock Holmes novels – as 'the person *for whom* the detective is a "subject supposed to know" by another subject'.[74] Copjec, whose analyses of film genres and popular culture have run parallel to Žižek's, gives the example of an episode from *Columbo* in which the guilty suspect – the analysand is indexed here as the guilty suspect – fails to entangle the detective in their game, or to elicit information about the analyst's relations with women; so when Columbo is asked what his wife's name is so that an autograph can be written for her, Columbo replies 'Mrs Columbo'.[75]

Who wants what?

In much of his writing Žižek uses film to illustrate psychoanalytic and philosophical concepts.[76] *Looking Awry* is one good, accessible example, but the translation between clinical categories – which is where Žižek has an edge on much 'Lacanian' cultural, literary and film theory – and popular culture also poses a big question: Is Žižek's 'analysis' of artefacts from popular culture a mere illustration of what we could expect to do for ourselves on the couch, or is it an analysis of the symbolic space we each traverse in our own particular idiosyncratic ways? We can address this question in two ways.

First, for all of the Hegelian reflexive gloss on the way the 'observer is already included, inscribed in the observed scene' when we gaze at the object that can only be seen 'anamorphically', from a particular position,[77] it is not at all certain that we are all included in the same way. There is always, for all of us perhaps, a sense that an object of desire has been lost, an object that may be located somewhere in an other, and this object – Lacan's *objet petit a* – is what we see in an other when we fall in love. But is this object that fascinates us in someone also seen by others? For Lacan, no. But, by contrast, take, for example, Žižek's contention that there is such a little object of fascination for an observer that draws them to Cindy Crawford but not to Claudia Schiffer. Even when he qualifies his claim by locating it for members of a particular culture, he does not solve the problem of translating between how it might operate for one particular individual and how it is assumed to operate within a culture: 'For Americans, at least, there is something all too cold in Claudia Schiffer's perfection: it is somehow easier to fall in love with Cindy Crawford because of her very small imperfection (the famous tiny mole near her lip – her *objet petit a*).'[78] What does it mean here to say that it is 'her' *objet petit a*, if that object is supposed to be something only visible from a particular position for a particular observer attracted to her?

The second way into the question is to note that there is evidently a mismatch between the uptake of Lacanian ideas as a resource for cultural political critique and the use of Lacanian concepts in clinical practice. In

Slovenia, for example, it may well be the case that 'the Lacanian movement was always on the side of the opposition',[79] but psychotherapists there still seem only to see 'Lacanian oriented theoreticians' as having 'played an important role in popularizing psychoanalytic concepts', only relevant to 'philosophy and the critique of ideology and art', as opposed to those practising clinically.[80] One might read this separation of personal self-understanding – the classical project of psychotherapy – from the relentless deconstruction of the self and ideology critique that Žižek engages in as itself symptomatic of a culture that separates individual from social change; as further evidence that 'psychoanalytic therapy is necessary only where it is not possible, and possible only where it is no longer necessary'.[81] This rather gloomy reading of the problem would mean that Lacanian psychoanalysis with individuals must always be consigned to the realm of a therapy that adjusted people to society. It would then not even be worth asking a key question for practice: whether Lacanian psychoanalysts may actually be doing ideology critique without knowing it;[82] there would be no way of linking the direction of the treatment with any collective project of social change. There is a paradox here, in that the grandiose claims that Žižek makes for Lacanian theory actually serve to obscure what is most radical about Lacanian clinical practice.

CLINIC OF THE WORLD

The Lacanian development of psychoanalysis as a clinical practice has wide-ranging consequences for how we think about treatment and where it leads, for interpretation and what it aims at, and for the position of the analyst in relation to the end-point of the work. Radical though it is, Žižek's characterisation of that end-point in some eruption of the truth of the subject in a 'psychoanalytic act' is so overblown as to be useless as a model of social change, as we shall see. In this respect, Žižek is not at all a 'Lacanian analyst'.

Direction of the treatment

The analyst does not guide the analysand, but does guide the direction of the treatment.[83] This is why the analyst needs a theoretical framework to make sense of how someone might take to the analytic work, or not. In the case of psychotic structure, the direction of the treatment will be towards the elaboration of a sense of self and symbolic reality, a work of construction rather than deconstruction. In the case of perverse structure one would not expect to find a question posed by the subject, because they will have installed a fetish of some kind through which they organise their enjoyment; for that reason a Lacanian does not expect someone of this kind – a subject

who knows well enough what they want and knows what the other wants
– to demand analysis.

In analytic work with those showing neurotic suffering around their
symptom it is important not to close down what has started to open up. To
guide the direction of the treatment is not to impose agendas or to suggest
how the work should be done, but to encourage a questioning and self-
questioning. The interventions of the analyst point to something beyond
what is said, to the fact that there is something 'unconscious', that
analysands do not have complete control over their words. The analysand
will be invited to follow the Freudian rule of 'free association' in order to
bring to light the role of the unconscious. As we have noted, an obsessional
strategy to avoid this rule would be to bring the analyst into the labyrinth
of choices and doubts that hold things in place. So here the analyst will be
contributing the kinds of questions and ambiguous comments that throw
this strategy off track. These interventions are designed to bring about a
'hystericisation' of the subject so that the direction of the treatment is then
all the more the direction of the analysand towards their truth. But the
'unconscious' can only be 'half-said' as a 'language structure' and so these
glimmering moments are then covered over again.[84] These moments in
Lacan's work, when the unconscious is characterised by Lacan as the
'emerging of a certain function of the signifier',[85] are an opening for Žižek
to treat psychoanalysis as a form of enquiry concerned with the operations
of discourse, with what Lacan analysed as 'the discourse of the
unconscious'.

It certainly seems at moments in Lacan's writing as if there is enough
warrant for us to link the bonds between individuals with what Lacan
describes as 'social bonds'. For Lacan, these social bonds operate in four
possible ways, in four discourses. To take the first two discourses: 'It is
when the master signifier is at a certain place that I speak about the
discourse of the Master; when a certain knowledge also occupies it, I
speak of that of the University.'[86] The spectre of the Hegelian master–slave
dialectic hangs over this description of discourse, and while it is most
clearly at work structuring the relation between the agent and other in the
discourse of the master – a relation of command and subservience – it is
still at work in the discourse of the university, which is why Lacanians try
to avoid this discourse and the way it turns analysis into a form of
education.[87] To move on to Lacan's next two discourses, the 'hystericisation' of the analysand in analysis means that 'when the subject in its
division, fundamental for the unconscious, is in place there, I speak about
the discourse of the Hysteric, and finally when *surplus enjoying* occupies
it, I speak about the discourse of the Analyst'.[88] This surplus enjoyment is
what is designated as the *objet petit a*, and then it does make sense for Žižek

to treat hysteria not as a function of particular individuals accusing others, but as 'always already a structure of discourse, in other words, a certain structuring of the social bond',[89] and for him to urge the 'critical intellectual' to occupy the position of *objet petit a* in the discourse of the analyst, a discourse which keeps things open for question.[90]

The analysand is the one who is speaking most of the time, the one who is analysing, and so the role of interpretation is to open the possibilities for the analysand to interpret. Again, there is a crucial question of the role of discourse here, and this has consequences for the position that the analyst adopts. The discourse of the master and the discourse of the university turn the analyst into someone who actually does know what the truth is that will be spoken by the analysand. This is precisely what Lacan noticed his colleagues in the Anglo-American tradition of psychoanalysis in the IPA resorting to. As Žižek points out, when the analysts start to believe that they can educate their analysands something very dodgy is happening. 'The "repressed" truth of this discourse is that behind the semblance of neutral "knowledge" that we try to impart to the other, we can always locate the gesture of the master.'[91] There is also a warning here, of course, against the lure of the 'metalanguage', the illusion that there is some superior vantage point, outside or beyond the network of relationships that make up the social, from which neutral judgement can be given. Žižek's particular attentiveness to this problem of the 'metalanguage', also formulated by Lacan as 'there is no Other of the Other',[92] is derived primarily from Hegel, and it is this 'reflexive determination' of theoretical judgment that makes Lacan's account of anamorphosis – a gaze on the object in which we are always necessarily included, invested – so attractive to him.

Against the discourse of the master and the discourse of the university, the relationship between analyst and analysand is itself marked by a kind of 'deadlock' in which the analyst provokes the analysand to question their part in the things they think about obsessively, or complain about as if they were a 'beautiful soul' independent of the disorder around them. The analyst positions themselves as the semblance of *objet petit a*, in the discourse of the analyst, while the hystericised analysand addresses their complaints to the analyst as master when they speak from within the discourse of the hysteric. It is then that the analysand – as divided subject, divided between the range of consciously apprehended statements about who they are and the unconscious truth of their own position which is usually repressed – is able to speak from the unconscious. The division opens up a space for the true 'subject of the enunciation' to be heard from within, and through and against the 'subject of the statement'. This is why Žižek's use of the distinction between the subject of the statement and the subject of the enunciation is so insidious when he applies it to the difference between Judaism and Christianity. The argument that one should be a Jew with respect to the contents of belief 'while retaining the Christian position of enunciation'[93] is not really so much of a balance between Judaism and Christianity as a sure judgement about what counts as the truth; it is the subject of the enunciation, which is usually hidden from view, that is privileged in Žižek's own statements – Christianity as the truth.

The analyst needs a theoretical framework not only to guide the direction of the treatment but also to know what place they have in it, and they need to ensure that it is the truth of the analysand that emerges and not merely their own knowledge. Entry into the symbolic brings about the sense that there is some access to power, perhaps power that has been lost, and that this is a power that is located in the symbolic around the phallus as the fantasy point of power, and so the analyst needs to be aware of the temptation to 'understand' exactly what the analysand is saying, which would mean getting drawn into the line of the imaginary. The analyst needs to notice how they are positioned by the analysand in the symbolic, to notice who the analysand is speaking to, transferentially speaking, and where they are speaking from. And the analyst needs to know how they will at points stand in the position of the lost object – *objet petit a* – for the analysand. For Lacan, desire is desire of the other,[94] but there are forms of mutual recognition in the analytic encounter that can lead to things getting stuck, or to a positive relationship flipping into a negative one. The analyst needs to shift the focus of recognition from imaginary mirror-like relations of identification or rivalry – which are the kinds of relations that face-to-face communication encourages – onto the broader questions of recognition of the other in the symbolic realm. The analysts are often asking themselves whether the chains of signifiers in analysis are running along the line of the imaginary or are opening the analysand into the symbolic.

The 'direction of the treatment' opens up the unconscious, gives space to truth to be said, albeit half-said, and perhaps it also leads to something more dramatic. But then, what is the end of analysis?[95] To answer this question with a neat formulation would close up the specific answers that each analysand may come to articulate. And a clear idea about what must transpire at the end of analysis, as an 'act' of some kind, drives Žižek's attempt to make psychoanalysis into a model for radical political action.

Ending with a bang

It is possible to specify two aspects of the end of analysis in very general terms. The first would concern the relation to the *objet petit a* anamorphically viewed by us, as something that fascinates us and operates as 'cause' of our desire. Instead of trying to find the one substantial thing that will give us power – a phallus – or tracking down that object of desire that we sense we lost, we discover how our particular fantasy of power and the nature of our object were constructed for us and by us. Žižek uses the motif of *objet petit a* to account for the way certain political communities are held in thrall by something that is really only important to them because it is viewed from a particular position, something that others cannot fathom as attractive in any way. The claim then follows that if they were able to give this object up – if Serbia were able to give up Kosovo as its fantasy object, for example – then they too would be free. This works as a fairly neat approximation of the Marxist dictum that 'any nation that oppresses another forges its own chains',[96] but it also draws attention to a crucial fantasy element and a prescription for some psychical working through, alongside a simple demand for 'troops out'.

The second specification concerns language. In analysis the analysand is confronted with the nature of language as the system of differences that makes them who they are, and so they also learn something about what language is. Lacan at one point formulates the desire of the analyst as 'a desire to obtain absolute difference',[97] and this involves more than bringing the analysand to the point where they become something like a pure Saussurean,[98] able to desubstantialise those things that have been reified so that they have come to operate for them as taken-for-granted things that constrain and inhibit them. The five-fold consequence of this attainment of absolute difference on the part of the analysand is: the understanding that there is no metalanguage, that there is no Other of the Other, that there is no sexual relationship, that the big Other does not exist – glossed by Žižek as 'the experience of the death of God'[99] – and that the analyst, installed by the analysand as subject supposed to know, can now be desupposed, dropped as semblance of *objet petit a*.

Žižek delights in the most extreme formulations of what the end of analysis might entail, with his favourite descriptions, derived from Lacan's writing, including 'traversing' or going through the fantasy, 'identifying' with the symptom, and facing 'subjective destitution'. It does seem as if the more bizarre and unappealing formulations are the ones that transfix him and operate as moral injunctions. And of all of these, the most problematic is the one he also uses as a model of social change. This is the psychoanalytic 'act' that changes the symbolic coordinates of a subject's life – something which can only be understood after the event, 'retroactively'. The retroactive making of sense then functions for Žižek as a further warrant for a rather intuitivist and spontaneist view of human agency, something which also bedevils his politics. Lacan's discussion of Antigone in his seminar on ethics[100] is mined many times by Žižek, and Antigone's decision to go against the state to bury her brother and bear the consequences of being buried alive is treated as if it were a moral example.

For Žižek, it is not at all surprising that Antigone, as such a powerful figure, is a woman who refuses to give ground relative to her desire. Lacan had argued that 'the only thing of which one can be guilty is of having given ground relative to one's desire',[101] and Žižek then seems to treat Antigone as an ethical example to be followed by others, interpreting having 'given ground' as not remaining true to desire. There is an extraordinary fascination in Žižek's writing with the figure of the woman as the exemplary subject of a true psychoanalytic act. The idealisation of woman as the prototypical ethical subject is also a way of retrieving Freud's claim that a woman's trajectory through the Oedipus complex means that she will have a weaker super-ego, that she will perhaps get by without such an agency. This retrieval and reversal of a minus to a plus appears in statements of the kind that 'women's lack of superego bears witness to their ethics',[101] and a fantasy of woman at least as potent as that of the Lady in courtly love is mobilised: 'Women don't need a superego, since they have no guilt on which the superego can parasitize – since, that is, they are far less prone to compromise their desire.'[102]

This is no mere lapse into an admiring gaze on the figure of Antigone as if she were an 'example' rather than, as she was for Lacan, an 'image' that was more a warning about transgression than an advertisement for ethical action.[103] In other places, Žižek goes further: perhaps Antigone is not really the most extreme and laudable example at all, and a better bet might be Medea. As an 'anti-Antigone', Medea kills those closest to her as an act of vengeance which throws her into the 'void of self-relating negativity', into the Hegelian 'negation of the negation' that Žižek reads as 'subjectivity itself'. Here, he concludes, there are 'two versions of femininity': while Antigone still stands for 'particular family roots against the universality of the public space of State Power',[104] he claims that Medea, on the contrary, 'out-universalizes Power itself'.[105] But why stop there? There are other more recent examples of women compounding their abject wretchedness – Žižek's horrified admiration of Sethe's 'act', the murder of her child which returns to haunt her, in Toni Morrison's *Beloved*, is one more case in point[106] – and these are recruited by Žižek as examples and lessons about what ethics is.

There are two clusters of problems here. The first is in the link between violence and femininity in these representations of the psychoanalytic act. The seam of imagery that Žižek works on in *Metastases of Enjoyment* concerning women as the traumatic 'cause' that disturbs the male subject, and as the subject with no super-ego who has some direct access to enjoyment, is one that runs under the surface of Lacanian psychoanalysis from the early days in the 1930s, when Lacan flirted with the surrealists.[107]

It is here that some of the most retrograde images of woman as figure of 'convulsive beauty' were mobilised, and now they are resurrected, put to work by Žižek.

The second cluster of problems is to do with the representations of psychoanalysis itself. The imagery of utter abjection is of individual subjects with no way out. Needless to say, this is not a terribly good advertisement for psychoanalysis, even if we are trying to stop it being assimilated to the images of stirring insight and happy outcomes popularised by many Hollywood films. Readings of psychoanalysis in film are what Žižek does so well in *Looking Awry*, but he is conveniently sidestepping the explicit location of these discussions about the 'psycho-analytic act' in psychoanalysis. Not only does he rip this notion out of a particular clinical domain in order to apply it to cultural and political domains, he also neglects to point out that this 'act' which may occur at the end of analysis is something that Lacan in his Seminar on this question describes as 'something belonging to the elective moment when psycho-analysand passes to psychoanalyst'.[108]

There is a significant difference between Lacan's own references to the 'act' and Žižek's. When Lacan describes an act in *Seminar XI*, it is to characterise something that marks out human activity as such and to draw attention to the real; 'an act, a true act, always has an element of structure, by the fact of concerning a real that is not self-evidently caught up in it'.[109] There is then a shift of emphasis that occurs in the work of the Millerians, and which picks up on Lacan's comments about the act in *Seminar XV*. There is an attention to the act as something that goes beyond analysand and analyst, and which still includes the moment by which an analyst is formed; 'This anticipated conclusion touches the real and is founded on a point of inexistence in the Other.'[110] The second shift, much more dramatic, is where Žižek turns this moment into something that is the model of proper political action; this makes the act into something that seems to combine aspects of Lacan's description of a psychotic '*passage à l'acte*', in which the subject cares nothing for the Other, and a hysterical 'acting out', which is staged for the Other. Lacan's seminars, addressed to psychoanalysts, are focused on clinical questions and clinical training, and the reading off from his writing into other spheres requires something a little less hasty and less dramatic than what we find in Žižek.

Žižek's sedimentation of psychoanalytic descriptions of sexual difference as immutable fixed points of impossibility between men and women, his slide from the level of the individual to the social, with prescription sub-stituting for critique, and his appeal to a certain reading of psychoanalytic change as the model for social transformation, have profound political consequences. It would, however, be a mistake to see these consequences as only flowing from psychoanalytic theory or a philosophical position. We know already from his history of political activity in Slovenia that motifs from Freud and Hegel are always used somewhat cynically by Žižek, and with that in mind we turn in the next chapter to the political choices and positions that he has adopted.

4
Politics – Repeating Marx

Why does Žižek tell us that 'Deep down I am very conservative; I just play at this subversive stuff',[1] and what are the consequences of his gloomy prognosis that 'a new Dark Age is descending on the human race'?[2] Why is it still so tempting to read his engagement with revolutionary socialist writers as a revindication of their ideas, and an indication that a healthy dose of Hegel and Lacan will enable us to revive Marxism?[3] Three deeply contradictory motifs in Žižek's writing often mislead his readers[4] and actually indicate that he is repeating Marx only within certain strict limits; the political coordinates he uses to guide his use of philosophy and psychoanalysis are quite pragmatic and opportunist. Žižek has been attractive to those working in the Marxist tradition, but for different reasons depending on the precise political projects of those reading him.

The first motif concerns his elaboration, from within the field of Marxist debates in the late 1970s and early 1980s, of a theory of ideology. Here Žižek struck a chord with 'post-Marxists' because he threw old certainties about class struggle into question and he seemed to take Left debates forward around the analysis of subjectivity as an ideological process. This analysis is the main burden of *The Sublime Object of Ideology*, Žižek's first book in English, published in the Laclau–Mouffe series of post-Marxist books reworking the Left project in terms of 'radical and plural democracy'. Ernesto Laclau and Chantal Mouffe had already been fairly influential in the intellectual milieu around the Communist Party of Great Britain, and their 1985 book *Hegemony and Socialist Strategy*[5] – which Žižek was initially very enthusiastic about[6] – had been a contributory factor in the disintegration of the remnants of the old party apparatus in Britain in the 1980s as it tried to escape its history of support for the Soviet Union, and instead lurched towards 'Eurocommunist' theories of hegemony (derived from the Italian Marxist Antonio Gramsci) to search for liberal pluralist alliances between 'progressive' representatives of Capital and Labour.[7]

Laclau's Preface to Žižek's book draws attention to two main features of 'the Slovene Lacanian School'; one being the use of Hegel as a reference point to read classical philosophical texts (which we have examined in some detail in Chapter 2), and the other being an account of ideology underpinned by fantasy as 'an imaginary scenario concealing the fundamental split or "antagonism" around which the social field is structured'[8] (which is where Lacan was brought into the equation). It was precisely the nature and depth of this 'antagonism' that was to explode the alliance forged between the Laclau–Mouffe group and Žižek. *The Sublime Object of Ideology* is still Žižek's best book, and his reading of Marx and Freud on commodities and dreams outlines an approach to ideological fantasy that is descriptively rich for those working in cultural studies or film theory. Whether it is politically useful is another matter, for there is no way out of the forms of ideology Žižek describes.[9]

The second motif is Žižek's broader appeal to Marxism, and his attempt to retrieve something radical in the history of Marxist thought from the debris of East European Stalinism. Here Žižek has been more appealing to those attempting to revive revolutionary Marxism around, for example, the journal *Historical Materialism*.[10] A lengthy rumination on these themes is to be found in 'Lenin's Choice', an 'afterword' to *Revolution at the Gates*, which brings together a selection of Lenin's writings from 1917. A version of the afterword had already circulated on the internet as 'Repeating Lenin',[11] and long sections of the article – around 5,000 words' worth – also appeared in a little book on the World Trade Centre attacks, *Welcome to the Desert of the Real!*[12] Žižek certainly likes to repeat himself, but the sense in which Marxism in general and Lenin in particular were to be 'repeated' is decidedly ambiguous.

Žižek declares that 'Lenin's legacy, to be reinvented today, is the politics of truth',[13] and, in a faithful repetition of his Lacanian-derived notion of antagonism around which the social field is structured alongside a Hegelian fusion of the universal and the particular, he refuses to abandon either universal truth or a partisan position. Rather, 'the *universal* truth of a concrete situation can be articulated only from a thoroughly *partisan* position; truth is, by definition, one-sided'.[14] This means that he has to oppose explicitly Lenin's self-styled 'materialist' claim that there are objects in the world outside consciousness, on the grounds that it was 'secretly idealist'.[15] But the break from Lenin is actually far more wide-ranging than that. Žižek claims elsewhere that he is 'careful to speak about not repeating Lenin';[16] after finding himself in a 'total deadlock' after World War I broke out, Žižek argues, 'Lenin had to think about how to reinvent a radical, revolutionary politics in this situation of total breakdown.'[17] What is needed now, in contrast to 'the old Marxist choice between private property and nationalization', is 'a complete reinvention of the political'.[18] The motif of 'repetition', then, is something that signals something other than Marxism.

The third motif concerns Žižek's characterisation of different forms of political organisation, where it might be possible to put Hegelian and Lacanian concepts to work, and he provides a handy sketch of how politics might be understood. Here Žižek is less appealing to revolutionary Marxists because he explicitly distances himself from Marxism as such, and he is also at odds with his old post-Marxist comrades because he seems to be swerving too far to some kind of non-Marxist ultra-leftism (the kind of ultra-leftism that can all too easily swing over to the right). Žižek's outline of six forms of politics – in which five of the options are but attempts to 'disavow' or 'foreclose' the 'proper logic of political antagonism'[19] – not only neatly displays Žižek's own political universe, but also makes explicit what he wants to avoid and what he hopes to aim for. He sets himself against the options of *parapolitics*, which reformulates antagonism as a depoliticised competition in which we play by the rules of the game; *post-politics*, that operates on a model of negotiation and incorporation of different strategic interests; *arche-politics*, operating on a quasi-medical model of enclosed organic community; and *ultrapolitics*, as a false radical-isation which reduces conflict to warfare between the community and enemies. The fifth option to be avoided is utopian socialist *metapolitics*, in which Marxism figures as an attempt to recognise political conflict but only as a 'shadow theatre' for economic processes.[20]

Only *politics proper*, which 'appeared for the first time in ancient Greece',[21] is able to realise his Hegelian dream of 'the inherent power of negativity'.[22] The problem is that, much as with ideology as such throughout his work, Žižek cannot avoid the first five options he inveighs against. And, just like the spectre of Marx he so often conjures with, he is haunted by the traces of the five forms of politics he claims to reject, as we shall see. If we do still take Marxism seriously as the theory and practice of collective struggle against contemporary capitalism, then Žižek turns out to be more of a liability than an asset to that political project.

AGAINST THE RULES OF THE GAME

Žižek shares with Marxists a profound ambivalence toward 'democracy', and this ambivalence can too easily be read as a sign to his readers that he too is a Marxist. Democracy is a signifier that both confirms present-day arrangements and offers the promise of something better than what exists today. But as Žižek steers a course between these different meanings of the term, and the kinds of politics that sabotage or succour democracy, he picks up some ideas that sit very uneasily with Marxism.

Parapolitics: democracy as ideology

On the one hand, democracy is often conflated in the popular imagination and academic commentary with the kind of rule exercised in capitalist society, and so to be in favour of democracy is to endorse politics in bourgeois ideology, in which it seems as if individuals freely choose their rulers in a collective decision-making process. This conflation might then be warrant enough for Marxists to refuse these rules of the game, and to refuse the lures of 'democracy', perhaps insisting that the dictatorship of the proletariat and the construction of socialist society will entail something qualitatively different. Sometimes Žižek seems drawn to this suspicion of 'democracy', even if he qualifies his hostility to it – in a little phrase that appears as if it were inserted later between hyphens – as a refusal of 'the way this term is used today': 'its minimal definition is the unconditional adherence to a certain set of formal rules which guarantee that antagonisms are fully absorbed into the agonistic game'.[23]

This adherence to the rules of the game is precisely the predicament we face in current modern forms of 'parapolitics', and Žižek uses that term to characterise forms of rule that depoliticise the social, as well as the various formal procedures set out by political theorists such as Jürgen Habermas and John Rawls that legitimise current arrangements through 'clear rules to be obeyed so that the agonistic procedure of litigation does not explode into politics proper'.[24] Žižek's account of ideology operates effectively as a form of Marxist critique when it is applied to the depoliticised subjectivity in thrall to some 'sublime object' in modern bourgeois society, whether it is directly and explicitly capitalist or was mediated by Stalinist bureaucratic rule in the former Yugoslavia. Žižek is following Lacan's account of sublimation here, in which sublimation is precisely the *process* by which we invest an object that attaches us to something, perhaps to 'democracy' itself, as a 'sublime object: a positive, material object elevated to the status of the impossible Thing'.[25] Here he also writes as a Marxist of some kind against democratic 'parapolitics'.

A most potent 'sublime object of ideology' is surely the elevation of democracy itself to some exalted position, so that it assumes such inexplicable and incomprehensible importance that it cannot be criticised. Under contemporary Western capitalism there is a corresponding elevation of the image of the individual subject as the thing prized by democracy, as free-thinking and able to choose political representatives uncontaminated by ideology. Žižek fleshes out the ideological fantasy that holds bourgeois ideology and individuals together in a closed reciprocal relationship so that any real political alternative is unthinkable. His theoretical reference points for this account of ideology are Lacan and the critical reflection on the limitations of the use of Lacan to specify the hold of ideology on individual subjects within 'Ideological State Apparatuses', outlined by Louis Althusser.[26] Like Laclau and Mouffe, Žižek's theoretical orientation is within the broad domain of 'post-Althusserian' theory, and this is one reason why Laclau and Mouffe initially found Žižek's critique and reworking of the Althusserian account so attractive.

Althusser's description of the way ideology 'interpellates' an individual – hooks a subject into position so that they recognise themselves in the categories of subjectivity structured into the ideological system – begs a question: What is there already as subject enough to be hooked? Žižek's answer is to say that before the subject is interpellated it has already been constituted in its very process of formation as a divided subject in relation to the *objet petit a*, and this object cause of desire – which becomes the sublime object of ideology – holds the subject in place in fantasy. This fantasy, for Lacan, is not the opposite of 'reality', but instead suffuses and shapes the very stuff of social relations, symbolic and imaginary. Ideology which holds us in thrall to the *objet petit a* is no mere illusion which can be dispelled by a good dose of reality testing, or of facts about the world given to us by Marxist analysis; far from offering us a point of escape, ideology offers us 'the social reality itself as an escape from some traumatic, real kernel'.[27]

The symbolic coordinates of fantasy are therefore at work well before we assume a position in ideology through interpellation, and those symbolic coordinates explain why the interpellation succeeds. Much of Žižek's description of the tightly-structured ideological apparatus that operates as a kind of machinery for the formation of subject positions before any particular individual comes to recognise themselves in it seems to apply better to Eastern Europe than to life under Western European and US capitalism, for which he has since had to augment his account. One might hazard a guess that his theoretical itinerary, from Yugoslavia through Austria and Germany to French Marxism and psychoanalysis, was a search for a space away from the grip of bureaucracy, but this theoretical terminus actually served more to confirm that this will always be the way things are; Ideological State Apparatuses could be detected by him under the surface in capitalist society because they were so overtly in place under actually existing Stalinism. Once this paradigm is adopted there seems to be only one way out, which is through approaching the real (and Žižek often advertises this option in his writings on the 'act'); and one way deeper in, in which we might disrupt the hold of ideology by taking it at its word through an enthusiastically knowing embrace of it in practices like 'over-identification'. But Žižek's problem is that the way out of those rules of the game is very risky and only temporary, and the idea that we should embrace ideology is already well-recuperated as a popular strategy in the games of cynical reason that have mutated out of modern parapolitics.[28]

There is a telling paradox at work in Žižek's hostility to the rules of the game, a paradox that might usefully be unravelled by looking at the times when he is actually prepared to participate and the times when he takes his distance. In a presentation and critique of the work of one of his political allies, Alain Badiou,[29] Žižek concludes his essay with a pincer-movement attack in which Badiou is accused both of failing to engage in a full revolutionary act[30] – which would presumably take him outside the domain of the symbolically acceptable political debate – and of refusing to engage with power by taking it and using it. Instead, he argues, Badiou is playing 'a game of hysterical provocation' rather than adopting 'the heroic readiness to endure the subversive undermining of the existing System as it undergoes conversion into the principle of a new positive Order that can *give body* to this negativity'.[31] There is perhaps something a little defensive in this claim, that it requires 'heroic readiness' to assume responsibility within a 'new positive Order'. We know very well that Žižek has participated in the Slovenian administration since independence, and that he has justified along the way the imposition of economic 'shock therapy' measures to jolt the economy into line with West European capitalism. It is not merely that he has had to endure the charge that he was, before independence, part of the 'inner party opposition',[32] complicit in the regime because he already benefited from it at the same time as he was criticising it, but that he is willing to play the rules of the game when he wants.

While he is most of the time resolutely against playing the rules of the game – against reducing antagonism to a simple agonistic competition between representatives of different political constituencies – he still holds onto a hope for a kind of political space in which it would be worth participating. The immediate aftermath of the Slovenian break from Yugoslavia was one example. Another case that clearly tempts him is the idea that there might be a shift in contemporary capitalism from struggles over property ownership to a form of 'class struggle' – for he holds onto the name if nothing else – between a hierarchical and an egalitarian 'post-property society'.[33] It is that prospect, that there might be a political setting in which something like the rules of the game required by parapolitics might be workable, that returns to haunt Žižek. Something from the domain of parapolitics – 'post-property society' – sticks to what he does even when he is so suspicious of its democratic pretensions.

There are good reasons to be suspicious of democracy, and Žižek is right to avoid blueprints for a future world, for they will always end up being drafted within the parameters of present-day society (and Marx, likewise, drafted no such blueprints). Democracy in contemporary society is a fake, predicated on an illusion that we are together making choices about how best to manage ourselves, an illusion that functions to obscure the fact that we vote for different individuals to exercise power in a state apparatus that is still dedicated to the efficient management of the capitalist economy. The imperatives of capitalism must always undermine democratic decision-making, and the term 'dictatorship of the proletariat' serves to indicate that the hollow democracy of the 'dictatorship of the bourgeoisie' must be replaced by a socialist democracy that realises the full potential of open collective self-management. Socialist democracy will be qualitatively different because it will at last be genuinely democratic. Sometimes Žižek seems to take this kind of stance towards 'fake participation' as the kind of 'participation of individuals in our post-modern political process', nicely metaphorised by him in the button that seems to close the door on an elevator but which actually has no effect at all: 'We are all the time asked by politicians to press such buttons. But some things are excluded. What is excluded from this participatory, multi-culturalist, tolerant democracy?'[34]

Postpolitics: cynical multinationalism

This twist on depoliticised modern parapolitics as one refusal of politics proper brings us to what Žižek terms postmodern 'postpolitics', in which 'the conflict of global ideological visions embodied in different parties who compete for power is replaced by the collaboration of enlightened technocrats (economists and public opinion specialists, for example) and liberal multiculturalists'.[35] Žižek is thus able to update his account of ideology to grapple with this new state of affairs but, apart from some of the slippage in psychoanalytic concepts he uses to describe what is 'disavowed' or 'repressed' and now 'foreclosed' from politics proper,[36] it now seems that what he opposes to postmodern postpolitics, and what he wants to redeem from it, is not Marxist at all.

Despite his insistence on the importance of antagonism as the real around which the social is structured, and the role of this notion of antagonism as a key motif in the break with Laclau, Žižek did already bring his own version of 'post-Marxist' politics to his encounter with Laclau and Mouffe – something that he now often expresses as outright anti-Marxism. In Žižek's debate with Judith Butler and Ernesto Laclau in *Contingency, Hegemony, Universality*,[37] Laclau declared that his 'sympathy with Žižek's politics are largely the result of a mirage'.[38] Žižek's response, after much goading by Laclau to define exactly what political programme he is advocating, declared that 'opting for the *impossible*' may mean terror and the ruthless exercise of power; 'if this radical choice is decried by some bleeding heart liberals as *Linksfaschismus* [Left fascism], so be it!'.[39] However outrageous this outburst might be, it does signal something of the allegiance that Žižek still has to the post-Marxist colleagues that visited him in Ljubljana in the mid-1980s – an acceptance of some underlying ground-rules of political analysis even at the same time as there is frustration with the political paralysis they produce. We can see this clearly in 'Lenin's Choice' from 2002, and there we find some of the themes already anticipated in *The Sublime Object of Ideology* back in 1989.

One of the paradoxes of the Laclau–Mouffe project to shift the Left from a supposedly Marxist fixation on the economy to an attention to struggles for hegemony – alliances to rearticulate signifiers like 'democracy' and 'nation' around progressive politics – was that their attack on certain forms of identity, particularly Marxism's identification with the working class (and the proletariat as a corresponding political category) opened the way for new forms of identity and identity politics. For Laclau, 'class struggle is just one species of identity politics, and one which is becoming less and less important in the world in which we live'.[40] For Žižek too, 'identity' is a dead-end. but it is not a mere theoretical problem; identity politics of any kind is worse than a diversion from what he imagines the real of 'class struggle' to be. He repeats his old complaints about the status given to the figure of the 'victim', for example, as another opportunity to inveigh against the reactionary evils of multiculturalism: 'The postmodern identity politics of particular (ethnic, sexual and so forth) lifestyles fits perfectly the depoliticized notion of society', one 'in which every particular group is accounted for and has its specific status (of victimhood) acknowledged through affirmative action or other measures'.[41]

This multiculturalist model of victimhood, with its claims for compensation or affirmative action, is, for Žižek, of a piece with another more dangerous, cynically reflexive use of categories of identity. One example that he often invokes is the violent skinhead who 'knows very well what he is doing, but he is nonetheless doing it'.[42] Here Žižek adapts descriptions of 'enlightened false consciousness',[43] in which subjects know very well what they are doing and cynically draw upon that awareness for a repertoire of justification for their actions, and he takes it further to describe how such cynical subjects are able to repeat the operations of ideological fantasy. They are able to take a 'cynical distance' from the fantasy, but in order to hold onto it, so that 'they know that, in their activity, they are following an illusion, but still, they are doing it'.[44] The explanation that such postmodern racists, who account for their actions in terms much-beloved by liberals who trade in identity politics – social insecurity, paternal and maternal absence, lack of warmth, and so on – is a cynical reflection, and 'the enlightened, tolerant, multiculturalist gets his own message in its inverted true form'.[45]

What Žižek still accepts, and thinks that he radicalises, from Laclau and Mouffe is the doctrine that society does not exist: 'society is not a positive field, since the gap of the Political is inscribed into its very foundations (Marx's name for the political which traverses the entire social body is "class struggle")'.[46] One can see why this formulation, that society doesn't exist, might be attractive to Žižek; it repeats the late Lacanian dictum that the woman doesn't exist and even, because 'woman' and 'man' are only signifiers, that there is no positive foundation for beings of a determinate sex who then imagine they can strike up a rapport with the other. By the same logic, this dematerialisation of the substance of woman (and man) and society can be extended to the point that 'Just as society doesn't exist, we should formulate the basic materialist thesis that "the world doesn't exist".'[47] Žižek's version of 'materialism' here – which he counterposes to Lenin's 'idealist' view that there are objects in the world independently of consciousness – leads him to an enthusiastic endorsement of an image of the social that operates as if it were able to dematerialise itself on demand. It is actually an image of the social that looks curiously like Žižek's image of contemporary capitalism itself, and so he is led to conclude that Marxism would remove the very condition for human productivity were it to succeed in overthrowing capitalism. Once again, a version of Hegel underpins this 'possible Lacanian critique of Marx'.[48]

This is how Žižek's argument works. What Marx overlooked in his attempt to release the full 'unbridled drive to productivity' that was hindered by capitalism, Žižek claims, is the way that the 'obstacle' or 'antagonism' that capitalism constitutes is not only the 'condition of impossibility' of this economic system but its very 'condition of possibility'. This means that if we were to remove this impediment we would therefore lose the very productivity that is generated by it, 'if we take away the obstacle, the very potential thwarted by this obstacle dissipates'.[49] So, we must abandon the Marxist vision of ceaseless, unbridled productivity released when private property ownership of the means of production has been displaced, and endorse instead a vision of capitalism dematerialised and reinvented, even though it is never clear exactly how this might work outside the frame of capitalism itself. The good news is that private property ownership is no longer the real issue: 'what matters is less and less the ownership of material objects, and more and more the ownership of "immaterial" formulas of experiences (copyrights, logos …)'.[50] If this is right, then all we might need from Lenin is what Žižek lamely offers at the end of the essay, 'more or less just the name itself'.[51] Even Žižek's generous acknowledgement of Trotsky as a revolutionary figure should be taken with a pinch of salt, for all he is really willing to take on here, again, is the name:

'perhaps the signifier "Trotsky" is the most appropriate designation of that which is worth redeeming in the Leninist legacy'.[52]

For all the scornful dismissal of Derrida's liberal evocation of Marxism, and critique of Derrida's conclusion that capital is *différance*,[53] Žižek gets drawn into the same kind of logic, finessed through reference to the ideological fantasy that keeps capitalism going, and to the dematerialisation of production through the emergence of a virtual economy in cyberspace,[54] but he is still keen to hold on to exactly the postmodern displacement of the economic process into the movement of language. What then haunts Žižek from the postpolitics he claims to surpass is an attachment to capitalism as a system of critical *différance* driving itself around an obstacle that cannot and should not be given up.

If Žižek rejects parapolitics, from which he takes the hope of an egalitarian post-property society, and postmodern postpolitics, from which he borrows the idea of dematerialised and re-energised capitalism, then what of more traditionalist alternatives, forms of politics that offer the hope of either organic closure or radical conflict?

COMMUNITY AND ENMITY

Systems of rule that claim to be democratic conceal within their ideological apparatus two deadly lures for those who try to resist, bait often taken by Marxists at times of exhaustion and desperation. Tired Marxists who have wished so hard for a world without class conflict can sometimes come to believe that we have already arrived there, and they then fall with relief into the folds of a community that offers closure and peace.[55] Impatient Marxists who are frustrated by the failure of the working class to overthrow capitalism can sometimes resort to measures designed to shake things up, and hope that through some extreme dramatic intervention the ideological ruses of the state can be exposed.[56] Žižek, too, is someone who at times seems to yearn for closure or needs to angrily kick out.

Arche-politics: medical corporatism

'Arche-politics', for Žižek, is that attempt to bring about closure – 'traditional, close, organically structured, homogeneous social space that allows for no void in which the political moment or event can emerge'[57] – and there are three examples of closure that are relevant here. The first lies in the East, in the 'non-political, corporate functioning of Japanese society',[58] for example, or in Singapore's 'paradoxical combination of capitalist economic logic with corporate communitarian ethics aimed at precluding any politicization of social life'.[59] Hong Kong under Chinese rule is also cited by him as moving in the same direction, 'albeit in a more

Americanized, multiculturalist, and pluralist spirit'.[60] By implication, this instantiation of corporate rule in closely controlled city-states may then function as one of the ways by which capitalism will become hegemonic, absorbing and neutralising opposition as it spreads through a mode of globalisation that blots out universalism. A second example lies in the forms of communitarian movement that recruit all members of the polity into close-knit loyalty organised around some essential though necessarily unspecifiable shared Thing. This, for Žižek, is the world of the Heideggerians, in which some authentic connection with Being might be forged through mystical organic unity between each and every expression of its underlying essence. Unpleasant though those oriental and volkish variants on the theme of organic closure and complete subjection to a community might seem, there is another, third, example of arche-politics that is, for Žižek at least, closer to home.

Here we can ask whether Žižek has taken his own good advice with respect to Lacanian psychoanalysis and has unreservedly given himself to the analytic community. This community is defined by him sometimes as a church, sometimes as an army, and sometimes as both. Apropos the militant struggle 'to demonstrate how Christianity effectively provides the foundations to human rights and freedoms', for example, Žižek claims that while the International Psychoanalytical Association (IPA) is the psycho-analytic church, 'we Lacanians are, on the contrary, the psychoanalytic army, a combative group working towards an aggressive re-conquest defined by the antagonism between us and them, avoiding, rejecting even the tolerant olive branch of the IPA'.[61] Žižek's formulation here, in 1999, repeats key themes of Jacques-Alain Miller's report for the General Assembly of the World Association of Psychoanalysis in Barcelona in 1998, in which Miller called for the Lacanians to 'quit the enclosure of the Latins' and asserted that 'It is now a question of bringing into effect the reconquest of the Freudian Field elsewhere, and specially in the countries of the English language.'[62]

If Žižek really does relate to the Lacanian psychoanalytic community in the way he says he does, there are political consequences that follow from this that pertain not only to the formal structure of political action but also to some questions of doctrine, particularly around sexual difference and feminist politics. Žižek insists that a Lacanian account of sexual difference should not be conceived as an ideal prescriptive norm, that it might actually come close to what Judith Butler is after in terms of a radical queering of sexual categories,[63] so that heteronormative binaries of male–female are seen as iterated and performed by subjects rather than as reducible to necessary biological or symbolic structures: 'Far from constraining in advance the variety of sexual arrangements, the Real of sexual difference is the traumatic cause that sets in motion their contingent proliferation.'[64]

However, as Butler points out elsewhere, the actual political position of some leading Lacanians on homosexuality does reveal a willingness to map available moral views about sexual difference as contents onto the formal grid that Lacan outlines in the formulae on sexuation. Jacques-Alain Miller, for example, generously acknowledges that homosexual relations could be given 'legal recognition', but balks at calling it 'marriage' on the grounds that the bond between two men is not the same as that between partners in a heterosexual couple: 'We do not find the demand for erotic, sexual fidelity that is introduced into the heterosexual couple by a certain number of factors – from the feminine side in a certain register; in another register by the demands of the male partner'.[65] This is bad, but it could be worse, and in some of Žižek's writing it is.

Žižek, in a footnote to 'Lenin's Choice', also smuggles in more conservative content to flesh out what is supposed to be the merely formal matrix of sexual difference in Lacanian theory. This appears, for example, in his comments about what he coyly calls 'the structural discontent/unease which pertains to lesbian subjectivity', and there is much hedging around this unease in Žižek's comments in order to avoid getting drawn into 'classic patriarchal wisdom'; 'One of the detrimental clinical consequences of the Cultural Studies Politically Correct stance', he says, is the prohibition on articulating this unease. He eventually arrives at the claim that 'the apparently "conservative" notion of homosexuality as relying on (or resulting from) some kind of "unnatural" derailment seems much more promising, theoretically as well as politically: it asserts homosexuality as the stance of courageously daring to take unexplored paths'.[66] Now, one issue here is how the notion of 'derailment' from some pre-symbolic sexual orientation might be useful theoretically, but this is really small change for Lacanians, for whom every form of sexual desire for a speaking being is always already necessarily a 'derailment'.[67] The other issue is how the categories of sexual difference are relayed by the symbolic at different cultural and historical periods to the individual subject – categories reinforced by psychiatry and medicalised psychoanalysis – and it is here that Žižek cannot resist invoking a 'clinical fact' to back up his stance in the 'structural discontent/unease' he is describing: 'the clinical fact that most lesbian relationships are characterized by an uncanny coldness, emotional distance, impossibility of love, radical narcissism, as well as unease with one's own position'.[68]

Surely what is being endorsed here is a position uncannily close to a form of what Žižek describes as arche-politics, which 'today usually has recourse to a medical model: society is a corporate body, an organism, and social divisions are illnesses of this organism'.[69] His articulation of 'unease' in relation to 'clinical facts' about female homosexuality is exactly of a piece with the rise of the conservative sexual political programmes of the 'new moral majorities' in Eastern Europe, including Slovenia, after the revolt against the Stalinist bureaucracies.[70] One is tempted to say that if the Lacanian movement was indeed a significant part of the opposition in Slovenia prior to independence, and it included such articulations of 'unease' about lesbian sexuality as part of its theoretical programme, then with the rise of the new moral majorities after independence the movement got its own message back in reverse true form; as if they had sent the message 'this is precisely how to articulate your unease about sexuality within our new community'.

There is, psychoanalytically speaking, something ironic about Žižek's faithful filiation with Jacques-Alain Miller; but faithful it is. He expresses his 'indebtedness and gratitude' to Miller in the acknowledgements to *The Sublime Object of Ideology*, but his references to Miller more than a decade later in 'Lenin's Choice' are more peculiar. There are echoes once more of the Hegelian figure of truth through error, but supplemented now with the element of terror that is also derived from Hegel. Miller, Žižek says, 'exerted a retroactive influence on Lacan himself, forcing him to formulate his position in a much more concise way', and he did this by 'introducing the reign of institutional terror'. In response to ex-Millerians who accuse Miller of Stalinism, Žižek then shrugs it off; he is 'tempted to reply' – and he then does – 'why not?'; this is not 'self-destructive terror' but something 'of a totally different order in the psychoanalytic community – here the Stalin figure is a "good" one'.[71]

In sum, even though Žižek loathes the arche-political option, he still seems often bewitched by the possibility that he may have access to and submerge himself in a particular form of Truth, as if it were taking shape as his own 'transferential object' embodied in the trinity of 'God, Analyst, Party'.[72] That avowed relation to Lacan and his representative on earth is but one index of this trace of the temptation of immersion into a community, a temptation that has profound political consequences.[73]

Ultrapolitics: decisionism and order

There is another traditionalist option Žižek toys with, that of 'ultrapolitics'. He is not explicitly endorsing ultrapolitics – 'the attempt to depoliticize the conflict by way of bringing it to extremes, via the direct militarization of politics'[74] – but, as they say when waste matter is flying around, although he is no real fan something sticks. And the matter in question here is the work of Carl Schmitt.[75] Schmitt, a German conservative political theorist between the First and Second World Wars, functions as one of the symptoms of the disintegration of 'post-Marxism' after the Althusserian and post-Althusserian attempts to re-orient the Left in the 1980s; his writing about the tension and intersection between 'order' and 'decision' from within the orbit of fascism fascinates those who have long abandoned their old political reference points and are searching for something to replace them. Different varieties of 'post' theoretical framework have been heavily influenced by cultural and moral relativism, even when their key theorists disavowed that relativism, and the spectre of ethical nihilism then hovered in the background. In much the same way as Heidegger seemed to some to offer an escape route, Schmitt appealed to others. One of those who have followed that post-Althusserian route out of the left argues that 'What led him [Schmitt] to collaborate with the Nazis from March 1933 to December 1936 was not, however, ethical nihilism, but above all a concern with order.'[76]

Žižek claims, in the same edited collection, that the core of Schmitt's argument is that 'the decision which bridges this gap [between 'pure normative order' and 'the actuality of social life'] is not a decision for some concrete order, but primarily a decision for the formal principle of order as such'.[77] Schmitt's 'decisionism' is thus set against a background of order in which an act of will opens up antagonism and then imposes a new order. The point to emphasise here is that Žižek is not actually advocating a Schmittian political position, but is trying to detect how that position reappears in the real as a form of politics – antagonism that calls for an act of truth – that has been 'foreclosed' from the symbolic coordinates of post-political debate. Žižek's assessment is that although Schmitt was 'radical', he was unable to recognise that antagonism runs through the social rather than simply between us, the community, and them, the enemies; with and against Schmitt, Žižek's argument is that 'true universalists are not those who preach global tolerance of differences and all-encompassing unity, but those who engage in a passionate struggle for the assertion of the Truth which compels them'.[78]

This necessarily one-sided assertion of Truth will, however, sometimes seem to draw the Right and Left together against what Žižek sees as 'liberal leftist "irresponsibility"' (advocating grand projects of solidarity, freedom, etc., yet ducking out when their price proves to be concrete and often cruel political measures)'.[79] Žižek often borrows the motif of 'terror' from Hegel at such points to assert what 'a true Leninist and an authentic political conservative have in common'.[80] Hegel had approvingly referred to the '*terror* of death' as the vision of 'negative nature of itself' that found expression in the French revolution,[81] and this logic of revolutionary terror is what Žižek has in mind when he uses the term; it has properly philosophical

reference points rather than directly political ones, but the use of those
reference points then has political consequences, when, for example, Žižek
says that 'In a political act, you do not choose what you will do, you do what
you must. You have definitely an element of Terror in this.'[82]

The role of 'terror' also is important when Žižek refers to Lenin and,
when pressed, offers some assessment of the role of Trotsky, who he does
not at all want to see as the cuddly-jumper alternative to the necessary terror
of the October Revolution. Trotsky has often been a rallying point for
those on the Left who refuse to accept the rule of the Stalinist bureaucracies as representative of the tradition of revolutionary Marxism. Trotsky's[83]
analysis of the degeneration of the Revolution under the impact of civil war
and the encirclement of Russia by imperialism, along with the justification
by Stalin of the imposition of a police state combined with peaceful
coexistence with the West as the construction of 'socialism in one country',
has also been read by many Trotskyists as a reassertion of socialist
democracy as a necessary aspect of Marxist politics.[84] Against this image
of Trotsky, Žižek responds that 'I am ready to assert the Trotsky of the
universal militarization of life, the Trotsky of the Red Army. That is the
good Trotsky for me.'[85] While Trotsky's 'logic was not Stalinist', he
argues, 'it was another logic of Terror'.[86] There is, then, a convenient and
only slightly more palatable chopping of 'terror' into 'bad terror' and
'good terror'; this is not a pretty choice for Marxists, but not such an
embarrassment for Žižek, since he uses Marxism tactically against other
political and theoretical systems, and not as a system to be endorsed as such.

Žižek argues that the key difference between fascism – for which Schmitt
provides theoretical warrant in analyses of politics as the realm of a
'decision' against and for 'order' – and Marxism is how the antagonism that
opens up politics is to be located. And this difference provides us with a way
of theoretically differentiating between an 'act' which confirms a totalitarian regime and an 'act' which undermines it; it provides a way of analysing
whether Antigone was a proto-totalitarian figure when she seemed to
transgress the law, or whether she was changing the symbolic coordinates
when she defied the state. On the one hand, Nazism was a 'psychotic'
system, in which there was a 'foreclosure' of antagonism and, as happens
when something has been foreclosed from the symbolic, the antagonism
reappeared in the real. The Nazi seizure of power therefore entailed, Žižek
claims, a 'disavowal/displacement of the fundamental social antagonism
("class struggle" that divides the social edifice from within) – with its
projection/externalization of the cause of social antagonisms into the figure
of the Jew'.[87] Marxism, on the other hand, attends to class struggle as a
form of antagonism that runs through the social, and so it informs an
'authentic act' which 'disturbs the underlying fantasy'; so an act 'does not

merely redraw the contours of our public symbolic identity, it also transforms the spectral dimension that sustains this identity'.[88] By 'spectral dimension' here, Žižek is referring to the domain of fantasy and its traumatic points of fixation, which in Nazi Germany would be the figure of the Jew (and in Milošević's Serbia would be the figure of Albanian threat in Kosovo).[89]

Žižek already departs from a Lacanian view of the psychoanalytic act in the clinic when he insists that in the sphere of politics there is some kind of suspension of the symbolic, that an act will take place outside the symbolic and thus change the symbolic coordinates. He now goes further to claim that not only can the symbolic be transformed by an act, but that the real itself can be touched and transformed: 'the true act is precisely, as Lacan puts it, that which changes the Real itself'.[90] This deliberate elision of claims for the act as something that can change symbolic coordinates and claims that it can change the real – presumably because it restructures the role of antagonism in the constitution of the social – is Žižek's way of reasserting Marxist notions of class conflict against fascism's foreclosure of the political in the service of capital.

There is a disturbing paradox at work in Žižek's use of Lacan here as a form of political intervention. Although this is the theoretical background for Žižek's specification of an 'authentic act', the moment of the act for him is still, psychoanalytically speaking, closer to a psychotic *passage à l'acte* than to the psychoanalytic act Lacan describes. For Žižek, 'This is the Lacanian act in which the abyss of absolute freedom, autonomy, and responsibility coincides with absolute necessity', one in which 'I feel obliged to perform the act as an automaton, without reflection (I simply *have* to do it, it is not a matter of strategic deliberation)'.[91] This is what seems to draw him to Schmittian ultrapolitics, and he tries to retrieve some authentic moment from it, as if he were trying to capture and symbolise a notion of decision in relation to order before it had been foreclosed from politics, before it appeared in the real as something akin to fascism. Whether 'decision' or 'act', political action is resolutely confined by Žižek to the individual, and the collective project of class consciousness and revolutionary change envisaged by Marxism is outside the frame of his political analysis.

So, when Žižek refuses arche-politics, from which he retains the temptation to give oneself over to a community of some kind, and ultrapolitics, from which he finds another resource for a radical decision without prior deliberation, where is left for him to go?

DID SOMEBODY SAY MARXISM?

One thing we surely have learnt from the fate of Marxism as official ideology of the state in various Stalinist regimes and as an academic approach in capitalist societies is that it is a disastrous mistake to develop a 'Marxist philosophy', 'Marxist sociology' or 'Marxist psychoanalysis'. Still more dangerous is the attempt to make these fill in for the truth in the service of any caste of theoreticians. Žižek's own political interventions – against the ruling party bureaucracy in Slovenia when it was part of the Socialist Federal Republic of Yugoslavia – were, of course, against a regime that claimed to be Marxist. The opposition movement there oscillated between a strategy of pitting the Marxist claims of the bureaucrats against themselves – a strategy of pragmatic immanent critique – and turning to other theoretical resources to critique Marxism itself. Those other resources – structuralist and so-called 'post-structuralist' theory from France that has since mutated in the US into 'post-colonial' and 'post-feminist' theory – also contained within their own frameworks, however, a tension between Marxist auto-critique and anti-Marxism, and this is what made the work of Laclau and Mouffe appealing to Žižek. The clash with Laclau in *Contingency, Hegemony, Universality* is fairly indicative of where Žižek stands now in relation to his old post-Marxist comrades. The point of conflict – around the role of 'antagonism' running through the social and its thematisation around 'class struggle' modelled on Lacan's description of sexuation – also serves to open up further the antagonism between Marxism and something else as the field of 'politics proper'.

Metapolitics: empires of meaning

From an account of contradiction *in* Marxist theory, we are now faced more and more in Žižek's writing with the motif of contradiction *against* Marxism. The realm of Marxist 'metapolitics' is thus seen by Žižek as warrant for the instrumentalisation of politics in the service of 'scientific knowledge' supposed to be able to disclose the economic processes at work beneath or behind the realm of the political. One way out of this for Žižek is to treat even that opposition between the political and the economic as a form of 'real' impossibility – perhaps mapped onto the opposition between the feminine as the place of the economic and the masculine as the realm of the political;[92] and then, after shifting the focus of 'class struggle' to a more abstract binary opposition – as 'the formal generative matrix of the different ideological horizons of understanding'[93] – to shift it back again to the realm of politics, even to conflict between the US and Europe.

Žižek's characterisation of the United States as a global society is designed to present it as the space of traditionalist arche-politics – a closure of difference between different sectors of the world, as the first world finally triumphs over the colonised and now post-colonial 'third world' and old 'second world' post-Stalinist states – as capitalism enforces economic and cultural globalisation. And, in the same breath, he presents the US as the epitome of post-modern multiculturalism, 'in which the global market and legal system serve as the container (rather than the proverbial melting pot) for the endless proliferation of particular group identities'.[94] The shift from one to the other is perhaps what is most emblematic in Žižek's political writing about the hegemony of US imperialism – which he strictly counterposes to the French republican tradition based on 'a universal notion of citizenship'.[95] This is what draws him to Hardt and Negri's account of this emerging world system as a new form of 'Empire'.[96]

It is the book *Empire* that Žižek resorts to after being goaded by Laclau to specify exactly what he has in mind as the fully anti-capitalist analysis to pit against the strains of liberal post-Marxism and feminist multiculturalism he detects in Laclau's and Butler's work; and his gloss on Hardt and Negri's book is indicative of how he wants to use it, as an analysis of globalisation as 'an ambiguous "deterritorialization"', in which 'triumphant global capitalism has penetrated all pores of social life, down to the most intimate spheres, introducing an unheard-off [*sic*] dynamics which no longer relies on patriarchal and other fixed hierarchical forms of domination, but generates fluid hybrid identities'.[97] Feminism actually counts for very little in Hardt and Negri's brief tour through various counter-cultural movements that have deterrorialised capitalism and produced new forms of 'multitude' that swirl in and around national borders, and Žižek reads this as further confirmation that movements dedicated to tackling patriarchy are now at best a diversion and at worst the warrant for depoliticised identity politics. Feminism is thus conveniently swept along with lesbian and gay and anti-racist politics – for which read 'multiculturalism' – into the dustbin of history.

Hardt and Negri's sprawling empire of a book trawls through every imaginable political reference point colonising and reframing existing Marxist analyses of imperialism, and in this, at least, it is a suitable companion in its grandiose sweep across the world of leftist theory to Žižek's own writing. There are other similarities too, in the way that its own space of analysis is institutionally embedded in first-world sectors of intellectual production, which indeed makes it possible to engage in perpetual 'deterritorialisation' and then to imagine that everyone else outside the academic empire also does this. To give credit to Žižek, he does recognise that there is a problem here, and two years after his first puff for the book he is more cautious, noting that the concrete demands Hardt and Negri pose at the end of the book are a bit of a let-down,[98] part of a broader problem that their book is 'pre-Marxist' insofar as it does not adequately analyse how 'the present socioeconomic process will create the necessary space for such radical measures'.[99] But does Žižek himself provide such an analysis? Methinks not.

Instead, what seems to attract Žižek to *Empire* is Hardt and Negri's suggestion that US globalisation repeats the dominance in 'the first centuries of our era' of (what he glosses as) 'the *global* "multicultural" Roman empire'; against which Žižek summons with heart-sinking predictability the struggle of the Christians against Rome. And once again he follows in Hegel's footprints when he insists that 'Christianity opposed itself to two types of discourses, the Greek discourse of philosophical sophistry and the Jewish discourse of obscurantist prophetism, like today's twin brothers of deconstructionist sophistry and New Age obscurantism.'[100] Hardt and Negri do indeed conclude *Empire* with an image to warm Žižek's heart when they evoke St Francis of Assisi's opposition to '*nascent capitalism*', '*identifying in the common condition of the multitude its enormous wealth*', an image to be repeated in '*postmodernity*' when they pose '*against the misery of power the joy of being*'; '*This*', they say in a final flourish, '*is a revolution that no power will control – because biopower and communism, cooperation and revolution remain together, in love, simplicity, and also innocence. This is the irrepressible lightness and joy of being communist.*'[101]

This image of the communist militant neatly connects the Marxist revolutionary tradition with a radical Christian message about the evils of commodification – the turning of relationships and the products of human creativity into things – under capitalism. It also repeats an attempt to connect Marxism and Christianity that has become popular recently in a variety of leftist traditions.[102] Žižek's own take on this connection is to take the old 'anti-humanism' of the Althusserians and post-Marxists in a certain direction of redemptive self-obliteration and combine it with one of the most dubious of Hegelian influences on Marx himself. In both cases, the connection functions to cut against Marxism rather than take it forward. With respect to the motif of anti-humanism we also find in Žižek a motif of the finding of wealth in poverty that reads more like a sermon than a call to revolutionary socialism: 'in love, *I am also nothing*, but as it were a Nothing humbly aware of itself, a Nothing paradoxically made rich through the very awareness of its lack'.[103] This is miles away from Marx's own call – in his 'Critique of Hegel's Philosophy of Right' – for the 'abolition of religion as the *illusory* happiness of the people' so that man 'will think, act and fashion his reality like a man who has discarded his illusions and regained his senses, so that he will move around himself as his own true sun'.[104]

With respect to the influence of Hegel, Marx tackles anti-semitism – in 'On the Jewish Question' – but unfortunately in such a way as to licence a reading of his call for the abolition of Jewish religion along with the abolition of all religion as itself anti-semitic. Marx's argument is that emancipation from Jewishness as such is also, for the Jew, necessarily emancipation from the position allotted to the Jew by capitalism, and Marx here is elaborating an analysis of structural anti-semitism under capitalism that does prefigure some of Žižek's own comments on the figure of the Jew as a fantasmatic anchoring point for contemporary ideology; that the Jew conspires and manipulates things behind the scenes is a comforting and paranoiac 'explanation' for the crises of capitalism.[105] However, there is a rapid slippage in Žižek's account of the fantasy of the Jew to an analysis of the Jewish religion as such, and here the problems pile up.

Žižek's analysis picks up on Hegel's framing of the historical sequence by which Christianity succeeds Judaism, a sequence that does also appear in Marx's writing. After noting that the way to make a religious opposition disappear is to 'abolish religion', Marx argues that the Jew and the Christian should 'recognise their respective religions as nothing more than *different stages in the development of the human spirit*, as snake-skins cast off by history, and *man* as the snake which wore them', and then 'they will no longer be in religious opposition, but in a purely critical and *scientific*, a human relationship'.[106] What Marx is aiming at here is a time when that historical sequence will be unimportant, but what Žižek always aims at is the sequence itself as the key to unlocking how it might be possible for the individual subject to move from law to love, from Judaism to Christianity. What Žižek actually takes from Marx, then, is not an analysis of political economy, still less of ownership of the means of production (which Žižek sees as historically redundant) but some abstract notion of historical development – social and individual – that repeats anti-semitic imagery.

Politics strict and proper

This, finally, is the space for 'politics proper' as 'something specifically "European"',[107] a political space in which St Paul's 'unconditional Christian universalism ... made him into a proto-Leninist militant'.[108] Žižek elaborates this 1998 formulation, which then includes Marx and Freud in the sequence of admirable figures, four years later in the essay on 'Lenin's Choice': 'Lenin did not just adequately translate Marxist theory into political practice – rather, he "formalized" Marx by defining the Party as the political form of its historical intervention – just as Saint Paul "formalized" Christ, and Lacan "formalized" Freud.'[109] The chain of figures Žižek specifies here is not accidental, for this repetition of the dialectical shift between 'the founding figure of a movement and the later figure who formalized this movement'[110] serves to confirm not only the Hegelian motif of truth arising through error but also the Lacanian return to the truth of Freud. This return, Žižek insists, is also necessarily a

'Christianising' of psychoanalysis, in the claim, for example, that 'Lacan accomplishes the passage from the Law to Love, in short, from Judaism to Christianity.'[111] It is also a fairly final, efficient severing of Marxism from the Jewish radical political tradition.

The first bizarre casualty of 'politics proper', then, is that the reframing of Marxism within an all-encompassing Hegelian theory of the development of religious belief systems also pathologises those traditions of Marxist 'metapolitics' that are not deemed to be properly European. Not only does this reintroduce some of the more unpleasant Christian motifs into politics, but it also leads to some decidedly odd suggestions about how to combat oppression. For example, Žižek argues that the gay man in the US army who killed a fellow soldier who was harassing him 'should first have *beaten himself up*, that is, got rid of *his own* libidinal investment in the rituals of his humiliation'.[112] This kind of 'radical self-degradation' is, he says, necessary if we are to adopt 'the position of the proletarian who has nothing to lose'.[113] Those on political demonstrations might also then take Žižek's advice when faced with police who are about to beat them: 'the way to bring about a shocking reversal of the situation is for the individuals in the crowd to start beating each other'.[114] Once again, there is a model from the history of psychoanalysis that Žižek is keen to draw into his argument. When Freud wrote *Moses and Monotheism*,[115] he did so, Žižek claims, as an act in which he gave up the precise quality that anti-semites attributed to the Jews – that they were a chosen people with a special link to God – by showing that Moses himself was an Egyptian, and that the existence of the Jews was itself a form of historical reconstruction.[116] It is as if Freud were beating himself up, a good Jew turning the other cheek to redeem himself.

The second casualty of Žižek's politics proper is the lesson he draws from ultrapolitics that a radical decision that has not been planned or thought through in advance might break a deadlock and open things up. This, we might say, is truth as the first casualty of the war of us against them that decisionist ultrapolitics demands. Truth is not something to be debated and argued through, but will appear in an 'act' which can only be accounted for and puzzled over after the event.

The third casualty is the temptation precisely to give oneself over to the logic of a revolutionary process, and it is here that Žižek's endorsement of the idea that one should give oneself over to the good Stalin – part-and-parcel of the domain of arche-politics – returns to haunt his account of politics proper. This is the domain of order as such that lures those who make a career out of seeming to reject everything.

Politics proper, for Žižek, also still retains from the domain of post-politics – as a fourth casualty of his version of the European tradition – an endorsement of the logic of capitalism. This is where he ends up with some of the most disappointing replays of arguments that capitalism has mutated into something for which old Marxism is no longer appropriate, so that when the signifier 'Marx' is retained it is as thoroughly dematerialised as the new virtual capitalism.

Finally, as a fifth casualty of politics proper, we find the traces in Žižek's proposals of a romantic vision of post-property society; perhaps even, in the most conservative versions of his writing on these themes, as something that we are able to detect emerging and worth supporting now. Even from the 'double disappointment' of the failed encounter between the West, which expected to find in Eastern Europe the reinvention of democracy as the shackles of Stalinist rule were shaken off, and the East, which looked to the West for the joys of free enterprise, Žižek finds something positive in the gap that separates the two: 'perhaps what transpires in the gap that separates the two perspectives is a glimpse of a Europe worth fighting for'.[117] At a time when the Europe that is being fought for necessarily includes drawing tight the boundaries around it as a Fortress Europe that will keep the non-Christian hordes at bay, this is not necessarily a progressive vision.[118]

What Žižek's position also accomplishes is a pathologisation of Marxist politics, for if Marxists do not follow the Christian trajectory from the law to love they will remain stuck in something limited and – when viewed from a Hegelian or Lacanian vantage point – regressive. Already Žižek had characterised the position of Marxists in the Stalinist states, and by implication any other Marxist who operates on a model of historical analysis and organised party opposition to capitalism, as expressing the problematic of 'perversion'. Whereas fascism operates according to the psychotic 'foreclosure' of antagonism, and will then see it return in the real around the fantasy figure of the Jew, Marxism in power under actually existing socialism was structured around the defence of 'disavowal' and the perverse subordination of the individual to the jouissance of the Other, so 'the Leninist revolutionary … occupies the properly perverted position of the pure instrument of historical necessity'.[119]

Marxist opposition to capitalism can also all too easily in Žižek's work be seen as a frantic attempt to make something happen, something obsessional and futile, or as hysterical complaint against what others are doing to us. In both cases, the neurotic (obsessional neurotic and hysterical) predicament of the activist is contained by, even provoked by, capitalism. One might also detect in Marxism a new twist on the 'interpassive' process by which we subordinate ourselves to others acting on our behalf, looking to the political process as a source of entertainment in much the same way as we watch a comedy show on television and rely on the canned laughter to enjoy the programme for us.[120] And Marxism can be seen as yet another replay of the attempt to find others who believe, as an easier, convenient replacement for our own belief. However important these warnings are, Žižek himself has succeeded in so thoroughly desubstantialising any political project that he ends up believing in nothing himself. Freud may have shown us something about the nature of symptoms that Marx already had detected in his analysis of commodities, but it seems that the overriding message Žižek wants to take from Lacan is that we must learn to enjoy these symptoms.

Žižek has woven Hegel, Lacan and Marx into such a tight theoretical knot that only a desperate 'act' of individual refusal is open to anyone who takes all this seriously. This kind of act might masquerade as something that will change the symbolic coordinates of a political system, but it actually leads us well away from any project of collective change. The thorough desubstantialisation of everyday life that Lacanian psychoanalysis, reconfigured as a worldview, encourages is then made compatible with an image of virtual capitalism; and this is then theoretically plugged into a classically idealist Hegelian focus on the realm of appearance as such. Only then might it indeed be possible to follow Žižek and to 'keep up appearances',[121] and only the appearance of Marxism. This is a dismal conclusion to what was supposed to be a radical theoretical intervention in political practice.

5
Culture – Acting Out

Now you know where Žižek is coming from and what he is up to. But before we move on to speculate about why he doesn't make much sense sometimes, it will be worth stopping for a moment to take stock, to review received images of Žižek and some critiques of his work. We can then find a way of grappling with some of the stylistic peculiarities of his writing, and the way it is as if 'substance becomes subject' for us in the course of his writing. Here we can explore how his cultural analyses – from art-house film to popular fiction – are the setting for theoretical work, and also how the formal properties of his writing display deadlocks in his use of theory. Žižek does not come from nowhere – the historical overview of the break-up of Yugoslavia in Chapter 1 was a way of exploring the ground-plan of his writing – and he always writes for an audience, addressing different constituencies and modifying his use of philosophical, psychoanalytic and political categories to suit.

Žižek makes himself appear to the gaze of the West, and now it is this appearance of the subject Žižek to us that we will focus on. What you need to know to read Žižek, then, is also precisely what Žižek needed to position himself within and against, as specific competing positions in a certain constellation viewed from Ljubljana and Paris.[1] That is why the review of Hegelian, Lacanian and Marxist resources in his work in the preceding chapters focused on the particular versions of those theoretical frameworks currently in circulation. A good way of beginning this assessment of Žižek is to go back and start again from scratch, now from the position of those who are encountering him for the first time.

Reader comments on one of his website articles[2] – on the war against Iraq[3] – include some quite revealing responses to his writing. 'Proud American' posted a reply from Kansas, for example, objecting to Žižek's article, commenting that 'it's no strange coming from a guy with rat name [*sic*]'.[4] Academic commentators have also rolled the name around, using its strangeness to them as the way in to a review of Žižek's ideas.[5] This kind of reaction renders quite understandable Žižek's own tetchy comments about the 'gaze of the West' on Slovenia, and about patronising lectures from liberals and leftists who tell him what he should or should not write about because of where he comes from.[6] For 'ROCKTIME', who went a little further in pinning down what the article on Iraq was about, Žižek was 'Obviously a philosopher from Eastern Germany, whose early years were influenced by the Soviet Union, carries a certain amount of paranoia.' This characterisation neatly disposes of political argument by pathologising the writer (a risk we will also be taking in the following pages).[7] The only critical response from a Left perspective complained that his article 'is little more than a plea to adapt to the "free Iraq" cabal. It obscures the central truth – that crocodile tears about the "Iraqi people" are the basest form of imperial contempt ... Democracy, as usual, has nothing to do with it.'[8] This perceptive response is a useful opening to some of the ways that Žižek has been read so far.

We will focus on the critiques of Žižek concerning politics, psychoanalysis and philosophy, and then turn to the way the particular interweaving of his positions in these different fields has led him into some peculiar deadlocks and worrying directions. As we shall see, it is precisely the deadlock in each of the readings he makes of theoretical frameworks that gives rise to the sudden shifts of direction in his writing, often paragraph by paragraph, sometimes sentence by sentence. Certain 'conditions of impossibility' operate at the substantive level – of the content of his claims – and at a stylistic level, so that the manner in which he writes mirrors what he writes about. This is what makes his writing so beguiling, and it sometimes seems designed to disturb those who like academic work to be built around evidence, inference and summative statements: 'The effect is that of a stream of non-consecutive units arranged in arbitrary sequences that solicit a sporadic and discontinuous attention.'[9] You think he is saying something, but then his argument veers off course and turns into the reverse. His writing on film in the edited *Everything You Always Wanted to Know About Lacan* or on cyberspace in *The Plague of Fantasies*, for example, provides the perfect setting for this sliding from claim to characterisation, and then sideways to another claim located in a completely different theoretical position, and his anecdotes and jokes often function as switch-points for a rapid transition from one kind of argument to another.

Žižek's work has been enthusiastically taken up by some writers in literary and cultural studies precisely because it breaks the traditional taken-for-granted opposition between 'high' and 'low' culture in line with the 'textual wing' of cultural studies, assuming that 'whatever analysis is made of particular uses made of cultural texts in determinate situations, the problem of textuality remains in any case – texts continue to be reproduced, re-used with a difference by other readers'.[10] Here questions of authorship and address need to be tackled carefully. This final chapter builds up an argument for seeing Žižek's work as a kind of 'machine' by which Lacan can be put to work sorting and combining Hegelian concepts, so that it can then be applied to culture as its object. Culture is treated by him in this process of application as if it were a politically charged superstructure. This machine, reiterated text-by-text, seems to work for Žižek as a way of reading Hegel, and the Lacan-machine-for-reading-Hegel then becomes a writing machine that holds things together, but in a way that also keeps them at a distance.

One way of accounting for the apparently wilful contradictoriness in Žižek's work is to put it down to 'carefully cultivated idiosyncrasies' underpinned by 'his tireless personal pursuit of publicity through provocation'.[11] Another tack is to pursue the thematic of madness further to account for why his writing seems so crazy.[12] But whether both claims are true or not, we now need to know how to disentangle ourselves from the seductive lures that hook us into his writing so we can still get something enjoyable and useful out of it. The critical responses to his work will show us something of the field of debate before we move in to pin him down.

HIS JUST DESSERTS

As Žižek swerves backwards and forwards between political, psychoanalytic and philosophical reference points, his critics within each of these domains have tried to fix him by exposing inadequacies in his readings of Marx, Hegel or Lacan, and the main critiques have been staged exactly where Žižek himself performs so well, in the domain of cultural analysis. It is in the difficult-to-define realm of 'culture' that we can see limits to his use of theory, and some deeper problems emerge in the interweaving of different theoretical frameworks which are designed to interpret, intervene and transform the symbolic coordinates of any given system of meaning. When we try to follow Žižek's attempt to combine the different theoretical frameworks, the real stakes of his work are ideological subjectivity, cultural analysis and political transformation.

Ideological subjectivity

The question of subjectivity is formulated by Žižek primarily with reference to the production of the divided subject of Lacanian theory held in thrall to the *objet petit a*. The fundamental fantasy of the subject precisely specifies that relationship and also, for Žižek, reveals the work of the 'sublime object' of ideology in pulling us back to something that feels deeper and earlier and more authentic to us. But subjectivity is also thematised and problematised in his work through the Marxist motif of 'false consciousness' and genuine 'class consciousness', an opposition that Žižek wants to avoid. Instead, the lure of any true full consciousness is treated as itself an ideological motif. In place of any future moment of full subjectivity that would overcome alienation and perhaps restore any past lost loving relation to others – a hope that one sometimes sees in Frankfurt School Hegelian Marxism – Žižek aims to keep subjectivity open to negativity; Hegel then becomes a theorist who refuses any closure or to repair the things that have been broken. Žižek's Hegel is the one who shows us how we are always already broken, and this is the baseline of Lacanian accounts of the subject and a reminder to Marxists not to hope for too much.

Russell Grigg notes that Žižek's rendition of Lacan is focused on the late Lacan, interpreted and formalised by Jacques-Alain Miller after Lacan's death,[13] but he also points out that what remains at work in Žižek's political analysis are themes from Hegel: 'this Hegelianism is pre-Oedipal in the true Lacanian sense'.[14] That is, beneath and behind a Lacanian account is a notion of subjectivity that corresponds to 'absolute negativity' in Hegel, and this will return to haunt Žižek when he turns to this absolute negativity as source and motor of revolutionary change. Absolute negativity does not always appear to Žižek's readers to provide the most immediately optimistic outlook, and Rosi Braidotti, for example, argues that 'Žižek stresses the gloomiest aspects of Lacan's theory of subjectivity, by applying it to ... an overdose of Hegelian dialectics'[15] (and here she cites Peter Dews' critique of Žižek's reading of Hegel, to which we will turn in a moment). As we have seen so far, even when Žižek is writing about Lacan, it is actually Hegel who is in command. We will be examining the implications of that privileging of Hegel later in this chapter.

For Braidotti there is a more serious problem, which is that Žižek's work 'represents an anti-feminist regression that reiterates the whole array of symbolic invisibility and specularity which feminists have been arguing against since the early days of Lacan's work'.[16] Braidotti's characterisation of Lacan is from the vantage point of a kind of feminism that thinks it knows what woman are, so she sets herself against any kind of 'performative' reading of subjectivity, quickly moving on to complain that 'a strange resonance has emerged between Žižek and Butler';[17] this presumably means that the debates in *Contingency, Hegemony, Universality* between Butler, Laclau and Žižek should be viewed with suspicion, as taking place on common ground that we should keep clear of.[18]

However, despite Braidotti's pessimism about Butler's ability to challenge Žižek, Butler herself does not actually let him so easily off the hook. Butler argues that his work 'tends to rely on an unproblematised sexual antagonism that unwittingly installs a heterosexual matrix as a permanent and incontestable structure of culture in which women operate as a "stain" in discourse'.[19] One of the key anchoring points for a psychoanalytic account of subjectivity is the notion of 'trauma' – that which is repressed, disavowed or foreclosed by the subject at the point of its assumption of a position in language – and trauma sometimes appears to be a way of holding the subject onto the past, gripping them so that they cannot move beyond it. For Butler, 'the very theoretical postulation of the originary trauma presupposes the structuralist theory of kinship and sociality',[20] and such theories of kinship and sociality are freighted with heteronormative assumptions (assumptions that Žižek does adhere to, and here Butler is quite right): 'What he's doing is consolidating these binaries as absolutely necessary. He's rendering a whole domain of social life that does not fully conform to prevalent gender norms as psychotic and unlivable.'[21] This is a real problem in his work.

A different tack on the role of 'trauma' in Žižek's work is taken by John Mowitt, who argues that 'Žižek's appeal to trauma is not really driven by a theoretical need to clarify the concept of the Real, but instead by a political need to forge a link between the Real and trauma'; this is so that psychoanalysis will have 'the last word about trauma'.[22] There are political stakes in this 'trauma envy', and Mowitt claims that the politics of trauma for Žižek do not at all lie in recovering or claiming some truth about what has happened in the past – to which it seems Žižek would happily agree – but in claiming a position for psychoanalysis as a master discourse which will speak the truth about trauma against other pretenders. The issue for Mowitt, then, is about the way an account of subjectivity is always implicated in the politics of theory.

Shifting up a gear in rhetorical abuse, Teresa Ebert points out that certain forms of subjectivity fit all too well with the ideological requirements of globalising capitalism, with cynicism operating nowadays as a 'logic of a pragmatism that opportunistically deploys ideas and beliefs in order to … get things done within the existing structures of access and privilege'.[23] Žižek's theoretical work is seen by her as fitting all too neatly into this ideological universe as a form of 'metacynicism', 'a cynicism that protects itself from being known as cynical by theorizing the cynical'.[24] As we have already seen, Žižek does indeed see traditional Marxism as out of date, no longer applicable to new conditions of global capitalism, and this does lead him back to Hegel, with Lacan offering a theory of 'difference' as a substitute for a genuinely Marxist thematic of class struggle.

Ebert is right on track, then, when she claims that 'Žižek *mimes* Marx in an effort to turn a materialist ideology critique upside down into a Hegelian idealism and dissolves class struggle into the symbolic surplus of the Lacanian Real.'[25] A similar point is made by Peter McLaren when he comments that Žižek's 'Lacanian Marxism' – rather a misnomer if Ebert and McLaren are right – 'proposes in some instances a fascinating yet not unproblematic Hegelian re-reversal of Marxism'.[26] Žižek's specifications for the nature of subjectivity already pre-empt any analysis that might be carried out, or any prospect of moving beyond interpreting the world to changing it.

Cultural analysis

Žižek is well-suited to trends in academic cultural theory that would like to restrict themselves to interpreting the world and to treat the idea of changing it as passé. But even then, his use of Hegel to produce analyses that insist on contradiction does make him a good deal more radical than someone who is content with merely identifying and describing structures in literary and cultural texts. Remember that for Žižek Hegel is the figure of perpetual negativity that owes much to Kojève's lectures in Paris in the 1930s. This means that any interpretation of Hegel here is already even more contested than the other various readings of his work.

These different interpretations also carry their own strange political baggage, as Dews points out in his critique of Žižek's reading of Hegel. Dews targets Žižek's argument that 'the identity of the subject consists in nothing other than the continual failure of self-reflection'.[27] One aspect of this problem is Žižek's claim that this is properly Hegelian – which Dews says it is not – and the other aspect is evident in the political consequences of Žižek's (mis)reading of Hegel. In the course of his critique, Dews tries to recover some notion of 'intersubjectivity' from Hegel, and he objects to Žižek's insistence that this is always subject to fracture and disintegration by negativity, something evoked by Hegel's brief comments on 'the night of the world' that haunts reason. Dews' critique of Žižek's reading of Hegel leads Dews to the conclusion that 'Žižek is ultimately a "Right Hegelian" masquerading – albeit unwittingly – as a "Left Hegelian".'[28] The Right Hegelian character of Žižek's work is apparent in the split between individual particularity – for which read classical bourgeois individualism – and a strong sense of tradition to secure order. This is fair and right enough as critique.[29]

Butler also lines up with Hegel – and in the tradition of the Left Hegelians – when she objects to some residues of Kantian formalism in Žižek's identification of formal structures in cultural phenomena. Her point is that 'we cannot identify such [formal] structures first and then apply them to their examples, for in the instance of their "application" they become something other than what they were'.[30] The problem with any appeal to universal formal structures, of course, is that they are also freighted with ideological content (as Butler's comments on the supposed link between trauma, kinship and heteronormativity in psychoanalysis make clear). The question that drives Butler's writing, and which it now becomes relevant to ask of Žižek, is how certain assumptions about formal structure are themselves a function of a particular historical conjuncture. Commenting on Žižek's example of Jaws as *point de capiton* for free-floating, inconsistent fears in which there is 'the return of the thing to itself',[31] Butler asks 'what is the place and time' of this 'performative operation', and she goes on to suggest that it may be 'restricted to the powers of nominalism within modernity'.[32] Butler finds an ally here when Laclau homes in on the same problem, noting that Žižek 'locates Lacan within the rationalist tradition of the enlightenment'.[33] There is no big problem with that as such, and other writers – Dews, for example – have also argued quite rightly that 'Lacanian theory is perhaps the most radical contemporary version of Enlightenment.'[34] The problem for Laclau lies in the way that Žižek 'has Lacanianized the tradition of modernity'.[35] It is not so much that psychoanalysis speaks to the universal in Žižek's work, but that he becomes one of the agents of the globalisation of the Lacanian rewriting of world history.

The issue here is not so much that Lacan is historically located, but that Lacan is used as a kind of grid to read all political phenomena; Žižek's 'discourse is schizophrenically split between a highly sophisticated Lacanian analysis and an insufficiently deconstructed traditional Marxism'.[36] Laclau complains that it is the Lacanian analysis that is in command, and he later concludes that 'Žižek's thought is not organised around a truly *political* reflection but is, rather, a *psychoanalytic* discourse which draws its examples from the politico-ideological field.'[37] In the same debate Laclau also points out that capitalism cannot be the real, as Žižek argues, because it operates as part of the symbolic. As Žižek has argued himself on many occasions, the Lacanian real is that which resists symbolisation, and Laclau's critique is useful insofar as it does draw attention to the problematic way that Lacanian discourse is mobilised by Žižek to read culture. As we shall see, what Žižek actually does is to use Lacan as a kind of machine to read Hegel, and then the Lacan-reading-Hegel-machine is applied to culture. That then gives rise to exactly the kind of disastrous conceptual errors that Laclau identifies and opposes in Žižek's work.

It has been claimed that Žižek has 'a somewhat idealized view of desire'.[38] There is some truth in this, but Žižek is also clear enough about the suffocating lure of desire, and he often resists the temptation of idealising it. Instead, it is more often the case that, taking his lead from Lacan after Seminar XI,[39] he idealises the drive instead. This is a problem that becomes more apparent when the psychoanalytic 'act' is used as a model of political change.

Political transformation

When Žižek refers to Marxism it is often in order to show the insufficiency of utopian socialist 'metapolitics' to a 'politics proper' that would be able to interpret, if not change, global virtual capitalism, and so when he speaks as a Marxist we cannot take this self-characterisation for granted. Žižek often seems most Marxist at those points in his writing when he claims to have gone beyond Marx in the name of Hegel and Lacan – in *The Sublime Object of Ideology* for example – and is least Marxist when he claims to 'repeat Lenin' in rhetorical flourishes that try to outflank his opponents from the Left. It sometimes seems that it is precisely at those moments when he tries to combine the different theoretical domains – philosophy, psychoanalysis and politics – that he fails, and it is at points when he insists that they cannot be combined that he is most faithful to Marx. However, as critics have pointed out when tackling Žižek on his supposed Marxism and on his relation to feminism and anti-racism, things are a little more complicated than this.

It could be said that Marxism 'has always been much more to the fore of Žižek's work than many of his commentators have cared to acknowledge',[40] and Sean Homer makes this point as a useful corrective to those who would prefer to overlook the Marxism. The problem, as Homer shows, is that Žižek's supposed shift from the earlier apparent 'post-Marxism' (during the time of his engagement with Laclau and Mouffe) to a more orthodox Marxism is itself rather illusory, and seems to be more of a performance for different kinds of audience than anything else: 'his thoroughgoing Lacanianism appears to rule out the possibility of any orthodox "understanding" of Marxism, or, indeed, the formulation of a clearly identifiable political project'.[41] The 'thoroughgoing Lacanianism' Homer objects to is actually less of a problem than the way Lacan is turned into a machine for reading Hegel, but Homer is quite right to insist that this has the effect of sidelining Marxist politics. Even Laclau – from the vantage point of a thoroughgoing 'post-Marxism' – was led to conclude, during the course of the three-way exchange with Žižek and Butler, that his 'sympathy with Žižek's politics was largely the result of a mirage'.[42] Whereas it was possible to debate with Butler, in the case of Žižek, 'The only thing one gets from him are injunctions to overthrow capitalism or to abolish liberal democracy, which have no meaning at all.'[43]

From a Marxist–feminist position, Ebert argues that Žižek's writings 'revive a regressive bourgeois idealism that suppresses the historical and revolutionary knowledges necessary for social transformation'.[44] It is not only the case that Žižek revives 'an idealized notion of capitalism as itself a permanent revolution',[45] but his insistence that enjoyment is the new bedrock against which all attempts to overthrow capitalism will come to grief is deeply flawed and reactionary. For Ebert, Žižek is thus just one of many 'ludic theorists' for whom desire becomes the new 'base', and – to repeat in a new key Ebert's scathing indictment of his cynical endorsement of prevailing cynical forms of subjectivity – 'Žižek thus makes the social symbolic reality synonymous with the modes of sense-making and subjectivities require by multicultural capitalism.'[46]

There is a certain queasiness about Žižek's rather repetitive critique of multiculturalism in McLaren's response to Žižek's work. All the same, McLaren neatly turns around Žižek's scornful dismissal of Western liberal romanticising of Native American culture, to question the formulation that they are 'as bad as we'; McLaren remarks that 'there is a danger that Žižek will disappear into the liberal multiculturalism that he so trenchantly contests'.[47] Although McLaren does also want to avoid notions of historical inevitability that sometimes appear in Marxist writing, he is not so happy with the notion that a 'sudden, unexpected irruption into everyday life' – an 'event' or act – offers a progressive alternative; this notion would seem to be 'powerered by a decisionism built around a … coupling of Schmittian Leninism to Alain Badiou's Maoist ontology'.[48] This worry, of course, chimes with the problems we have identified in the previous chapter with respect to Žižek's writings on 'decision' and the 'act'.

One of the main ways political transformation is thematised by Žižek is not from within Marxism at all, but from a reading of Lacan on the act. As we have already seen, Grigg draws attention to the problematic role of the Hegelian motif of 'absolute negativity' lying in the background of Žižek's reading of Lacan, and this motif comes to the fore in a somewhat romanticised reading of Lacan on the 'act'. As Grigg – who comes at this question as a committed Millerian – points out, 'from the point of view of political change there would also appear to be a very disturbing implication of this view of an act: its radical indeterminacy, which implies that *all* political action is gratuitous'.[49] There is then a further problem, which is that the figures that Žižek hails as exemplifying some step into absolute freedom are themselves closely tied to the law. Antigone, for example, 'presents as the epitome of manic hysterical behaviour [and] has become a hero of, a martyr to, the father's desire'.[50] Her refusal to adhere to the demands of the state 'is entirely consistent with, and binds her to, her family destiny and paternal law'.[51] This reading of Antigone, incidentally, is closer to Hegel's own reading, as Judith Butler notes in her attempt to reclaim Antigone for feminism and queer theory.[52]

Lacan is clear enough in his discussion of Antigone, as Yannis Stavrakakis points out, that while she knows what she is doing in facing death, her decision was never an 'act' that was designed to 'effect a displacement in the status quo'.[53] This is already against Žižek's own spontaneist version of what a true psychoanalytic 'act' is, and even by Žižek's own standards, then, 'one has to conclude that this makes her unsuitable as a model for transformative ethico-political action'.[54] Once again, the problem lies in the way Lacan is turned from being a tool for political analysis – something Stavrakakis has no problem with[55] – into a model for political change.

ASYMMETRY: MACHINE, OBJECT, APPLICATION

The critical responses to Žižek we have reviewed so far draw attention to his partisan readings of canonical texts and to some of the disturbing political consequences of the peculiar way he weaves his readings of Marx, Hegel, and Lacan. But those critiques do not yet go far enough, on two counts, and these two outstanding issues provoke two questions.

Taking Žižek at his word, twice

Žižek does not pretend to provide an empirically correct reading of any text, and his warnings about the deadlock of representation that sabotages any political project aiming at consensus and shared debate applies equally well to his own work. Every attempt to capture what he is really doing, as if it would be possible for someone else to be a 'Žižekian', will fail. The point he makes time and again from within each different framework is about the nature of the real and the impossibility of sealing it over. Whether by a standpoint that is not inflected by class position, a position that is not reflexively implicated in the presuppositions it makes about its object or a metalanguage that pretends to escape the contours of the symbolic, this impossibility marks something of the truth of what it is to be a human subject. That is, there is no harmonious resolution of political conflict, no clear view of world history and no unassailable position from which to declaim and educate other benighted souls.

We need to take Žižek at his word here in order to tackle the supposition that sometimes appears among his readers, if it is not deliberately produced in the texts themselves, that there is a system of thought being elaborated, an overarching theoretical framework into which each of the other three and more[56] systems he discusses and utilises can be absorbed. That is, the too-easy counterpart to the charge that he is opportunistically misreading a theory or cultural phenomenon without any consistent rationale for distorting it is the charge that he must really have a master-plan which –

were we able to discover it through constructing an accurate picture of his idiosyncratic pathological engagement with Western European culture, his intellectual development from Heideggerian phenomenology or the project of the 'Slovene Lacanian School' – would enable us to discover and map each of the apparently accidental but actually deeply-motivated mistakes he seems to make. As if. This leads us to the first question. There is no theoretical system as such in Žižek's work, but it often seems as if there is one. How do we account for that?

The second reason the existing critiques do not go far enough is that they do not account satisfactorily for the dynamic interplay between the different theoretical frameworks he uses and his rapid movement between these frameworks. An all-too-tempting way of accounting for the rush we get when we are whirled along in a Žižek text is to imagine that the speed of the journey is simply an expression of the speed of writing, to say he just writes too much too fast, and that perhaps that is why it does not always make sense. One of the keys to unlocking this image of Žižek the author – who writes too fast and skims through different theories so that we end up with as little idea of where he is going as he has – lies in the form of his own writing. The point he makes about the illusory consistency of the subject and the work of the unconscious, in disrupting as well as reproducing the symbolic networks in which a subject speaks, leads us to some different ways to think about what we imagine him to be as the author of the texts that bear his name.

We need to take Žižek at his word again here, when he tells us that in his work nothing is as it seems. There is indeed a performance for each different kind of audience that introduces an element of motivated inconsistency, and so we need to take seriously the rapid transitions from one theoretical frame to another in Žižek's writing, and the sometimes jerky movement from theory to its exemplification in culture or politics and back again, as well as Žižek's own scornful refusal to be pinned down. So, to take him at his word we also need to treat every explanation he gives as untrustworthy as a guide to his work. And we need to do this in a way that grasps something of the movement of his work over time, rather than treating the shifts as yet more evidence that there are flaws in the theoretical architecture of his work that are being repaired as it undergoes renovation.[57] So, the second question. There is an impression of chaotic movement in his writing which belies the lucid elaboration of a theoretical argument. How do we account for that?

These two questions – how we account for the illusion that there is an underlying rationale, and how not to get fixated on the image of Žižek the magpie for whom it seems that it does not really matter that none of it really hangs together – lead us to one little grid for making sense of where Žižek is going. But you should treat this as only one grid, and as riddled by exceptions. The grid includes the supposition that there is a theoretical system and the supposition that there is an erratic author. Treat those suppositions as stepping stones, not as sedimented 'truths', as if they could really be seen lying underneath the surface of the text or as somehow embodied in the figure of Slavoj Žižek (within whom we could diagnose a certain pathological condition which would explain our confusion).

For these purposes, and only these, I will try to account for how the shape of Žižek's theoretical 'system' has developed through its publication and dissemination in the English language. Here, of course, is a further limitation to this exercise which we should treat as one of the very conditions for being able to read and interpret what Žižek says in any particular article in relation to the rest. What we know about the other writing that appears under Žižek's name in other languages also frames this account – work that ranges from the 1988 book on Hegel and Lacan that Jacques-Alain Miller declined to publish[58] to material for a German newsletter discussing sermons for priests.[59] We will also, in this process, be supposing something about the author of the texts that comprise this system, but we need to be particularly careful to keep in mind that this author is one who appears for us behind the texts as a function of those texts. We turn to that issue of authorship when we examine the thematic of escape in his writing, but first we will lay out the asymmetrical structure of the writing as an evolving system of work.

Systemic asymmetry

The different elements in Žižek's writing simply do not cohere. This is not necessarily a problem, for perhaps it would be worse if they did lock together. The critical comments on his work reviewed so far in this chapter sometimes focus on his misreading of particular theorists, but there is always also some puzzlement about how it is possible to put the pieces of the jigsaw together. In fact, it is precisely because of the deadlock that Žižek arrives at in his rendering of each framework that he jumps out of that framework into another one. And the jumping backwards and forwards is accomplished all the more artfully when he is able to shift into detailed description of a film-narrative (or plot of a book or opera). This serves not only to divert attention from the nature of the deadlock – when he has reached as far as he can go within one theoretical frame – but also to compound the problem and mystify the reader by evoking a sensation that we are now lost but that it must all really make sense. This deadlock now brings us to the question of where the different elements stand in relation to each other.

The three main theoretical components of Žižek's theoretical system – organised around the signifiers Marx, Lacan and Hegel – are asymmetrically weighted. As we have seen, Žižek renders Hegel in a certain distinct way that has a close relation to the Hegel presented to Lacan and other French intellectuals by Kojève in the 1930s; Žižek's Lacan is a version of late Lacan distilled by Jacques-Alain Miller in the 1980s, and his Marx is not much more than a foil for his attempt to move beyond Marxist 'metapolitics' to a 'politics proper' appropriate to global virtual capitalism. The three components designed to open up and elaborate an interpretation of history, of the subject and of politics do not always carry equal weight, for sure, but complaints by Marxists, Hegelians or Lacanians that he does not do justice to their own favourite theorist miss the point about this weighting. This is because the more important issue is that these frameworks play different roles in his work. Hegel is read through Lacan, and it seems that Lacan is interesting to Žižek only insofar as Lacanian psychoanalysis operates as a system for reading Hegel: 'If I look really deep into my heart, my focus is not Lacan, my focus is not even politics, my ultimate focus is Hegel and Schelling.'[60] So, that first relationship between the two is asymmetrical, to the extent that we can say that Lacan is a kind of machine for reading Hegel.[61]

This means that when you read about Hegel in Žižek it is interesting and useful – you learn something about German idealism, some new interpretation of Hegel – but this entails a retroactive positing of presuppositions, the discovery after the event of Lacanian motifs in Hegel. The other, complementary, effect of this elaboration of Lacan as a machine for reading Hegel is that Lacan himself is reconfigured so that psychoanalysis is tuned to certain frequencies in Hegel. In this respect, the simple charge that Žižek is merely late-Lacanian (or Millerian) is not enough to account for how Lacan has been remade by him to do a certain kind of work on Hegel. A consequence of this is that when we read Lacan through Žižek, in Žižek's lucid but second-hand account, we are reading a Lacan who is useful and interesting only for certain cultural-political purposes. The clinical frame for Lacan's writing is used by Žižek as a warrant for interrogating subjects who may be characterised by different structures – neurotic, perverse, psychotic – and for whom the treatment may be directed towards the traversing of their fundamental fantasy – identification with the symptom and subjective destitution – but the clinical content of Lacan's work is stripped out and replaced with abstract formulations about the nature of the subject. The other various elements of Lacan's work that Žižek then draws upon – four discourses, sexuation, the psychoanalytic act, for example – are also then retooled in order to make the Lacan-machine-for-reading-Hegel more efficient. When we turn to Marx and Marxist politics there is a further significant asymmetry. Žižek is working with an understanding of the political domain that takes Marxism as a conceptual 'matrix' for theorising class struggle, independently of any particular empirical analysis of the ownership of the means of production. In this respect he does indeed follow the 'poststructuralist' shift of attention from the economy to the cultural domain, a domain that he treats as if it were a kind of signifying superstructure without any determinate signified or referent. Even the 'economy' is then evoked as a point of the real in and against – as the constitutive limit of – that superstructure. This also means that some Hegelian work has already been done on the material that Marxism concerns itself with, such that the appearance of things can be treated as itself the essence, rather than as a 'shadow theatre' for another realm behind it which can be scientifically disclosed to the experts. Politics and culture are certainly treated by Žižek as sites of intervention but also, more importantly, as sites of application. Politics is but one domain, but also perhaps the key cultural domain – the key reference point against which his analyses of cultural material are measured – for the application of the Lacan-on-Hegel machine.

Žižek writes on detective fiction, art-house cinema or high opera as domains of culture that are assumed to be always politically textured in a certain way – a domain of appearance as the fantasy-infused reality for individual subjects – and so the objects of his analysis are thus already rendered into things that the Lacan-reading-Hegel machine can be applied to. This means that you will learn something about politics and a Marxist tradition in politics – quasi-Stalinist with tinges of Maoism most of the time – in Žižek's work. But you should never imagine that there is a direct identification here between Žižek and his domain of application. Even his quick response to the question of what a good social order is for him, namely 'communism', is accompanied by a cynical taunting gloss on the answer, that this means 'egalitarianism with a taste of terror'.[62] However, the asymmetry between the Lacan-reading-Hegel machine, on the one hand, and its domain of application as politically textured culture, on the other, means that there is a double distortion at work.

Asymmetric anamorphic applications

There is in Žižek's writing a particular kind of application to the domain that frames politics in Lacanian terms, and another that frames it in Hegelian terms, and it is that second asymmetry that makes the political lens of the machine and object very fragile, at least prone to serious symptomatic distortions. The second asymmetry – Lacan-reading-Hegel as the machine, and culture treated as a politically textured superstructure as the domain of application – means that it is not at all the case that Žižek follows Lenin in putting politics in command. Politics is indeed a constant domain of application for Žižek, but his politics is susceptible to radical, even disastrous shifts as the lens is knocked. With theoretical work, just one little knock of the lens will change the view we have of the whole social field.

One striking example of this anamorphic shift of perspective concerns the relationship between psychoanalysis and culture, specifically psychoanalysis as a cultural practice made possible by the position of Freud as a Jew at one and the same moment in and against the dominant secular, but still by default Viennese Christian, culture. The characterisation of psychoanalysis as a 'Jewish science' is not a mere fantasy of the Nazis, but also draws attention to the importance in Freud's work of the Jewish religious, mystical and cultural tradition as infusing the texture of debate. This internally heterogeneous and marginalised tradition constituted psychoanalysis as a practice in a particular relation to talk and text, drawing on an intellectual culture in which apprenticeship is organised through an oral tradition which is devoted to re-readings of the Torah, the Talmud and a host of Rabbinical commentaries.[63] It would be possible to say that psychoanalysis is also constituted in a particular relation between the law – the Oedipal relation that the child must negotiate to enter civilisation, the symbolic that enters into the constitution of the unconscious as the infant becomes a speaking subject – and love. Love is brought to play in the transference enacted in analysis as the repetition of relations to earlier love objects, and the love of knowledge is experienced as appearing in the subject supposed to know. This is why Lacan's work is properly psychoanalytic insofar as it retains that link with the broad cultural tradition of secularised Judaism.

The Christian thematic in Lacan's work is most of the time subdued, mainly submerged within the broader Judaic tradition of psychoanalysis,[64] and the Hegelian European worldview is often tempered in Žižek's writing until the late 1990s. However, now that his more explicit discussions of the figure of Christ – a little bit of the real, a fragile figure of lack, the one who assumes the burden of our interpassive relation to the Other – have assumed centre-stage, it is possible to go back and find the same underlying reference points in Žižek's first English-language books, and it is then tempting to assume that this one position underpins each of his successive interventions in philosophy, psychoanalysis and politics since the 1980s. We also need to attend, though, to the change of focus in his work, in order to understand how the lens of the Lacan-reading-Hegel machine has been knocked so as to give rise to some quite different political effects.

There is then – when the lens is knocked – an unfortunate retroactive reframing of the Lacanian tradition so that the participation of many

Jesuits in the founding of Lacan's own school in 1964, after his 'excommunication'[65] from the IPA, for example, stands as evidence for some kind of revolt of the Christians against the new English-speaking psychoanalytic empire, and for what Žižek likes to see as the 'Christianising' of psychoanalysis. It should be noted – especially for readers from within Anglican or Protestant cultural traditions – that Žižek's radical historical counterposition of Judaic Law, as the rule of an omnipotent terrifying God, to Christian Love, as the offer of redemption under the guidance of Christ as fragile shepherd, is actually simply a repetition of one of the stories Catholic children are told over and again about the Jews in Sunday-school. Žižek's image of Judaism is a Catholic image, and it is being revived by him now exactly at a time when Catholic Slovenia is reasserting its Christian heritage against both the formerly, formally atheist Yugoslavia, and the current revival of the Orthodox Church in Serbia. Although Žižek makes a distinction in *The Puppet and the Dwarf* between the 'perverse' ideological universe of 'really existing Christianity' and the redemptive new beginning promised by Christ that he aims to retrieve from that universe, his favourite texts are those of reactionary Catholic writers like G. K. Chesterton and C. S. Lewis – and he draws attention with great delight, as he had already ten years back (in EYW), to the fact that Hitchcock too was an English Catholic.

Psychoanalytic Stalinism

The use of Lacan as a machine for reading Hegel with its domain of application as politics thus careers off the tracks of the quasi-Marxist project of the 1960s; Jacques-Alain Miller had been active in those days as a Maoist, so Žižek could then easily have come to imagine that this 'good Stalin' really did want to turn psychoanalysis to the Left, and now Žižek is one of the driving forces for a re-orientation towards some kind of 'Pauline materialism'. On the one hand (a grim prognosis for Lacanian psychoanalysis), Žižek is not alone, for he is accompanied by comrades like Alain Badiou, also writing about the 'event' that was St Paul, and the choice of Carl Schmitt – speaking for the worst of the Christian Right – over Jacques Derrida's reworking of Judaic liberalism[66] is another bad omen. On the other hand, Žižek does not wield much influence on Miller, whose political ambitions are much more cautious and cryptic.[67]

In fact, Žižek's relationship to the psychoanalytic community, which he proudly characterises as Stalinist, is uncannily close to the position of Leftist fellow-travelling artists and intellectuals in relation to the Communist Party apparatus when it enjoyed power in Eastern Europe. In 'Lenin's Choice', for example, Žižek praises Bertholt Brecht in terms that draw attention to some close identification with his subject alongside a res-

urrection of the Neue Slowenische Kunst motif of overidentification:
'Brecht was unbearable to the Stalinist cultural establishment because of
his very "over-orthodoxy".'[68] Presumably we are supposed to include in
manifestations of this radical orthodoxy Brecht's own diary account –
which Žižek cites two pages earlier – of waving at the column of Soviet
tanks on their way to crush the Berlin workers' uprising of 1953. It sure is
similar to Žižek's tale of sitting eating strawberry cakes in Prague in 1968
while watching the Soviet tanks deal with the demonstrators.[69]

Brecht's ostensible 'over-orthodoxy' then prompts Žižek to insert a
footnote about the six-category classification of literature by the Stalinist
regime in the German Democratic Republic. In this classification Brecht
figures as one of the '"problematic" authors who, although committed
Marxists, were not totally controlled by the Party, and were thus always
under suspicion and tightly controlled.'[70] This 'problematic' category,
along with the category of anti-communist authors who were simply
ignored, was not, Žižek claims, even referred to publicly, and the four
categories that were used by the nomenklatura – 'Communist classics,
great progressive humanists, tolerated authors and prohibited authors' – thus
served to sideline troublesome characters like Brecht without having to
confront them head-on.

Žižek's own position in relation to the Millerian 'psychoanalytic army'
seems to be exactly of this kind; there have been occasional meetings
where he is wheeled out for the US audience, but he is not a trustworthy
part of the apparatus.[71] Žižek's references to the Slovene Lacanian 'inner
party circle'[72] also draw attention to a marginal status that he seems for now
to revel in. Where Žižek moves next with the Lacan machine for reading
Hegel, applied to culture as some kind of self-sufficient, politically charged
superstructure, will therefore eventually also pose a question for where he
stands in relation to psychoanalysis as an institution, and it may well not
be decided by him. Will he indeed slide from the unacknowledged category
of problematic authors into one of those who are simply ignored? This will
be determined mainly by the context of his writing, but there are also key
issues of form that need to be tackled. We now move on to more risky
territory in order to try and account for the stylistic properties of his writing.

THE WRONG MAN

In the course of a discussion of the phenomenon of 'interpassivity' – in
which we give ourselves over to something or someone to act in our
place[73] – Žižek extends the remit of the well-known Lacanian formula for
transference, as the installation by the analysand of a 'subject supposed to
know' that stands for them in the place of the analyst. Beyond analysis,

Žižek argues, there is already in place a 'subject supposed to believe' which is 'the fundamental, constitutive feature of the symbolic order'.[74] Our most fundamental beliefs, then, are from the start imputed to some other, and this 'universally and structurally necessary' phenomenon is the original grounding point from which we develop a relation to belief. One can see here a replay of Žižek's account of the symbolic order as an ideological machinery which already contains a system of beliefs and positions for the divided subject, organised around an indefinable 'sublime object'. To become a Marxist, then, is also to find a system in which there are others who believe, and then to participate in the ritualised reproduction of those beliefs so that one eventually is able to believe the system oneself.

As Žižek freely admits, this is an elaboration and correction of the Althusserian account of interpellation that mimics a definition drawn from Pascal[75] of how one comes to religious faith. There is, he claims, in addition to the 'subject supposed to believe' – as a further function of the super-egoic imperative to 'enjoy!' (the obscene reverse of the superegoic prohibition on enjoyment) – the production of a 'subject supposed to enjoy', someone else who will relieve us of the pressure of having to enjoy ourselves. So now it seems reasonable to step into Žižek's frame of belief to ask what subject supposed to believe we impute to the texts we read by him, and what subject supposed to enjoy appears to us as readers as some kind of ghostly phantom.

The grid I have outlined so far provides one view of the asymmetrical relation between the components of this symbolic system – Žižek's writing – and we have moved a little closer to some kind of understanding of what it is that could be going on in his work. But we still need to go a little further to explain why things are set up in this way and what might happen next. One way of doing that is to reconstruct his trajectory around questions and breaking points, and treat these as the conditions of impossibility that structure his work. Three motifs in his writing are key for plotting this trajectory, and for outlining coordinates for making sense of his style of writing.

Post-colonial edginess

First, there is what could be termed post-colonial edginess. What do we learn about what it is to become a subject in post-Second World War Yugoslavia? What we learn from Žižek is a very specific narrative about being at the edge of power. The only child of parents who were members of the Communist Party, as he also was to be, but in an apparatus that was itself at the edge of the edge; Slovenia as a small Catholic country on the edge of a state that presented itself as a socialist self-management regime on the edge of the Soviet bloc. Žižek's writing on cynicism as a key component of the functioning of ideology exactly traces that position of being on the edge, but also of being personally implicated – dependent on parents for support after an academic post was refused him, and then dependent on the party apparatus during his time taking minutes for the very bureaucrats he would indict. This edginess is also replicated in his astute commentaries on West European and US culture, in an insistence that Europe – with the advent of 'politics proper' in Greece – is the point of opening and of resistance against the new global Empire of post-political rule, and in an attention to what is going on inside the Empire that is sharper than that of many of its own inhabitants.

There are two paradoxes of centre and periphery under contemporary global capitalism that are neatly captured in 'post-colonial' theory.[76] One paradox is that while those who like to think of themselves as being at the centre are increasingly uncertain about who they are and where they are going, they project that sense of fragmentation onto the periphery. The 'Third World' and post-Stalinist Eastern Europe can then become the romanticised sites in which non-rational divided subjects seem to live and enjoy diverse and contradictory but, at the same time, more organically natural lifestyles, and this is one way that post-structuralism hooks up with New Age evocations of something spiritual (something Žižek himself notices and comments upon, of course).

The second intersecting paradox is that the gazed-upon subjects of this supposedly new post-colonial condition, those on the edges, have been very well schooled in old colonial culture, for they were made to learn it as a condition for being thought civilised enough to participate in intellectual debate. The message the post-colonial subject returns – in reverse true form – to the colonial centres, then, is that indeed it is the case that you have lost your old culture, and we know that better than you. This is the message we get back from Žižek about Hitchcock films, for example. He tells us he has seen all of them, and tells us what is going on in them unbeknownst to us. In this sense we could say that Žižek appears to us as a perfect post-Stalinist post-colonial subject; that he knows more about us than we know about ourselves and that he knows that our fascination with him as an exotic character is license for games in which he tells us lies that we treat as truth.[77]

Embrace or escape

The second motif is an oscillation between embrace and escape, a polarity in which there is a recurring fear and temptation of complete immersion in a symbolic system on the one hand and a hope, on the other, that there might be some way of leaping out of it so that one is free of all that is laid down and all that is expected. What do we learn about language, the law and ideology from Žižek? That there is a perpetual threat that they will enclose and envelop the individual subject so that there is no way out. The tension between ideology as all-enveloping and the hope that there is an alternative is clearly at work in Žižek's writing on politics. But we find the same tension at work throughout his writing. Do we need to try frantically to get out – with an impossible 'act' as the only way to change the symbolic coordinates – or can we sink relieved into the system of language? Is it really the case that Žižek was ever so thoroughly against the bureaucracy in Slovenia at all, and was there not always a temptation to relax and enjoy being part of the inner party opposition?

There is even a nostalgic tinge to this formulation when Žižek repeats the joke about the bureaucrats in Russia riding about in limousines 'while in Yugoslavia, *ordinary people themselves ride in limousines through their representatives*',[78] for 'by submitting myself to some other disciplinary machine, I, as it were, transfer to the Other the responsibility to maintain the smooth run of things and thus gain the precious space in which to exercise my freedom'.[79]

Against the complaint in Žižek's writing on ideology – that there is complete closure, no space for thinking against it – there is also, then, a claim that the symbolic is not at all a totally regulated intersubjective space where everything is closed down. Žižek makes the point against Butler, for example, that she mischaracterises the symbolic when she treats it as something that is imposed to limit the movement of the subject. For Žižek (following Lacan quite faithfully) it is the imaginary that fixes us in a relation to the other, and the entry into the symbolic that opens up space to move around in. There is, then, always something like the hope that 'by surrendering my innermost content, inclusive of my dreams and anxieties, to the Other, a space opens up in which I am free to breathe'.[80] There is thus an opposition structuring Žižek's writing, an opposition between the option of moving in or moving out. This opposition sets out a forced choice: an embrace of the way things are as the conservative option, or escape from everything, as the ultra-left option. One option is the cracked mirror of the other.

The knot of writing culture

The third stylistic motif in Žižek's work is the way he writes culture as a way of knotting things together, so that we then suppose that something is holding all of these contradictory texts together. The temptation to be avoided here is to assume that when Žižek moves from one position to another he is solving the contradictions, or improving the narrative so that it reads more seamlessly. Rather, we should notice what changes in his writing and what stays the same. What changes is the content of his critical description of cultural phenomena. At one point the concern might be with the process of interpellation in Marx, and the spectre of an ideological machine that pulls the subject into it without any meaning offered in return, the predicament of the subject in Kafka's *Trial*.[81] At another point the concern might be with the process by which the police system incriminates a subject, and the prospect that someone who is innocent will be at the mercy of the law, the predicament of Henry Fonda in Hitchcock's film *The Wrong Man*.[82] And at yet another point, the concern may be with a new symbolic system luring the subject into it with the promise that everything will be laid open, but which is actually shutting things down around it, the predicament of the subject too close to things in cyberspace.[83]

What stays the same is the horrific idea that something or someone will capture and toy with the subject. This idea is something that, Žižek argues, 'translates the logic of Hitchcock's "sadist" playing with the viewer' in which the trap of 'sadistic identification' is laid: 'Hitchcock closes the trap by simply realising the viewer's desire: in having his/her desire fully realised, the viewer obtains more than he/she asked for.'[84] This logic is homologous to when cyberspace closes the gap between subject and symbolic; 'the distance between the subject's symbolic identity and its phantasmatic background; fantasies are increasingly immediately externalized in the public symbolic space',[85] and so 'the phantasmatic intimate kernel of our being is laid bare in a much more direct way, making us totally vulnerable and helpless'.[86] And – this is the crucial point – Žižek keeps space free from all of this by writing culture.

This is where the Lacan-machine-for-reading-Hegel becomes a writing machine that will hold things together in a way that also keeps them at a distance. And it keeps them at a distance by re-representing them to the Other. One telling example Žižek throws into his discussion of the staging of things for the desire of the Other is that of a comedy film about Western tourists in the GDR. The tourists see brutal dogs and beaten children – the full horror of life under communism as they expected to see it – but when they move on the scene changes and the children get up and dust themselves down, 'in short, the whole display of "Communist brutality" was laid on *for Western eyes*'.[87] Žižek knots things together in his writing so that they seem to hold together, and he always produces that writing as a display for an audience. In this sense he is leading us on again when he says that things are the opposite of what they seem, for his writing is actually a triumph of representation; things are actually as they appear.

The present, to wrap him up

These coordinates for reading Žižek – post-colonial edginess, immersion–escape dualism, writing culture as the knot of his work – lead us to make a leap from the torrent of books and papers to some figure lying behind them. If we were to think that we really are capturing and characterising something of what is going on inside his head, we would be making a big mistake. What we have to keep focused on is the way that gap between the texts we read and the author is itself an artifice, an artful game in which, as he tells us, everything is the opposite of what it seems. In that game he gives us enough clues to mislead us, perhaps even to read the writing as an elaborate system of defences that would indeed confirm the diagnosis he often provides of himself – that this is the work of obsessional neurosis. And we should also take care not to fall into the trap of imagining that the psychoanalytic machine for reading Hegel applied to Marxist themes is a knot of writing culture that will lead us to a more certain diagnosis of 'Žižek-the-*sinthome*'.[88]

The *sinthome* – among other things the term is a homophone in French for 'saintly man' – is a formulation of the symptom in late Lacan as, in Žižek's words, 'a particular, "pathological", signifying formation, a binding of enjoyment, an inert stain resisting communication and interpretation'.[89] For Lacan, the *sinthome* was a conceptual device for pinning James Joyce down, for identifying the role of Joyce's writing as the place where things were held together, perhaps as a way of circumventing psychosis. For Žižek, this symptom with which the subjects must identify themselves at the end of analysis is 'a stain which cannot be included in the circuit of discourse, of social bond network, but is at the same time a positive condition of it'.[90]

This would be a neat enough way to end a book on Žižek; to move through 'two stages of the psychoanalytic process: [1] *interpretation of symptoms* – [2] *going through the fantasy*',[91] and so conclude that he is an inert stain resisting communication and interpretation. But once again we need to give another little reflexive twist to the narrative, to include some Hegelian reflexive determination in the story, to include us as implicated in the gaze of the West (wherever we are), reading Žižek, trying to map the conditions of impossibility that will make his work more readable. For Žižek, the underlying primary position of the subject is as hysteric,[92] and capitalism is a form of hysterical social bond. It incites complaining and questioning about what is being done to us and where we are in all this, as men or women. And this hysterical condition of the subject as historically located in certain economic conditions does not so much provoke a psychotic *passage à l'acte* as 'acting out'. The crucial difference between the two kinds of act, remember, is that a *passage à l'acte* – which Žižek takes as his exemplar for an act that will escape immersion in a symbolic system that has come too overwhelmingly close – is completely outside the frame of the Other. Acting out, on the other hand, is always staged for the Other – a display of hysterical challenge that accuses and refuses. So, when he accuses and refuses his readers he also does so as someone who knows something more than ourselves about what we enjoy. That is why it does not need to make sense, and then it could be said that Slavoj Žižek is acting out, for us, and that is why we like it.

Abbreviations

These abbreviations are for the main Žižek texts cited in this book. See the bibliography for full details of the titles.

CHU   *Contingency, Hegemony, Universality: Contemporary Dialogues on the Left* (co-authored with Judith Butler and Ernesto Laclau)

DSST   *Did Somebody Say Totalitarianism? Five Interventions in the (Mis)use of a Notion*

ES   *Enjoy Your Symptom: Jacques Lacan In Hollywood and Out*

EYW   *Everything You Wanted to Know About Lacan (But Were Afraid to Ask Hitchcock)*

FA   *The Fragile Absolute – or, Why is the Christian Legacy Worth Fighting For?*

FTKN   *For They Know Not What They Do: Enjoyment As a Political Factor*

IR   *The Indivisible Remainder: An Essay on Schelling and Related Matters*

LA   *Looking Awry: An Introduction to Jacques Lacan through Popular Culture*

ME   *The Metastases of Enjoyment: Six Essays on Woman and Causality*

OB   *On Belief*

OWB   *Organs without Bodies*

PD   *The Puppet and the Dwarf: The Perverse Core of Christianity*

PF   *The Plague of Fantasies*

RG   *Revolution at the Gates: A Selection of Writings from February to October 1917*

SOI   *The Sublime Object of Ideology*

TN   *Tarrying with the Negative: Kant, Hegel, and the Critique of Ideology*

TS   *The Ticklish Subject: The Absent Centre of Political Ontology*

Notes

CHAPTER 1 YUGOSLAVIA – TO SLOVENIA

1. For a discussion of the difference between Foucault and Lacan on the historicist reduction of ideas to their specific contexts see Joan Copjec (1993) *Read my Desire: Lacan Against the Historicists* (Cambridge, MA: MIT Press).

2. 'The key "reversal" of the dialectical process takes place when we recognize in what at first appeared as a "condition of impossibility" – as a hindrance to our full identity, to the realization of our potential – the *condition of possibility* of our ontological consistency.' FTKN, p. 70.

3. http://www.ff.uni-lj.si/filo/english/staff/zizeka.htm (accessed 13 January 2003).

4. See, for example, the references to the 'mighty socialist revolution' and a 'workers and peasants government' (from a US American quasi-Trotskyist position) in George Fyson, Argiris Malapanis and Jonathan Silberman (1993) *The Truth About Yugoslavia* (New York: Pathfinder Press), and allusions to Yugoslavia being viewed as a communist state with a difference by a generation of radicals after the Second World War (from a British feminist standpoint) by Meg Coulson (1993) 'Looking behind the violent break-up of Yugoslavia', *Feminist Review*, 45, pp. 86–101.

5. Churchill's account of a meeting with Stalin in the Kremlin in October 1944 indicates how quickly Stalin agreed by ticking with a blue pencil the half sheet of paper on which was sketched out the apportionment of the countries of the buffer-zone. See Robert Black (1970) *Stalinism in Britain: A Trotskyist Analysis* (London: New Park Publications), p. 193.

6. See Branka Magaš (1993) *The Destruction of Yugoslavia: Tracking the Break-up 1980–92* (London: Verso), p. 26.

7. 'The Ustashe, an extreme Croat nationalist movement fostered by Italian fascism in the thirties and numbering no more than a few hundred supporters, were hoisted to power by the invading German army.' Magaš, *The Destruction of Yugoslavia*, p. 43.

8. Žižek discusses Lenin's break from this conception of history in his afterword to *Revolution at the Gates*. The most far-reaching Marxist critique of this stagist position was Trotsky's 1906 *Results and Prospects*, elaborated in the theory of permanent revolution in1929. Leon Trotsky (1969) *The Permanent Revolution and Results and Prospects* (New York: Pathfinder Press).

9. See Black, *Stalinism in Britain*.

10. For a Marxist analysis of this degeneration see Trotsky's 1936 account, in Leon Trotsky (1973) *The Revolution Betrayed: What is the Soviet Union, And Where is it Going?* (London: New Park Publications).

11. See Tim Wohlforth (1964) 'The theory of structural assimilation', in Wohlforth, T. and Westoby, A. (1978) *'Communists' Against Revolution: Two Essays on Post-War Stalinism* (London: Folrose Books).

12. The report of a 1976 delegation to Albania of the Communist Party of Britain (Marxist-Leninist), for example, enthusiastically described how the education system was built

on 'the revolutionary triangle of learning, physical labour and military training'. New Albania Society (1970s, n.d.) *Albania, The Most Successful Country in Europe* (London: New Albania Society), pp. 19–20.

13. Wohlforth, 'The Theory of Structural Assimilation', p. 59.

14. See Edvard Kardelj (1978) *Democracy and Socialism* (London: Summerfield).

15. See Misha Glenny (1993) *The Rebirth of History: Eastern Europe in the Age of Democracy*, second edition (Harmondsworth: Penguin).

16. 'Self-management could not have functioned without prior denationalisation, without separation of economic subjects (enterprises) from the state.' Janez Šmidovnik (1991) 'Disfunctions of the system of self-management in the economy, in local territorial communities and in public administration', in Simmie, J. and Dekleva, J. (eds) (1991) *Yugoslavia in Turmoil: After Self-Management* (London and New York: Pinter Publishers), p. 17.

17. Sigmund Freud (1930) *Civilization and Its Discontents*, in Freud, S. (1964) *The Standard Edition of the Complete Psychological Works of Sigmund Freud, Volume XXI (1927–1931)* (London: Hogarth Press), p. 124.

18. See Michel Foucault (1975) *Discipline and Punish: The Birth of the Prison*, translated by Alan Sheridan, 1979 (Harmondsworth: Penguin).

19. Karl Marx noted after the 1845 events in France that 'Each overturn, instead of breaking up, carried this machine to higher perfection. The parties, that alternately wrestled for supremacy, looked upon the possession of this tremendous governmental structure as the principal spoils of their victory.' Karl Marx (1869) *The Eighteenth Brumaire of Louis Bonaparte*, http://www.e-bookshop.gr/gutenberg/files/mar1810.pdf (accessed 17 June 2003), p. 168.

20. See the interview in Robert Boynton (1998) 'Enjoy your Žižek!: An excitable Slovenian philosopher examines the obscene practices of everyday life – including his own', *Linguafranca: The Review of Academic Life*, 7 (7), http://www.linguafranca.com/9810/zizek.html (accessed 15 May 2001).

21. Boynton, 'Enjoy your Žižek!'.

22. Kusturica 'unknowingly provides the libidinal economy of the Serbian ethnic slaughter in Bosnia'. PF, p. 64. Žižek points out that Kusturica himself has claimed that 'in the Balkans, war is a natural phenomenon, nobody knows when it will emerge, it just comes, it's in our genes', in Geert Lovink (1995) 'Civil society, fanaticism, and digital reality: A conversation with Slavoj Zizek', http://www.ctheory.com/article/a037.html (accessed 8 May 2001). See also Igor Krstic (2002) 'Re-thinking Serbia: A psychoanalytic reading of modern Serbian history and identity through popular culture', *Other Voices*, 2 (2), http://www.othervoices.org/2.2/krstic/ (accessed 14 June 2002).

23. Avtah Brah (1993) 'Re-framing Europe: En-gendered racisms, ethnicities and nationalisms in contemporary Western Europe', *Feminist Review*, 45, pp. 9–28.

24. Lepa Mladjenovic and Vera Litricin (1993) 'Belgrade feminists 1992: Separation, guilt and identity crisis', *Feminist Review*, 45, pp. 113–19.

25. Renata Salecl (1994) *The Spoils of Freedom: Psychoanalysis and Feminism After the Fall of Socialism* (London: Routledge).

26. I refer to 'Kosovo' in this account, following the spelling used in most mainstream and opposition Yugoslav literature, though it should be noted that the preferred self-designation of the place by many Kosovars is 'Kosova'. See Geoff Ryan (ed.) (1994) *Bosnia 1994: Armageddon in Europe* (London: Socialist Outlook).

27. Magaš, *The Destruction of Yugoslavia*, p. 18. (Magaš, who is from Croatia, uses the term 'Moslem'.)

28. The 1974 Constitution also recognised as 'nationalities' Bulgarians, Czechs, Gypsies, Italians, Romanians, Ruthenians, Slovaks and Turks, and 'ethnic groups' of Austrians, Greeks, Jews, Germans, Poles, Russians, Ukrainians and Vlahs. Coulson, 'Looking behind the violent break-up of Yugoslavia', p. 88.

29. Magaš, *The Destruction of Yugoslavia*, p. 18.

30. *Bradstvo i jedinstvo* in Serbo-Croat.

31. Ryan, *Bosnia 1994.*

32. See Magaš, *The Destruction of Yugoslavia* for an account of these changes in the line of the Yugoslav Communist Party.

33. A claim made by some Croats interviewed by Magaš, *The Destruction of Yugoslavia*.

34. Jože Mencinger (1991) 'From a capitalist to a capitalist economy?' in Simmie and Dekleva, *Yugoslavia in Turmoil*.

35. Ibid., p. 83.

36. Ryan, *Bosnia 1994.*

37. And so, 'the struggle among the different republican and provincial bureaucracies soon becomes translated into a struggle between different "natural and authentic" national interests'. Miha Kovač (1988) 'The Slovene spring', *New Left Review*, 171, pp. 115–28, (p. 119).

38. Slavoj Žižek (1990) 'Eastern Europe's Republics of Gilead', *New Left Review*, 183, pp. 50–62, (p. 60).

39. Magaš, *The Destruction of Yugoslavia*, pp. 30–1.

40. Ibid., p. 34.

41. Ibid., p. 46.

42. The petition is reproduced in Magaš, *The Destruction of Yugoslavia*, pp. 49–52.

43. Salecl, *The Spoils of Freedom*, p. 28.

44. Stalin, in fact, revoked rights to abortion and divorce instituted during the 1917 October revolution in the Soviet Union and revived reactionary images of the nation and the family. Lucio Colletti (1970) 'The question of Stalin', *New Left Review*, 61, pp. 61–81.

45. A Network of Yugoslav Feminists was founded in Ljubljana in 1987, but by the 1990s 'conflicts over nationalism were far too strong in dividing women and there was no way to go on'. Mladjenovic and Litricin, 'Belgrade feminists 1992', p. 117.

46. Salecl, *The Spoils of Freedom*, p. 25.

47. Ibid., p. 22.

48. Ibid., p. 29.

49. *Praxis International* appeared in 1981 as a successor to *Praxis*, which had been published from 1964 to 1975. At that point, although 'the theoretical orientation of *Praxis* was always clearly Marxist and its commitment to democratic socialism explicit, the journal came under increasingly strong attack by political authorities'. Richard Bernstein and Mihailo Marković (1981) 'Why *Praxis International?*', 1, 1, pp. 1–5 (p. 1). For a history of the group see Mihailo Marković and Robert Cohen (1975) *The Rise and Fall of Socialist Humanism: A History of the Praxis Group* (Nottingham: Spokesman Books). A representative text of the Praxis group was Mihailo Marković (1974) *The Contemporary Marx: Essays on Humanist Communism* (Nottingham: Spokesman Books). The open letter defending the 1986 appeal from Zagorka Golubović, Mihailo Marković and Ljubomir Tadić to the Editorial Collective of *Labour Focus on Eastern Europe* is reproduced with a reply by Magaš (writing as 'Michelle Lee') in Magaš, *The Destruction of Yugoslavia*, pp. 55–61.

50. There had been one report of murder of a Slav in Kosovo in the previous five years, the outcome of a dispute between neighbours that the judicial investigation decided had

not been committed out of national hatred. The level of rapes was not higher than in other parts of Yugoslavia, and 'the figures do not show any particular national bias: the overwhelming majority of both perpetrators and victims are Albanian'. Magaš, *The Destruction of Yugoslavia*, p. 62.

51. Cited in Magaš, *The Destruction of Yugoslavia*, p. 41.
52. Vamik Volkan (2001) 'Transgenerational transmissions and chosen traumas: An aspect of large-group identity', *Group Analysis*, 34, 1, pp. 79–97 (p. 92).
53. Ibid.
54. Ibid., p. 93.
55. This is apropos what he sees as Chomsky's errors on Kosovo, in which he claims that Chomsky's narrative was that 'we shouldn't put all the blame on Milosevic, that all parties were more or less to blame, and the West supported or incited this explosion because of its own geopolitical goals'. Žižek, in Doug Henwood (2002) 'I am a fighting atheist: Interview with Slavoj Žižek', *Bad Subjects*, 59, http://eserver.org/bs/59/zizek.html (accessed 3 June 2002).
56. Ian Parker (1997) *Psychoanalytic Culture: Psychoanalytic Discourse in Western Society* (London: Sage).
57. For an enthusiastic account of this view of classes see David MacGregor (1984) *The Communist Ideal in Hegel and Marx* (Toronto: University of Toronto Press), p. 30.
58. For one of the latest formulations of this fantasy of a 'third way', in which owners and employees would work together in a common interest, see Anthony Giddens (1998) *The Third Way: The Renewal of Social Democracy* (Cambridge: Polity Press).
59. Bogomir Kovač (1991) 'Entrepreneurship and the privatisation of social ownership in economic reforms', in Simmie and Dekleva, *Yugoslavia in Turmoil*.
60. See, for example, Milovan Djilas (1966) *The New Class: An Analysis of the Communist System* (London: Allen and Unwin).
61. Žižek, 'Eastern Europe's republics of Gilead'.
62. The phrase 'theft of enjoyment' is borrowed from Jacques-Alain Miller's 1986 lecture '*Extimité*', published in English in M. Bracher, M. M. W. Alcorn, R. J., Corthell and F. Massardier-Kenney (eds) (1994) *Lacanian Theory of Discourse: Subject, Structure and Society* (New York: New York University Press).
63. Žižek, 'Eastern Europe's republics of Gilead', p. 59.
64. Ibid., p. 54.
65. Ibid., p. 58.
66. For example, in the account by Krstic, 'Re-thinking Serbia'.
67. Žižek, 'Eastern Europe's republics of Gilead', p. 62.
68. The Slovenian Government website now glosses the activities of the student and youth resistance during the 1980s as a 'push towards freedom of speech, democratisation of society and market oriented reforms', http://www.uvi.si/eng/slovenia/facts/international-relations/ (accessed 13 January 2003).
69. Jože Mencinger (1991) 'From a capitalist to a capitalist economy?' in Simmie and Dekleva, *Yugoslavia in Turmoil*.
70. Kovač, 'The Slovene spring'.
71. 'Yugoslavia was not over with the secession of Slovenia. It was over the moment Milosevic took over Serbia. This triggered a totally different dynamic. It is also not true that the disintegration of Yugoslavia was supported by the West. On the contrary, the West exerted enormous pressure, at least until 1991, for ethnic groups to remain in Yugoslavia', Žižek in Henwood, 'I am a fighting atheist'.

72. Now written as 'overwhelming victory by the Slovene Territorial Defence Forces' on the Slovenian Government website, http://www.uvi.si/eng/slovenia/facts/international-relations/ (accessed 13 January 2003).

73. Žižek in Henwood, 'I am a fighting atheist'.

74. 'The British government abandoned its publicly stated opposition to diplomatic recognition of Croatia and Slovenia under German pressure on 16 December 1991, in exchange for German support for the British right to "opt-out" from European monetary union and the Social Chapter of the Maastricht Treaty.' James Petras and Steve Vieux (1996) 'Bosnia and the revival of US hegemony', *New Left Review*, 218, pp. 3–25 (p. 12).

75. As one commentator put it a few months after the June ten-day stand-off, 'It is as yet uncertain whether this attack was intended to keep Slovenia in Yugoslavia, or to drive it out altogether.' Magaš, *The Destruction of Yugoslavia*, p. 333.

76. Kovač, 'The Slovene spring'.

77. Ibid.

78. Miha Kovač had been editor of *Mladina*, the weekly journal of the Association of Socialist Youth of Slovenia (that is, what is known in other accounts as the 'Slovene Socialist Youth Alliance'). Ibid.

79. Kenneth Mackendrick (2001) 'Slovene Lacanian school', in Winquist, C. and Taylor. V. (eds) *Encyclopaedia of Postmodernism*. London: Routledge. Ernesto Laclau describes the 'Slovenian Lacanian school' in his preface to Žižek's *The Sublime Object of Ideology*.

80. Salecl, *The Spoils of Freedom*.

81. Alenka Zupančič (2000) *Ethics of the Real: Kant, Lacan* (London: Verso).

82. For work by Dolar and Božovič on film, as well as by Salecl and Zupančič, see Žižek's edited *Everything You Always Wanted to Know about Lacan (But Were Afraid to Ask Hitchcock)*.

83. Kovač, 'The Slovene spring'.

84. Ibid.

85. Tomaž Mastnak (1991) 'From the new social movements to political parties' in Simmie and Dekleva, *Yugoslavia in Turmoil*, p. 45.

86. *Mladina*, established in 1943 as the paper of the Communist Youth Organization, is still going, and now looks back on the days of disintegration of the Yugoslav state apparatus with some nostalgia that still carries the traces of old Popular-Front Stalinism: 'Those were happy days for Slovenia: fascists and anarchists holding each others' hands and reading Mladina', http://yellow.eunet.si/yellowpage/0/mediji1/ml-info.html (accessed 27 May 2003). Their rather cruel caricature of Žižek wearing a bib with a picture of Stalin on is at http://www.mladina.si/projekti/duplerice/slavoj-zizek/ (accessed 27 May 2003).

87. Kovač, 'The Slovene spring', p. 117.

88. Joanne Richardson (2000) 'NSK 2000? Irwin and Eda Cufer interviewed by Joanne Richardson', http://subsol.c3.hu/subsol_2/contributors/nsktext.html (accessed 3 January 2003).

89. Ibid.

90. Ibid.

91. For one influential take on this see Ernesto Laclau and Chantal Mouffe (1985) *Hegemony and Socialist Strategy* (London: Verso).

92. Mastnak, in Simmie and Dekleva, *Yugoslavia in Turmoil*, p. 49.

93. Ibid., p. 53.

94. Ibid., p. 51.

95. Živko Pregl (Vice-President of the Federal Executive Council of the SFRY) in the Foreword to Simmie and Dekleva, *Yugoslavia in Turmoil*.

96. Meanwhile, Serbia has sought and failed to win approval from the West for its efforts at privatisation. Zoran Djindjic, the Serbian prime minister assassinated in March 2003, had tried to please the West and hardline nationalists. His trajectory from being a member of the Praxis Group and doctoral student under Jürgen Habermas to posing with Radovan Karadžić is symptomatic of the recent state of Serbian state politics.

97. Salecl, *Spoils of Freedom*, p. 147.

98. Mastnak, in Simmie and Dekleva, *Yugoslavia in Turmoil*, p. 61.

99. Žižek, in Lovink, 'Civil society, fanaticism, and digital reality'. This kind of comment does fuel the suspicion among Žižek's former allies in Slovenia that he is willing to endorse at least 'soft nationalism'; the movement for 'civil society' was in the early 1990s a faction on the left of his Liberal Democratic Party that was opposing nationalist agendas. See Nikolai Jeffs (1995) 'Transnational dialogue in times of war: The peace movement in ex-Yugoslavia, *Radical Philosophy*, 73, pp. 2–4.

100. Žižek, 'Eastern Europe's republics of Gilead', p. 62.

101. The charge that the 'heedless egoism' of the Slovenes 'did so much to wreck the old Federation' by the editor of *New Left Review* would seem to be a case in point. Robin Blackburn (1993) 'The break-up of Yugoslavia and the fate of Bosnia', *New Left Review*, 199, pp. 100–19 (p. 119).

102. Žižek in Lovink, 'Civil society, fanaticism, and digital reality'.

103. Slavoj Žižek (1999) 'Against the double blackmail', *New Left Review*, 234, pp. 76–82 (pp. 81–82). A longer version of the same article, with the same title, also appeared for a mainly US audience on the 'Lacan.com' website. Slavoj Žižek (1999) 'Against the double blackmail', http://www.lacan.com/kosovo.htm (accessed 23 September 2000).

104. The version I have was dated 9 April 1999. There is a discussion of the motif of hesitation in Sean Homer's '"It's the Political Economy Stupid!"': On Žižek's Marxism', *Radical Philosophy*, 108, pp. 7–16.

105. Žižek in Lovink, 'Civil society, fanaticism, and digital reality'.

106. Žižek in Boynton, 'Enjoy your Žižek!'.

CHAPTER 2 ENLIGHTENMENT – WITH HEGEL

1. The significant date of publication for Freud's formulation was 1933, the year the Nazis seized power in Germany.

2. Sigmund Freud (1933) *New Introductory Lectures on Psychoanalysis* (Lecture XXXI: The Dissection of the psychical personality), in S. Freud (1964) *The Standard Edition of the Complete Psychological Works of Sigmund Freud, Volume XXII (1932–1936)* (London: Hogarth Press), p. 80.

3. One characterisation of this standard view, which is then carefully unravelled in one of the best biographies of Hegel, runs as follows:

> Hegel is one of those thinkers just about all educated people think they know something about. His philosophy was a forerunner to Karl Marx's theory of history, but unlike Marx, who was a materialist, Hegel was an idealist in the sense that he thought that reality was ultimately spiritual, and that it developed according to the process of thesis / antithesis / synthesis. Hegel also glorified the Prussian state, claiming that it was God's work, was perfect, and was the culmination of all human history. All citizens of Prussia owed unconditional allegiance to that state,

and it could do with them as it pleased. Hegel played a large role in the growth of German nationalism, authoritarianism, and militarism with his quasi-mystical celebrations of what he pretentiously called the Absolute. Terry Pinkard (2000) *Hegel: A Biography* (Cambridge: Cambridge University Press), p. ix.

4.   Note that the formulation here – 'I am thinking, therefore I am, or I exist' – is a little different from the standard phrase in English ('I think, therefore I am'). The more processual designation of 'thinking' is preferred by Žižek, and is in the John Cottingham translation. René Descartes (1641) *Meditations on First Philosophy with Selections from the Objections and Replies*, translated by John Cottingham, 1996 (Cambridge: Cambridge University Press), p. 68.
5.   TN, p. 232.
6.   TN, p. 1.
7.   Žižek uses a theme from Wagner's *Parsifal* in TN (and in a number of other books) to describe how it is the very thing that we pose as the cause of our misery that may eventually come to be seen as the condition of our release: that 'The wound is healed only by the spear that smote you.'
8.   OB, p. 151.
9.   Hegel was a key reference point for T. H. Green and F. H. Bradley in England in the early nineteenth century, and became popular towards the end of the nineteenth century in the United States, where his work operated as background assumptions in the pragmatism of Dewey and Mead, and in the motif of 'recognition' among therapists influenced by Carl Rogers.
10. Žižek refers to this book in TS, p. 13.
11. Alexandre Kojève (1969) *Introduction to the Reading of Hegel* (New York: Basic Books).
12. Vincent Descombes (1980) *Modern French Philosophy* (Cambridge: Cambridge University Press).
13. Elisabeth Roudinesco (1990) *Jacques Lacan & Co.: A History of Psychoanalysis in France, 1925–1985* (London: Free Association Books), p. 135.
14. Descombes, *Modern French Philosophy*, p. 7.
15. Žižek, in Doug Henwood (2002) 'I am a fighting atheist: Interview with Slavoj Žižek', *Bad Subjects*, 59, http://eserver.org/bs/59/zizek.html (accessed 3 June 2002).
16. Fredric Jameson (1972) *The Prison-House of Language: A Critical Account of Structuralism and Russian Formalism* (New Jersey: Princeton University Press).
17. Terry Pinkard (1994) *Hegel's Phenomenology: The Sociality of Reason* (Cambridge: Cambridge University Press), p. 361.
18. '[T]he sensuous This that is meant *cannot be reached* by language', G. W. F. Hegel (1807) *Phenomenology of Spirit* (Oxford: Oxford University Press), p. 66.
19. TN, p. 142.
20. Hegel, *Phenomenology of Spirit*, p. 172.
21. 'While the one combatant prefers life, retains his single self-consciousness, but surrenders his claim for recognition, the other holds fast to his self-assertion and is recognised by the former as his superior. Thus arises the status of *master and slave*', Hegel, *Phenomenology of Spirit*, p. 173.
22. Hegel, *Aesthetics*, quoted in Pinkard, *Hegel's Phenomenology*, p. 401.
23. Hegel, quoted in TS, pp. 29–30.
24. TN, p. 142.
25. IR, p. 98.
26. Ibid.

27. Pinkard, *Hegel's Phenomenology*, p. 400.
28. Ibid., p. 217.
29. Hegel, *Aesthetics*, quoted in Pinkard, *Hegel's Phenomenology*, p. 401.
30. Pinkard, *Hegel's Phenomenology*, p. 251.
31. Cornelius Castoriadis – a practising Lacanian psychoanalyst as well as a Marxist – made this central to his account of the project of autonomy, and his arguments about the centrality of Greece in the history of European culture are picked up and endorsed, to take one case in point, by Renata Salecl (1996) 'See no evil, speak no evil: Hate speech and human rights' in Joan Copjec (ed.) (1996) *Radical Evil* (London: Verso).
32. TS, p. 88.
33. Ibid., p. 89.
34. Hegel, *Phenomenology of Spirit*, p. 170.
35. Pinkard, *Hegel*, pp. 49–51.
36. Pinkard, *Hegel's Phenomenology*, p. 436. There is an interesting discussion of Foucault, which traces the way writers after Kojève tried to open up the bloody struggle again and reconfigure it along Nietzschean lines as unending and as always viewed from within a history written by the victors. Michael Roth (ed.) (1988) *Knowing and History: Appropriations of Hegel in Twentieth Century France* (Ithaca: Cornell University Press).
37. David MacGregor (1984) *The Communist Ideal in Hegel and Marx* (Toronto: University of Toronto Press), p. 36.
38. Slavoj Žižek (2002) 'The interpassive subject', http://www.lacan.com/interpass.htm (accessed 2 December 2002). Žižck borrows the notion of 'interpassivity' from the Austrian philosopher and art theoretician Robert Pfaller. Robert Pfaller (1997) 'Philosophie und spontane philosophie der kunst-schaffenden / Philosophy and the spontaneous philosophy of the artists', *95/97 Projekte, Archimedia*, pp. 171–82. Robert Pfaller (1998) 'The work of art that observes itself: Eleven steps towards an aesthetics of interpassivity', *Presencias en el Espacio Publico Contentemporaneo, Universitat de Barcelona*, pp. 229–40.
39. Žižek, OWB, p. 204.
40. Descombes, *Modern French Philosophy*, p. 10.
41. Jean-Paul Sartre (1960) *Critique de la Raison Dialectique*, quoted in Descombes, *Modern French Philosophy*, p. 10.
42. Ibid., p. 148.
43. Immanuel Kant (1784) 'An answer to the question: What is enlightenment?', http://www.english.upenn.edu/~mgamer/Etexts/kant.html (accessed 24 February 2003).
44. A Kantian phrase, which Foucault adopts. For a discussion of this, and for Foucault's discussion of Kant's essay, see Hubert Dreyfus and Paul Rabinow (1982) *Michel Foucault: Beyond Structuralism and Hermeneutics* (Brighton: Harvester Press).
45. Kant, quoted in OB, p. 134.
46. Ibid., p. 135.
47. 'The "infrastructural" condition of possibility of an entity is at the same time the condition of its impossibility, its identity-with-itself is possible only against the background of its self-relationship – of a minimal self-differentiation and self-deferment which opens a gap forever hindering its full identity with itself', FTKN, p. 70.
48. TN, p. 128.
49. Ibid.
50. Kant, *Religion within the Limits of Reason Alone*, quoted in Copjec, *Radical Evil*, p. xiv.
51. Copjec, *Radical Evil*, p. xiv.

52. Gilles Deleuze (1994) *Masochism: Coldness and Cruelty* (New York: Zone Books), p. 83. Also quoted in Copjec, *Radical Evil*, p. xv.

53. Žižek does pay his respect to Joan Copjec in a footnote in *Tarrying with the Negative*, enough to say that the book is 'a token of my theoretical debt to her'. TN, p. 250. This is where he acknowledges that his discussion of Kant and Lacan's formulae of sexuation draw on Copjec's (1994) *Read My Desire: Lacan Against the Historicists* (Cambridge, MA: MIT Press). OWB has the dedication 'To Joan Copjec, with the coldness and cruelty of a true friendship'.

54. Copjec, *Radical Evil*, p. xviii.

55. Ibid., p. xiv.

56. Žižek's phrase to describe her, in ME, p. 213.

57. Jacques Lacan (1989) 'Kant with Sade', *October*, 51, pp. 55–104.

58. Alenka Zupančič (2000) *Ethics of the Real: Kant, Lacan* (London: Verso), p. 81.

59. Ibid., p. 90.

60. Lacan, 'Kant with Sade'.

61. Žižek, 'Foreword: Why is Kant worth fighting for?', in Zupančič, *Ethics of the Real*.

62. Zupančič, *Ethics of the Real*, p. 82.

63. OB, p. 135.

64. Josefina Ayerza (1992) 'Hidden prohibitions and the pleasure principle [interview with Žižek]', http://www.lacan.com/perfume/zizek.htm (accessed 25 February 2003).

65. This argument, outlined by Kant in *Religion Within the Limits of Reason Alone* (1793) is discussed in Joan Copjec, *Radical Evil*.

66. TS, p. 13.

67. However, for a review of the problems the Praxis Group faced, including in Slovenia, see Mihailo Marković and Robert Cohen (1975) *The Rise and Fall of Socialist Humanism: A History of the Praxis Group* (Nottingham: Spokesman Books).

68. Žižek, in Peter Dews and Peter Osborne (1991) 'Lacan in Slovenia: An interview with Slavoj Žižek and Renata Salecl', *Radical Philosophy*, 58, pp. 25–31 (p. 25).

69. TS, p. 13.

70. Ibid.

71. Ibid.

72. Ibid., p. 14.

73. Ibid., p. 20.

74. Eric Hobsbawm and Terence Ranger (eds) (1983) *The Invention of Tradition* (Cambridge: Cambridge University Press).

75. Žižek, in Ayerza, 'Hidden prohibitions'.

76. SOI, p. 155.

77. TN, p. 4.

78. Nathan Rotenstreich (1963) *The Recurring Pattern: Studies in Anti-Judaism in Modern Thought* (London: Weidenfeld and Nicolson).

79. Žižek, in Henwood, 'I am a fighting atheist'.

80. Ibid.

81. Žižek, in Ayerza, 'Hidden prohibitions'.

82. Ibid.

83. Žižek, in Henwood, 'I am a fighting atheist'.

84. OB, p. 11.

85. PD, p. 154

86. TS, p. 89.

87. TN, p. 285.

88. Žižek, in Henwood, 'I am a fighting atheist'.

89. OB, p. 106.

90. Ibid.
91. Castoriadis, quoted by Salecl, in Copjec, *Radical Evil*, p. 163.
92. OB, p. 106.
93. Ibid., p. 133.
94. Islam is, 'in spite of its global expansionism', one of the 'other "particularistic" religions', OB, p. 143. Even so, Žižek still refers to the 'truly dangerous power of Catholic ideology' as a threat to the old Yugoslav regime and, despite (or because of) Slovenia being a Catholic country, cites some of the most reactionary Catholic writers as warrant for his supposedly radical re-reading of the Christian legacy. PD, p. 49.
95. OB, p. 133.
96. Ibid., p. 129. On the other hand, 'Buddhist (or Hindu for that matter) all-encompassing Compassion has to be opposed to Christian intolerant, violent love'. PD, pp. 32–3.
97. In Judaism there is 'the tendency to perceive God as the cruel superego figure'. OB, p. 142.
98. Ibid. p. 132.
99. Ibid., p. 106.
100. Ibid., p. 89.
101. Ibid., pp. 89–90.
102. Ibid., p. 132.
103. Ibid., pp. 132–3.
104. Ibid., p. 141.
105. TN, p. 237.
106. Dialectically speaking, we then reach the point where we can apprehend 'absolute negativity' as the foundation not only of our own enlightenment but also of 'Hegel's break with the Enlightenment tradition'. ME, p. 145.

CHAPTER 3 PSYCHOANALYSIS – FROM LACAN

1. Sigmund Freud (1900) *The Interpretation of Dreams*, in S. Freud (1953) *The Standard Edition of the Complete Psychological Works of Sigmund Freud, Volume V (1900–1901)* (London: Hogarth Press), p. 437.
2. Bruno Bettelheim (1985) *Freud and Man's Soul* (London: Flamingo) argues that '*A Search for the Meaning of Dreams* or *An Inquiry into the Meaning of Dreams*' would have been a translation of *Die Traumdeutung* more in keeping with what Freud was aiming at (p. 70). Bettelheim's discussion of the other mistranslations of Freudian terms in the English *Standard Edition of the Complete Psychological Works of Sigmund Freud*, including the now notorious rendering of *Trieb* as 'Instinct' rather than 'Drive', has to be borne in mind while engaging in any interpretation of what Lacan was up to. Other examples include the rendering of Freud's everyday German words *Ich*, *Über-Ich* and *Es* (the 'I', 'above-I' and 'it') into the more technical English-speaking psychoanalytic vocabulary as 'ego', 'superego' and 'id'. The mistranslations have not been as drastic in the French editions of Freud's writing, and so there is already a conceptual and cultural gap between our English Freud and the 'return to Freud' in Lacan's work. Žižek is, in this respect, at least two steps ahead of us insofar as he comes to Freud through the German 'original' and then through the French debates.
3. Freud, in a letter to Jung, quoted in the epigraph to Bettelheim, *Freud and Man's Soul*.
4. TN, p. 4.
5. The Hegelian term for this simultaneous improvement and supercession is *Aufhebung*, part of a dialectical process in which concepts are retained and appear again on a higher level.

6. Deconstruction is one example of the relativist arguments in French philosophy that Lacan encountered, and a fairly late one, elaborated by Jacques Derrida in detail in the 1960s, but it is emblematic of the attempt to dissolve the subject into culturally local forms of language and the turn to deconstruction among Derrida's followers (if not for Derrida himself), which brought to a head certain sets of problems that psychoanalysis had to address. This is presumably why Žižek, in *Tarrying with the Negative*, names 'deconstruction' as the threat that Lacan tackled and surmounted.

7. Jacques Derrida (1983) 'Letter to a Japanese Friend', in David Wood and Robert Bernasconi (eds) (1988) *Derrida and* Différance (Evanston Il: Northwestern University Press). The reference to *Destruktion* here is to Heidegger's radical questioning of the conceptual architecture of Western philosophy, a notion that Derrida then sought to 'translate and adapt' for deconstruction (p. 1). The Heideggerian and Derridean notions open up and resituate concepts, and it is in this sense that we could think of psychoanalysis as a form of deconstruction.

8. Jacques Lacan (1975) *On Feminine Sexuality, The Limits of Love and Knowledge, 1972–1973: Encore, The Seminar of Jacques Lacan, Book XX*, translated with notes by Bruce Fink, 1998 (New York: Norton).

9. 'On the one hand, you can redeem Hegel or Kant through Lacan, but on the other hand, I claim that by reading them through Lacan you get another approach to Lacan himself. What you get this way is precisely the philosophical foundations of Lacan, and the social/critical dimensions of Lacan become much clearer if you combine the two.' Žižek, in Andrew Long and Tara McGann (1997) 'Interview with Slavoj Žižek', *Journal for the Psychoanalysis of Culture and Society*, 2, (1), pp. 133–7 (p. 137).

10. Jacques Lacan (1973) *Four Fundamental Concepts of Psycho-Analysis*, translated by Alan Sheridan, 1979 (Harmondsworth: Penguin).

11. Holbein's painting, together with a discussion of its place in anamorphic art, can be found at http://mason-west.com/Art/holbein.shtml (accessed 14 April 2003).

12. Žižek, in Long and McGann, 'Interview with Slavoj Žižek', p. 133.

13. David Stafford-Clark (1967) *What Freud Really Said* (Harmondsworth: Penguin) is one book that should be avoided; it includes terms like 'Electra complex' that Freud took pains to distance himself from.

14. One example is Bernard Burgoyne and Mary Sullivan (eds) (1997) *The Klein–Lacan Dialogues* (London: Rebus Press). Another is the exchange between the then president of the IPA, Horacio Etchegoyan, and Jacques-Alain Miller in 1996, www.ilimit.com/amp/english/vertex.htm (accessed 12 February 1999).

15. An indicative position statement of the Frankfurt School reading of 'Freud's developmental theory as an *empirical concretization* of the Kantian practical philosophy' is to be found in Joel Whitebook (1994) 'Hypostatizing Thanatos: Lacan's analysis of the ego', *Constellations*, 1, (2), pp. 214–30 (p. 215). This is in explicit opposition to Lacan, a deeply mistaken reading which also emphasises that it is 'an historical fact, not a piece of Eurocentrism, that this breakthrough [self-questioning in Kant and then Freud] occurred in the West' (p. 216).

16. Lacan (1973) *Four Fundamental Concepts of Psycho-Analysis*.

17. The notorious mistranslation of *Trieb* as 'instinct' rather than 'drive' has been noted by many writers, and is now acknowledged as such by most English-speaking psychoanalysts. However, there are a range of other mistakes in the translation that mean that English-speaking 'Freudians' still often turn to natural-scientific language to describe their practice.

18. It is usually Hegel, and at times Schelling, that operate as the proto-psychoanalytic predecessors to Lacan, and sometimes in these accounts Freud is bypassed altogether.

See Slavoj Žižek, 1996, *The Indivisible Remainder: An Essay on Schelling and Related Matters* (London: Verso).

19. One example is the discussion of Freud's brief comment about the non-analysable Slovene in *For They Know Not What They Do* as a hook to open the book, and another is the terrific in-depth account of Freud's theory of the dreamwork as homologous with Marx's account of commodities in *The Sublime Object of Ideology*.

20. Žižek, in CHU, p. 250. For a review of this Hegelianising of Freud by Žižek, and also by Butler and Laclau in *Contingency, Hegemony, Universality*, see Ian Parker (2003) 'Lacanian social theory and clinical practice', *Psychoanalysis and Contemporary Thought*, 26, (2), pp. 51–77.

21. ME, Chapter 1. For a discussion of the allegiances of psychoanalysis to the left, wiped out by the rise of fascism in Central Europe and by anti-communism and medicalised psychoanalysis in the US, see Russell Jacoby (1983) *The Repression of Psychoanalysis* (New York: Basic Books).

22. ME, p. 72.

23. Noreen O'Connor and Joanna Ryan (1993) *Wild Desires and Mistaken Identities: Lesbianism and Psychoanalysis* (London: Virago).

24. Michel Foucault (1976) *The History of Sexuality, Volume 1: An Introduction*, translated by Robert Hurley, 1981 (Harmondsworth: Pelican).

25. ME, p. 171.

26. Žižek usually allies himself on these matters with the World Association of Psychoanalysis headed, as 'Delegate General', by Jacques-Alain Miller, Lacan's son-in-law. The split at the Barcelona conference in 1998 led to the emergence of the Forums of the Freudian Field around Colette Soler, which is only one of the many dissident Lacanian groups. There have been indications recently that Žižek is distancing himself from Miller (with whom he was in analysis for a year), and his participation in a book edited in the US by Bruce Fink which includes two chapters by Soler (but without any Millerian input, unlike the first two volumes in this series of books 'reading' Lacan's Seminars) sends some kind of message about the degree to which he has actually 'irrevocably' given himself to this particular analytic community. See Suzanne Barnard and Bruce Fink (eds) (2002) *Reading Seminar XX: Lacan's Major Work on Love, Knowledge, and Feminine Sexuality* (New York: State University of New York Press).

27. Despite Foucault's suspicion of psychoanalysis in *History of Sexuality, Volume 1*, he did attend Lacan's seminar, and the description of 'care of the self' in a later volume of the *History of Sexuality* he was working on when he died is sometimes read by Lacanians as compatible with the project of psychoanalysis. Michel Foucault (1984) *The Care of the Self: The History of Sexuality Volume 3*, translated by Robert Hurley, 1990 (Harmondsworth: Penguin). See Jacques-Alain Miller (1989) 'Michel Foucault and psychoanalysis', in T. J. Armstrong, (ed.) (1992) *Michel Foucault: Philosopher* (New York: Harvester Wheatsheaf). Žižek's objection to Foucault's account of 'power' and 'confession' is that it avoids the notion of fantasy as a 'formal matrix' that provides the structuring principle of the subject's position in social relations. ME, p. 198.

28. Radostin Kalaianov (2001) 'Hegel, Kojève and Lacan – The metamorphoses of dialectics – Part II: Hegel and Lacan', www.academyanalyticarts.org/Kalo2.html (accessed 9 October 2001).

29. Lacan's formulation is that 'the symbol manifests itself first of all as the murder of the thing'. Jacques Lacan (1977) *Écrits: A Selection*, translated by Alan Sheridan (London: Tavistock), p. 104. Sometimes the phrase 'the word is the murder of the thing' is attributed to Hegel, which is an interesting retroactive construction.

30. Lacan, *Écrits: A Selection*, translated by Alan Sheridan, p. 193. Another formulation, in a recent alternative translation is 'the unconscious is the Other's discourse', Jacques Lacan (2002) *Écrits: A Selection*, translated by Bruce Fink (New York: W. W. Norton and Company), p. 183.

31. This object, which appears in Lacan's earlier writing and is elaborated in Seminar VII on Ethics as 'The Thing' (with some deliberate evocation of the Kantian noumenal 'thing'), is reworked as Lacan's distinctive and perhaps most important conceptual innovation as *objet petit a*, discussed in detail in Jacques Lacan, *Four Fundamental Concepts of Psycho-Analysis*. See Jacques Lacan (1986) *The Ethics of Psychoanalysis 1959–1960: The Seminar of Jacques Lacan Book VII*, translated with notes by Dennis Porter, 1992 (London: Routledge). We will discuss *objet petit a* further below.

32. For an elaboration of this argument see Ian Parker (1997) *Psychoanalytic Culture: Psychoanalytic Discourse in Western Culture* (London: Sage).

33. 'For Lacan "discourse" refers to the social bond – "le lien social". In order for someone to be hysteric, the whole intersubjective space must be structured in a certain way – it is in this sense that one can say that capitalism is "hysterical".' Žižek, in Peter Dews and Peter Osborne (1991) 'Lacan in Slovenia: An interview with Slavoj Žižek and Renata Salecl', *Radical Philosophy*, 58, pp. 25–31 (p. 30).

34. Lacan, *On Feminine Sexuality*, p. 12.

35. ME, p. 108.

36. Ibid., p. 90.

37. Ibid., p. 75.

38. Ibid., p. 56.

39. Lacan, *On Feminine Sexuality*, p. 39.

40. Lacan, *On Feminine Sexuality*, p. 81. This is actually the closest Lacan gets in *Seminar XX: Encore* to the oft-repeated phrase attributed to him, that 'Woman does not exist'. Another formulation of this problematic relation between Woman and language two years earlier has it that 'the woman, I mean the woman in herself, the woman – as if one could say *all the women* – the woman – I insist, who does not exist – is precisely the letter', Jacques Lacan (1971) *The Seminar of Jacques Lacan, Book XVIII, On A Discourse That Might Not Be A Semblance*, translated by Cormac Gallagher from unedited French manuscripts, 17 March, p. 16.

41. Ibid.

42. Renata Salecl (1994) *The Spoils of Freedom: Psychoanalysis and Feminism After the Fall of Socialism* (London: Routledge).

43. Salecl, *The Spoils of Freedom*, p. 133.

44. ME, p. 141.

45. Ray Monk (1990) *Ludwig Wittgenstein: The Duty of Genius* (New York: The Free Press).

46. Sigmund Freud (1905) *Three Essays on the Theory of Sexuality*, in S. Freud (1953) *The Standard Edition of the Complete Psychological Works of Sigmund Freud, Volume VII (1901–1905)* (London: Hogarth Press), p. 143. Freud later commented that Weininger (who was homosexual) 'was completely under the sway of his infantile complexes; and from that standpoint what is common to Jews and women is their relation to the castration complex'; what Freud is drawing from this 'highly gifted' but 'sexually deranged' writer is an insight into the way that as a function of images of circumcision as the feminising of Jews the 'castration complex is the deepest unconscious root of anti-semitism'. Sigmund Freud (1909) *Analysis of a Phobia in a Five-Year-Old Boy*, in S. Freud (1955) *The Standard Edition of the Complete Psychological Works of Sigmund Freud, Volume VII (1909)* (London: Hogarth Press), p. 36.

47. ME, p. 144.
48. Ibid., p. 145.
49. Lacan, *On Feminine Sexuality*, p. 94.
50. Renata Salecl (2000) 'Introduction' in R. Salecl (ed.) (2000) *Sexuation* (Durham, NC: Duke University Press), p. 9.
51. She has Judith Butler in her sights here, in Joan Copjec (1993) *Read My Desire: Lacan against the Historicists* (Cambridge, MA: MIT Press).
52. Jacques Lacan (1986) *The Ethics of Psychoanalysis 1959–1960: The Seminar of Jacques Lacan Book VII*, translated with notes by Dennis Porter, 1992 (London: Routledge).
53. ME, p. 108. A more unfortunate consequence of this argument is that it also folds into some of the most misogynistic motifs in patriarchal ideology when 'Christian love' is stirred into the narrative: 'Love is violence not (only) in the vulgar sense of the Balkan proverb "If he doesn't beat me, he doesn't love me!" – violence is already the love choice as such, which tears its object out of its context, elevating it to the Thing.' PD, p. 33.
54. ME, p. 153. This repeats a connection between Lacanian sexuation and Kantian antinomies that was rehearsed in *Tarrying with the Negative*, where it was borrowed, with due acknowledgement, from the then unpublished manuscript of Copjec's *Read My Desire*.
55. Simone de Beauvoir (1949) *The Second Sex*, 1968 (London: Jonathan Cape).
56. Lacan, *On Feminine Sexuality*.
57. ME, p. 31.
58. Juan-David Nasio (1992) *Five Lessons on the Psychoanalytic Theory of Jacques Lacan*, translated by David Pettigrew and François Raffoul, 1998 (New York: State University of New York Press).
59. ES.
60. Jacques-Alain Miller (1986) *Extimité*, in M. Bracher, M. W. Alcorn, R. J. Corthell and F. Massardier-Kenney (eds) (1994) *Lacanian Theory of Discourse: Subject, Structure and Society* (New York: New York University Press).
61. Jacques Lacan (1987) *Television*, *October*, 40, pp. 7–50.
62. Antonio Quinet, 1999, 'The functions of the preliminary interviews', *Journal of European Psychoanalysis*, 8–9, http://www.psychomedia.it/jep/number8–9/quinet.htm
63. LA, p. 25.
64. LA, p. 179.
65. As Ernesto Laclau points out in his preface to *The Sublime Object of Ideology*, it is then possible to see the *point de capiton* as 'the fundamental ideological operation', for it also fixes the subject in relation to certain objects of fantasy. SOI, p. xi.
66. Whether there is actually a 'subject' present in cases of psychotic structure is a moot point in Lacanian theory. On the one hand, something like analysis proceeds for whoever comes with a demand for analysis, and the analysand of whatever structure is accorded full ethical weight as a subject. On the other hand there are more brutal formulations in the Lacanian clinical literature now appearing, such as 'if there is no unconscious in psychosis, there is no being, no subject, and no desire, strictly speaking'. Bruce Fink (1997) *A Clinical Introduction to Lacanian Psychoanalysis: Theory and Technique* (Cambridge, MA: Harvard University Press), p. 255. For a review of this book and problems in the US uptake of Lacan's clinical work see Ian Parker (1999) 'Clinical Lacan: Review essay on Bruce Fink's *A Clinical Introduction to Lacanian Psychoanalysis: Theory and Technique*', *PS: Journal of the Universities Association for Psychoanalytic Studies*, (2), pp. 69–74.

67. Antonio Quinet (1999) 'The functions of the preliminary interviews', *Journal of European Psychoanalysis*, 8–9, http://www.psychomedia.it/jep/number8–9/quinet.htm (accessed 5 August 2002). This first period of work before the analysis proper gets going (work which is also described by Freud as the 'preliminary meetings') raises questions about what exactly Žižek was doing in his year of 'analysis' with Jacques-Alain Miller.

68. LA, p. 58.

69. This would be the case for analysts working in the tradition of Melanie Klein – in the UK drawing on the work of Wilfred Bion, and in the US drawing on the work of Herbert Rosenfeld (both of whom were analysed by Klein). For an overview of these frameworks see Neville Symington (1986) *The Analytic Experience: Lectures from the Tavistock* (London: Free Association Books).

70. There is some ambiguity about this, and some psychoanalysts still (as Freud often did) refer to 'normal' and 'non-neurotic' types, as if there were subjects who had entered language in such a way as to escape pathology. The predominant Lacanian, and Žižekian, position is that we should not be asking whether we are pathological or not but in what ways we are pathological.

71. Jacques Lacan (1966) 'Position of the unconscious: Remarks made at the 1960 Bonneval colloquium rewritten in 1964', translated by Bruce Fink, 1995, in Richard Feldstein, Bruce Fink and Maire Jaanus (eds) (1995) *Reading Seminar XI: Lacan's Four Fundamental Concepts of Psychoanalysis* (New York: State University of New York Press).

72. Obsessional neurosis is distinguished from hysteria, but it is also described by Freud and Lacan as a 'dialect' of hysteria, organised through certain modes of defence that need to be tackled for the analysis to proceed so that the analysand can engage in the hysterical questioning of the other and him- or herself.

73. LA, p. 62.

74. Ibid.

75. The trick that Copjec misses here, though, is that Columbo reproduces, as do many analysts in tiny clues for their analysands – engagement or wedding rings perhaps – a relation to woman that is disturbingly or reassuringly heterosexual, organised around an assumed binary of sexual difference (and Columbo solves the problem by making it appear that his woman doesn't exist), Copjec, *Read My Desire*, p. 179.

76. There has not been space here to review Žižek's writing specifically focused on modern directors, ranging from David Lynch to Krzysztof Kieslowski, for which see, for example, his (2000) *The Art of the Ridiculous Sublime: On David Lynch's* Lost Highway, and (2001) *The Fright of Real Tears: Kieslowski and the Future*.

77. LA, p. 91.

78. RG, p. 215.

79. Salecl, in Dews and Osborne, 'Lacan in Slovenia', p. 26.

80. Janko Bohak and Miran Možina (2002) 'Psychotherapy in Slovenia', http://marela.uni-mb.si/skzp/Srecanja/SloScena/StudDneviSKZP/Zborniki/Rogla2001 (accessed 3 January 2003).

81. ME, p. 15.

82. Leslie Chapman (2002) 'Ideology and Psychoanalysis: Žižek in the clinic?', paper at Centre for Freudian Analysis and Research, London, October, unpublished ms.

83. Jacques Lacan (1958) 'The direction of the treatment and the principles of its power', in J. Lacan (2002) *Écrits: A Selection*, translated by Bruce Fink (New York: W. W. Norton and Company).

84. Lacan, *The Seminar of Jacques Lacan, Book XVIII, On a Discourse That Might Not Be a Semblance*, 13 January, p. 16.

85. Ibid.
86. Ibid., 20 January, p. 3.
87. Ian Parker (2001) 'What is wrong with the discourse of the university in psychotherapy training?', *European Journal of Psychotherapy, Counselling and Health*, 4, (1), pp. 1–17.
88. Lacan, *The Seminar of Jacques Lacan, Book XVIII, On a Discourse That Might Not Be a Semblance*, 20 January, p. 3.
89. Žižek, in Dews and Osborne, 'Lacan in Slovenia', p. 30.
90. This is the way Žižek specifies the position of the 'critical intellectual' as the hole in the Romanian flag during the overthrow of Ceauçescu. TN, p. 1.
91. LA, p. 131.
92. Lacan, *On Feminine Sexuality*, p. 81.
93. OB, p. 141.
94. This formulation about desire being desire of the other has a long pedigree in Hegelian philosophy, especially in France where, under the influence of Kojève, it became a catch-cry not only for Lacanian psychoanalysts but also for existentialists after Jean-Paul Sartre (1943) *Being and Nothingness: An Essay on Phenomenological Ontology*, translated by Hazel Barnes, 1969 (London: Methuen).
95. For one Lacanian account see Anne Dunand (1995) 'The end of analysis (II)'. In R. Feldstein, B. Fink, and M. Jaanus (eds) *Reading Seminar XI: Lacan's Four Fundamental Concepts of Psychoanalysis* (New York: SUNY Press).
96. Karl Marx and Frederick Engels (1971) *Ireland and the Irish Question* (Moscow: Progress Publishers), p. 163.
97. Lacan, *Four Fundamental Concepts of Psycho-Analysis*, p. 276.
98. Ferdinand de Saussure was the founder of what came to be known as structuralism, and his account of the formation of signs through signifier and signified was useful for Lacan as a reformulation of Freudian theory. Much has been made of the influence of Saussure on Lacanian psychoanalysis, perhaps too much, and that is one reason why his work has not been foregrounded in the account of Lacan's clinical practice in this chapter. See Ferdinand de Saussure (1915) *Course in General Linguistics*, translated by Wade Baskin, 1974 (Glasgow: Fontana/Collins).
99. ME, p. 42.
100. Lacan, *The Ethics of Psychoanalysis*.
101. ME, p. 69.
102. Ibid.
103. Marc de Kesel (2002) 'Is not Antigone a proto-totalitarian figure? On Slavoj Žižek's interpretation of Antigone', paper at Globalization … and beyond' conference, Rotterdam, June, unpublished ms.
104. OB, p. 158. The point that Žižek makes here repeats Hegel's view of Antigone, and the claim for the realm of the family against that of the state is also cause for feminists to be wary about seeing Antigone as their heroine. See Judith Butler (2000) *Antigone's Claim: Kinship Between Life and Death* (New York: Columbia University Press).
105. OB, p. 158.
106. 'One bears witness to one's fidelity to the Thing by *sacrificing (also) the Thing itself.*' FA, p. 152. Nevertheless, even after these alternative more radical examples of an act, it is Antigone who is still the reference point at the end of Žižek's discussion of 'revolutionary cultural politics' in his 2004 book on Deleuze: 'it is theoretically and politically wrong to oppose strategic political acts, as risky as they might be, to radical "suicidal" gestures à la Antigone, gestures of pure self-destructive ethical insistence with, apparently, no political goal'. OWB, pp. 204–5.

107. David Macey (1988) *Lacan in Contexts* (London: Verso).
108. Jacques Lacan (1967–68) *The Seminar of Jacques Lacan, Book XV, The Psychoanalytic Act*, translated by Cormac Gallagher from unedited French manuscripts, Annex 3, p. 1.
109. Lacan, *Four Fundamental Concepts of Psycho-Analysis*, p. 50.
110. Véronique Mariage (2003) 'The psychoanalyst: An effect of the act', *Psychoanalytical Notebooks: A Review of the London Society of the New Lacanian School*, 10, pp. 79–86 (p. 85).

CHAPTER 4 POLITICS – REPEATING MARX

1. Žižek, in Robert Boynton (1998) 'Enjoy your Žižek!: An excitable Slovenian philosopher examines the obscene practices of everyday life – including his own', *Linguafranca: The Review of Academic Life*, 7 (7) http://www.linguafranca.com/9810/zizek.html (accessed 15 May 2001).
2. Slavoj Žižek (2003) 'Too much democracy?', http://www.lacan.com/toomuch.htm (accessed 22 April 2003).
3. For an argument that Hegel anticipates Marx and then leads us to a social-democratic 'third way', see David MacGregor (1984) *The Communist Ideal in Hegel and Marx* (Toronto: University of Toronto Press). Yannis Stavrakakis (1999) *Lacan and the Political* (London: Routledge) makes a case for Lacan as a resource for re-energising Marxism more in line with the Laclau-Mouffe political project.
4. The error of presenting Žižek as a Marxist is made by both Sarah Kay (2003) *Žižek: A Critical Introduction* (Cambridge: Polity Press) and Tony Myers (2003) *Slavoj Žižek* (London: Routledge). It is perhaps only for tactical reasons that some Marxists have cited Žižek's recent commentaries on Lenin and Lukács as evidence that he has shifted to the Left from his previous 'post-Marxist' stance; 'as eloquent and original [a] writer as Zizek is a powerful and welcome recruit to the anti-capitalist struggle'. Alex Callinicos (2001) 'Review of *The Ticklish Subject* and *Contingency, Hegemony, Universality*', *Historical Materialism*, 8, pp. 373–403.
5. Ernesto Laclau and Chantal Mouffe (1985) *Hegemony and Socialist Strategy* (London: Verso).
6. Žižek's response to *Hegemony and Socialist Strategy*, 'Beyond Discourse-Analysis', is reprinted in Ernesto Laclau's (1990) *New Reflections on the Revolution of Our Time* (London: Verso).
7. Cf. Ernest Mandel (1978) *From Stalinism to Eurocommunism: The Bitter Fruits of 'Socialism in One Country'* (London: New Left Books).
8. Laclau, 'Preface', in SOI, p. xi.
9. The one positive, hopeful formulation offered at the end of the book is Christianity read through Hegel, in which 'human freedom is finally conceived as a "reflexive determination" of this strange substance (God) itself'; the other negative, hopeless formulation is derived from (a version of) a Lacanian view of 'the final stage of the psychoanalytic process: "subjective destitution"', in which the subject 'accepts the Real in its utter meaningless idiocy', SOI, p. 230.
10. See Matthew Beaumont and Martin Jenkins (2000) 'An Interview with Slavoj Zizek', *Historical Materialism*, 7, pp. 181–97 (p. 195).
11. Slavoj Žižek (2001) 'Repeating Lenin', http://www.lacan.com/replenin.htm (accessed 27 March 2001).
12. Slavoj Žižek (2002) *Welcome to the Desert of the Real! Five Essays on September 11 and Related Dates* (London: Verso).
13. RG, p. 176.

14. RG, p. 177.
15. RG, p. 183.
16. 'I am not an idiot. It wouldn't mean anything to return to the Leninist working class today.' Žižek, in Doug Henwood (2002) 'I am a fighting atheist: Interview with Slavoj Žižek', *Bad Subjects*, 59, http://eserver.org/bs/59/zizek.html (accessed 3 June 2002).
17. Žižek, in Henwood, 'I am a fighting atheist'.
18. RG, p. 295.
19. Slavoj Žižek (1998) 'A leftist plea for "Eurocentrism"', *Critical Inquiry*, 24, (2), pp. 988–1,009. The complaint about 'multiculturalism', which Žižek bitterly inveighs against in many other places, is rehearsed at length in Slavoj Žižek (1997) 'Multiculturalism, or, the cultural logic of multinational capitalism', *New Left Review*, 225, pp. 28–51. An interview with Žižek shortly after the September 11 World Trade Center attacks again makes the point that multiculturalism and fundamentalism are two sides of the same coin. Sabine Reul and Thomas Deichmann (2001) 'The one measure of true love is: you can insult the other', http://www.spiked-online.com/Articles/00000002d2C4.htm (accessed 19 November 2001).
20. Žižek, 'A leftist plea', p. 992.
21. Ibid., p. 988.
22. Ibid., p. 997.
23. Žižek, 'Too much democracy?'.
24. Žižek, 'A leftist plea', p. 992.
25. SOI, p. 71.
26. Louis Althusser (1971) *Lenin and Philosophy, and other Essays* (London: New Left Books).
27. SOI, p. 45.
28. Peter Sloterdijk (1988) *Critique of Cynical Reason* (London: Verso).
29. See Jason Barker (2002) *Alain Badiou: A Critical Introduction* (London: Pluto Press).
30. Slavoj Žižek (1998) 'Psychoanalysis in post-Marxism: The case of Alain Badiou', *The South Atlantic* Quarterly, 97, (2), pp. 235–61. Žižek refers to a 'full revolutionary *passage à l'acte*' (p. 258), which is curious given that for Lacan this kind of act would characterise psychosis. Presumably Žižek is willing to risk this because he thinks it is the only way to move outside all symbolic coordinates. In this way, once again, Zizek elides the difference between Lacan's account of an act as hysterical 'acting out' staged as complaint and provocation for the analyst (for the Other) and a genuine psychoanalytic act that might occur at the end of analysis (which also marks a quite different relation to the Other and a 'desupposition' of the analyst's knowledge).
31. Ibid., p. 259.
32. Slavoj Žižek (1996) 'Postscript' [to an earlier interview], in Peter Osborne (ed.) (1996) *A Critical Sense: Interviews with Intellectuals* (London: Routledge), p. 43.
33. RG, p. 295.
34. Slavoj Žižek (1999) 'Human Rights and its discontents', http://www.bard.edu/hrp/zizektranscript.htm (accessed 7 June 2002).
35. Žižek, 'A leftist plea', p. 997.
36. Žižek says that we are dealing with a new form of 'denegation' of the political in post-politics, and he describes this as 'foreclosure' (the defence which characterises psychotic structure in Lacanian theory); this contrasts with the form of defence that, he says, underpins parapolitics, which at one point he refers to as 'disavowal' (the defence which characterises perverse structure) and at another 'repression' (which characterises hysteria and obsessional neurosis). Perhaps he is using these terms very loosely here, but at other points, in *The Sublime Object of Ideology* for example, he

insists on their specific application and their very different consequences for politics (contrasting the perverse Stalinist regimes, psychotic Nazism, and neurotic bourgeois democracies).

37. For a review of the importance of antagonism for the three contributors to this book see Ian Parker (2003) 'Lacanian social theory and clinical practice', *Psychoanalysis and Contemporary Thought*, 26, (2), pp. 51–77.

38. Laclau, in CHU, p.292.

39. Žižek, in CHU, p. 326.

40. Laclau, in CHU, p. 203.

41. Žižek, 'A leftist plea', p. 1006.

42. Ibid., p. 1000.

43. 'Well-off and miserable at the same time, this consciousness no longer feels affected by any critique of ideology; its falseness is already reflexively buffered', Sloterdijk, *Critique of Cynical Reason*, p. 5.

44. SOI, p. 33.

45. Žižek, 'A leftist plea', p. 1,001. Elsewhere he evokes Hegel to make a similar point about the paralysis of European social-democratic governments faced with the election of Jörg Haider in Austria; Slavoj Žižek (2000) 'Why we all love to hate Haider', *New Left Review (II)*, 2, pp. 37–45: 'Is not Haider himself the best Hegelian example of the "speculative identity" of the tolerant multiculturalist and the postmodern racist?', p. 44; 'For New Right populism is the necessary supplement of the multiculturalist tolerance of global capital, as the return of the repressed', p. 45; and 'the Third Way gets its own message back in inverted form.', p. 45.

46. RG, p. 183.

47. Ibid., p. 182.

48. Ibid., p. 275.

49. Ibid.

50. Ibid., p. 289.

51. Ibid., p. 312.

52. Ibid., p. 306.

53. Žižek is having a go at Jacques Derrida's (1994) *Spectres of Marx: The State of the Debt, the Work of Mourning, and the New International* (London: Routledge), where Derrida calls for a virtual 'New International' and for a return to Marx (a return which is about as substantial as Žižek's call for us to 'repeat Lenin').

54. 'Socialism = free access to the internet + *the power of the Soviets*', RG, p. 294. Žižek emphasises that the 'second element is crucial, since it specifies the only social organization within which the Internet can realize its liberating potential', but if he is actually referring to the power of the Soviets as the 'second element' here rather than free access to the internet he does not tell us how this might be brought about.

55. This is the story of many ex-Marxists who embrace a new stage of capitalism which renders conflict unnecessary, but also of fellow-travellers who wistfully look to other parts of the world – today for some that is Cuba or North Korea – that seem to have successfully made a revolution to live at last in bliss.

56. This is the story of ultra-leftists who are so sick of being marginalised that they turn to terrorist tactics to wake up the working class – a dead-end strategy that includes the activities of the Red Army Fraction in Germany and Sendero Luminoso in Peru.

57. Žižek, 'A leftist plea', p. 991.

58. Ibid.

59. Ibid., p. 1008.

60. Ibid.

61. Slavoj Žižek (1999) 'Human Rights and its discontents', http://www.bard.edu/hrp/zizektranscript.htm (accessed 7 June 2002).

62. Jacques-Alain Miller (1998) 'Report for the General Assembly in Barcelona – 23 July 1998', *Psychoanalytical Notebooks of the London Circle*, 1, pp. 117–52 (p. 141). It is a curious paradox that Žižek's insistence that Lacan Christianized psychoanalysis and that Miller formalised Lacan as the good Stalin – Lacan as Lenin, and Freud as Marx – is at a time when Miller, who is Jewish, has succeeded Lacan (his father-in-law), who was brought up Catholic and once sought an audience with the Pope. See Elisabeth Roudinesco (1990) *Jacques Lacan and Co.: A History of Psychoanalysis in France, 1925–1985* (London: Free Association Books).

63. Judith Butler (1990) *Gender Trouble, Feminism and the Subversion of Identity* (London: Routledge). See also Butler's elaboration of her argument in relation to Žižek (and Laclau) in CHU.

64. Žižek (2002) 'The Real of sexual difference', in Suzanne Barnard and Bruce Fink (eds) (2002) *Reading Seminar XX: Lacan's Major Work on Love, Knowledge, and Feminine Sexuality* (New York: State University of New York Press), p. 72. Once again, Žižek signals his indebtedness here to Joan Copjec's (1994) *Read My Desire: Lacan against the Historicists* (Cambridge, MA: MIT Press).

65. Quoted in Butler, CHU, p. 180. Butler herself does not advocate gay or lesbian marriage because that would also reproduce a heteronormative institution, but her qualms are of a different political order than Miller's.

66. RG, p. 323.

67. For a good, useful review of the Freudian (and Lacanian) conception of the relation between biology and sexuality, see Ona Nierenberg (1998) 'A hunger for science: Psychoanalysis and the "Gay Gene"', http://www.apres-coup.org/Papers/ONierenberg-GayGene.htm (accessed 11 February 2003).

68. RG, p. 323.

69. To be fair, the quote runs on in a slightly different direction, condemning arche-politics as proposing that 'what we should fight, our enemy, is a cancerous intruder, a pest, a foreign parasite to be exterminated if the health of the social body is to be reestablished', Žižek, 'A leftist plea', p. 993. Žižek is articulating 'unease' which can too easily be medicalised when he invokes 'clinical facts', but he is not at all advocating extermination of forms of sexuality that are non-normative.

70. Renata Salecl (1994) *Spoils of Freedom: Psychoanalysis and Feminism After the Fall of Socialism* (London: Routledge).

71. RG, p. 316.

72. Ibid., p. 188.

73. This, perhaps, also explains why he reverses Marx's dictum in Thesis 11 on Feuerbach – see Karl Marx (1845) 'Concerning Feuerbach', in K. Marx (1975) *Early Writings*, translated by Rodney Livingstone and Gregor Benton (Harmondsworth: Pelican) – that philosophers so far have only interpreted the world while the point is to change it, to claim that 'the first task today is precisely *not* to succumb to the temptation to act, to intervene directly and change things', RG, p. 170. Žižek's injunction here flows not only from the worry that any act will be within certain 'hegemonic ideological coordinates' but also from his hope that some more subtle shift might occur that would ameliorate things so that the exercise of state power might be possible to support, as in his weak plea for justice after September 11: 'America should learn humbly to accepts its own vulnerability as part of this world, enacting the punishment of those responsible as a sad duty, not as an exhilarating retaliation', RG, p. 244.

74. Žižek, 'A leftist plea', p. 992.

75. See Chantal Mouffe (ed.) (1999) *The Challenge of Carl Schmitt* (London: Verso), in which Mouffe argues that 'In spite of his moral flaws, he is an important political thinker whose work it would be a great mistake to dismiss merely because of his support for Hitler in 1933', p. 1. It is worth pointing out that all of the English-language articles listed in the Schmitt bibliography included in Mouffe's book are from the journal *Telos*, which lurched from Frankfurt School Leftism across the political spectrum to the Right in the 1980s.

76. Paul Hirst (1999) 'Carl Schmitt's decisionism', in Mouffe, *The Challenge of Carl Schmitt*, p. 8.

77. Žižek (1999) 'Carl Schmitt in the age of post-politics', in Mouffe, *The Challenge of Carl Schmitt*, p. 18.

78. Žižek, 'Carl Schmitt in the age of post-politics', p. 35.

79. Žižek is here aiming this barb at Badiou, in Žižek, 'Psychoanalysis in post-Marxism', p. 259.

80. Ibid.

81. Georg Wilhelm Friedrich Hegel (1807) *Phenomenology of Spirit*, translated by A. V. Miller, 1977 (Oxford: Oxford University Press), p. 361. Žižek refers to this passage, a little more critically, in 'A leftist plea', p. 994.

82. Žižek, in Beaumont and Jenkins, 'An interview with Slavoj Zizek', p. 195.

83. Leon Trotsky (1973) *The Revolution Betrayed: What is the Soviet Union, And Where is it Going?* (London: New Park Publications).

84. Ernest Mandel (1978) *From Stalinism to Eurocommunism: The Bitter Fruits of 'Socialism in One Country'* (London: New Left Books).

85. Žižek, in Beaumont and Jenkins, 'An interview with Slavoj Zizek', p. 196.

86. Ibid.

87. CHU, p. 124.

88. Ibid.

89. Žižek's discussion of the work of Giorgio Agamben's (1998) *Homo Sacer: Sovereign Power and Bare Life* (Stanford: Stanford University Press) also lurches into some worrying territory. Agamben draws on Schmitt's decisionist theory of politics and uses the image of the Nazi concentration camp as the defining image of contemporary political division between the living and the living dead; the Jews in the camps existed as 'bare life'. Žižek then takes this motif of *Homo Sacer* to call for Jews in Israel to respect Palestinians as 'other' rather than as bare life stripped of political rights. See Slavoj Žižek (2002) 'Are we in a war? Do we have an enemy?, *London Review of Books*, 24 (10), www.lrb.co.uk/v24/n10/zize2410.htm (accessed 30 May 2002).

90. Žižek, in Beaumont and Jenkins, 'An interview with Slavoj Zizek', p. 192.

91. Žižek, 'The Real of sexual difference', p. 69. Even 'in a truly radical political act, the opposition between a "crazy" destructive gesture and a strategic political decision momentarily breaks down'. OWB, p. 204.

92. RG, p. 329. This argument is explicitly turned against Badiou on p. 271.

93. Ibid., p. 190.

94. Žižek, 'A leftist plea', p. 1,007.

95. Ibid.

96. Michael Hardt and Antonio Negri (2000) *Empire* (Cambridge MA: Harvard University Press).

97. It is 'the model of an analysis of capitalism close to what I have in mind ... a book which tries to rewrite *The Communist Manifesto* for the twenty-first century'. Žižek, in CHU, p. 329.

98. The three demands Hardt and Negri come up with are for 'global citizenship' (p. 400), a 'social wage' (p. 403) and the 'right to reappropriation' (p. 406). The third demand is possibly the most radical but least fully elaborated, as 'having free access to and control over knowledge, information, communication and affects' (p. 407); this, before musing over how the 'multitude' might come to 'political autonomy' as a new 'posse'. As Žižek correctly notes, 'the problem with these demands is that they oscillate between formal emptiness and impossible radicalism', RG, p. 331.

99. RG, p. 331.

100. Žižek, 'A leftist plea', p. 1,007.

101. Hardt and Negri, *Empire*, p. 413. Emphasis in original (in the final section on 'Militant', pp. 411–13).

102. See, for example, Andrew Collier (2001) *Christianity and Marxism: A Philosophical Contribution to Their Reconciliation* (London: Routledge). For a historical survey of attempts to connect the two traditions in European thought see James Bentley (1982) *Between Marx and Christ: The Dialogue in German-Speaking Europe 1870–1970* (London: New Left Books).

103. Žižek, 'The Real of sexual difference', p. 61.

104. Karl Marx (1843–44) 'A contribution to the critique of Hegel's Philosophy of Right. Introduction', in Marx, *Early Writings*, p. 244.

105. SOI, pp. 96–7.

106. Marx (1843) 'On the Jewish question', in Marx, *Early Writings*, p. 213.

107. Žižek, 'A leftist plea', p. 991.

108. The list is continued with Marx, Freud and de Gaulle, who in 1940 introduced a 'radical split' between those who would follow him to resist the German occupation of France 'and those who preferred the collaborationist fleshpots of Egypt'. Žižek, 'A leftist plea', p. 1,002. The same formulation is repeated in Žižek's essay, 'Carl Schmitt in the age of post-politics' (p. 35), albeit with the phrase 'Egyptian fleshpots' placed in quote marks, which does not really make it any more illuminating.

109. RG, p. 191.

110. Ibid.

111. Žižek, 'The Real of sexual difference', p. 68.

112. RG, p. 226.

113. Žižek also applauds the scene in *Fight Club* where Edward Norton beats himself up as exemplary of this self-degradation in the face of the other. RG, p. 252.

114. Ibid., p. 253.

115. Sigmund Freud (1939) *Moses and Monotheism: Three Essays*, in S. Freud (1964) *The Standard Edition of the Complete Psychological Works of Sigmund Freud, Volume XXIII (1937–1939)* (London: Hogarth Press).

116. For a more nuanced Lacanian account of this reconstruction of history and identity by Freud see Eric Santner (1999) 'Freud's *Moses* and the ethics of nomotropic desire', in R. Salecl (ed.) (2000) *Sexuation* (Durham, NC: Duke University Press).

117. Žižek, 'A leftist plea', p. 1,004.

118. It should be said, however, that Žižek is quite clear with respect to the US-led invasion of Iraq that the 'attack was wrong', even though this is augmented by the Lacanian observation that the call for an attack was 'false with regard to the position from which it is enunciated' (that is, that the charges of abuse of human rights by the regime were driven by an economic imperative to control oil and a political attempt to ensure that dictators installed by the US remained obedient to their masters). Slavoj Žižek (2003) 'The Iraq war: Where is the true danger?', www.lacan.com/iraq.htm (accessed 24 March 2003).

119. Žižek, 'A leftist plea', p. 994.
120. Zizek, 2003, 'The interpassive subject', www.lacan.com/interpass.htm (accessed 2 December 2002).
121. Žižek, 'A leftist plea', p. 996.

CHAPTER 5 CULTURE – ACTING OUT

1. This is not at all to pretend that these things viewed from Manchester are now available to the reader undistorted and as they really are. There is no neutral perspective on any of the issues Žižek discusses, and the critique elaborated in this book is from a partisan position that is also Marxist, Lacanian and Hegelian.

2. Within a week of the article appearing there were over 50, mainly enthusiastic, reader comments on Žižek's (18 March 2003) article 'Today, Iraq. Tomorrow ... Democracy?' in the US-based leftist magazine *In These Times*, http://inthesetimes.com/comments.php?id=119_0_1_0_C (accessed 26 March 2003). A curious thing about the string of responses is the way that – despite Žižek not having introduced the topic and there being no indication that the readers knew of his recent preoccupations with spirituality – the discussion turned quite quickly into a squabble about what Jesus said and whether George Bush was a good Christian. This is symptomatic of the world into which Žižek is writing, one all too receptive to his work and well able to recuperate it.

3. Ibid. This article consists of extracts from the longer 'The Iraq War: Where is the true danger?', dated 13 March 2003 on www.lacan.com/iraq.htm (accessed 24 March 2003).

4. 'Proud American' – one of the two right-wing responses – clearly specified 'rat' here in the message, and his line was that Bush should 'carpet-bomb iraq, kill those iraqui rats and their descendents, and take the oil that is rightfully ours'.

5. Robert Miklitsch (1998) '"Going through the fantasy": Screening Slavoj Žižek', *The South Atlantic Quarterly*, 97 (2), pp. 475–507. This annoying article also plays with the X of 'X-Yugoslavia', pointing out that 'Žižek hails of course from the East' and commenting that 'The x here – like the Slavic vs and zs – indicates the uncanny status of Slovenia for most Americans (p. 476). It is worth displaying these perceptions so we can see what Žižek is up against.

6. The examples include anecdotes about audiences in the US telling him that he should not talk about film when Bosnia was in flames. See, for example, 'Introduction: From Sarajevo to Hitchcock ... and back' in *Metastases of Enjoyment*.

7. The most horrible example of this I witnessed at an academic conference was at the 'Globalization ... and beyond' meeting devoted to Žižek's work in Rotterdam in June 2002, where some of the speakers and audience gleefully mimicked Žižek's gestures (what they clearly saw as slightly manic fidgety movements) after he left the conference. This contemptible display was indeed an example of an evil gaze which sees evil, here aimed at a scruffy, successful East-European intellectual with a beard.

8. Peter Anestos posted this on 18 March 2003 from San Francisco.

9. Geoffrey Galt Harpham (2003) 'Doing the impossible: Slavoj Žižek and the end of knowledge', *Critical Inquiry*, 29 (3), pp. 453–85 (p. 485). Sarah Kay (2003) *Žižek: A Critical Introduction* (Cambridge: Polity Press) is a little too generous when she tries to solve this problem of style by putting it down to the invitation to undergo 'psycho-analytic therapy' and to puzzle about lack of fit between examples and themes in the writing while Žižek reveals his 'persona' to us.

10. Antony Easthope and Kate McGowan (1992) 'Introduction', in *A Critical and Cultural Theory Reader* (Buckingham: Open University Press), pp. 2–3.

11. Peter Osborne (2003) 'Interpreting the world: September 11, cultural criticism and the intellectual Left', *Radical Philosophy*, 117, pp. 2–12 (p. 3).

12. Some accounts of Žižek's work which do risk playing with motifs of madness to describe his writing are Denise Gigante (1998) 'Toward a notion of critical self-creation: Slavoj Žižek and the "vortex of madness"', *New Literary History*, 29 (1), pp. 153–68, and Bran Nicol (2000) 'Normality and other kinds of madness: Žižek and the traumatic core of the subject', *Psychoanalytic Studies*, 2 (1), pp. 7–19.

13. Russell Grigg (2001) 'Absolute freedom and major structural change', *Paragraph*, 24 (2), pp. 111–24 (p. 111).

14. Ibid., p. 112.

15. Rosi Braidotti (2002) *Metamorphoses: Towards a Materialist Theory of Becoming* (Cambridge: Polity Press), p. 54.

16. Ibid.

17. Ibid., p. 56.

18. The original working title of *Contingency, Hegemony, Universality* – as of 14 June 2002 still present on the image of the cover of the book on www.amazon.co.uk – was *Agonistic Universality: A Dialogue on the Theory of Hegemony*. Butler argues in her opening contribution to the book that all three co-authors agree 'on the continuing political promise of the Gramscian notion of hegemony' (CHU, p. 13), but by the end of the book it did not at all seem clear that Žižek agreed with this at all.

19. Butler (1993) *Bodies That Matter: On the Discursive Limits of 'Sex'* (London: Routledge), p. 21.

20. Butler, CHU, p. 142. Against this, Butler's position is that 'The formal character of this originary, pre-social sexual difference in its ostensible emptiness is *accomplished* precisely through the reification by which a certain idealized and necessary dimorphism takes hold', Butler, CHU, p. 145.

21. Butler, in Peter Osborne and Lynne Segal (1993) 'Gender as performance: An interview with Judith Butler', *Radical Philosophy*, 67, pp. 32–9 (p. 37).

22. John Mowitt (2000) 'Trauma envy', *Cultural Critique*, 46, pp. 272–97 (p. 287).

23. Teresa Ebert (1999) 'Globalization, internationalism, and the class politics of cynical reason', *Nature, Society, and Thought*, 12 (4), pp. 389–410 (p. 400).

24. Ibid., p. 402.

25. Ibid., p. 406.

26. Peter McLaren (2002) 'Slavoj Žižek's naked politics: Opting for the impossible, a secondary elaboration', *Journal of Advanced Composition Quarterly*, 21 (3), pp. 614–37 (p. 620). McLaren goes on to argue that 'Žižek's psycho-Marxism relies too heavily on a theory of language that focuses on the erotogenic body and ignores the toiling body' (p. 638).

27. Peter Dews (1995) *The Limits of Disenchantment: Essays on Contemporary European Philosophy* (London: Verso), p. 239.

28. Ibid., p. 252.

29. However, Dews' attempt to recover a notion of 'intersubjectivity' from Lacan to repair the damage done by Žižek's reading of Hegel, on the other hand, will only work if Lacan's later writings – the main source of Žižek's development of Lacanian theory – are ignored.

30. Butler, in CHU, p. 26. That 'Exemplification entails a reductive formulation of theory that keys the decoding of popular culture in reiterable slogans that circularly serve as theory's illustrations' is a point neatly made and elaborated against Žižek by Dianne

Chisolm (2001) 'Žižek's exemplary culture', *Journal for the Psychoanalysis of Culture and Society*, 6 (2), pp. 242–52.

31. The phrase Žižek is citing here is taken from Hegel, and so this introduces a further question about the applicability of formulae from Hegel to all places and all times.

32. Butler, in CHU, p. 27.

33. Laclau, in CHU, p. 75.

34. Dews, *The Limits of Disenchantment*, p. 238.

35. Laclau, in CHU, p. 75.

36. Ibid., p. 205. Laclau's own position is that traditional Marxism does need to be deconstructed: 'class struggle is just one species of identity politics, and one which is becoming less and less important in the world in which we live' (ibid., p. 203). Lacan may be useful as part of this process, but it would not be helpful if 'Lacan' was to turn into a new master signifier.

37. Ibid., p. 276.

38. Grigg, 'Absolute freedom and major structural change', p. 122.

39. Jacques Lacan (1973) *Four Fundamental Concepts of Psycho-Analysis*, translated by Alan Sheridan, 1979 (Harmondsworth: Penguin).

40. Sean Homer (2002) '"It's the Political Economy Stupid!" On Žižek's Marxism', *Radical Philosophy*, 108, pp. 7–16 (p. 7).

41. Ibid.

42. Laclau, in CHU, p. 292.

43. Ibid., p. 290.

44. Teresa Ebert (1996) *Ludic Feminism and After: Postmodernism, Desire, and Labor in Late Capitalism* (Ann Arbor: The University of Michigan Press), p. 58.

45. In this way, Ebert argues, Žižek also turns Trotsky's notion of permanent revolution 'into a strategy of crisis management for capitalism itself to produce another comforting narrative of the permanence of capitalism as unstranscendable' (ibid., p. 61).

46. Ibid., p. 62.

47. McLaren, 'Slavoj Žižek's naked politics', p. 629.

48. McLaren, 'Slavoj Žižek's naked politics', p. 635.

49. Grigg, 'Absolute freedom and major structural change', p. 118.

50. Ibid., p. 120.

51. Ibid., p. 121.

52. 'Although not quite a queer heroine, Antigone does emblematise a certain heterosexual fatality that remains to be read'. Judith Butler (2000) *Antigone's Claim: Kinship Between Life and Death* (New York: Columbia University Press), p. 72.

53. Yannis Stavrakakis (2003) 'The lure of Antigone: Aporias of an ethics of the political', *Umbr(a)*, pp. 117–29 (p. 118).

54. Ibid., p. 119. There is a reply to all the 'false attributions' to him by Žižek which actually serves to compound rather than clarify the problems Stavrakakis raises. Slavoj Žižek (2003) '"What some would call…": A response to Yannis Stavrakakis', *Umbr(a)*, pp. 131–5. A similar worry about the political consequences of taking Antigone as an example are voiced by Marc de Kesel (2002) 'Is not Antigone a proto-totalitarian figure? On Slavoj Žižek's interpretation of Antigone', paper at 'Globalization … and beyond' conference, Rotterdam, June, unpublished ms.

55. See Yannis Stavrakakis (1999) *Lacan and the Political* (London: Routledge).

56. Žižek's detailed discussions of Benjamin, Kant and Deleuze (see OWB) are often yet more opportunities to stage debates between Marx, Hegel and Lacan on the terrain of cultural theory, and this is really where 'culture' becomes a fourth frame for his writing. Žižek clearly tackles more than three theoretical frameworks, and his own

reading of each of those frameworks has the effect of dividing and multiplying them into more than three.

57. This mistake – the idea that Žižek clarifies and tidies up his mistakes as his work develops – runs through other 'introductions' to his work, and sometimes there is a search for the theory that might be responsible for the limitations on how far he can go; in Tony Myers (2003) *Slavoj Žižek* (London: Routledge), all the blame is laid on Lacan, for example.

58. The book was Žižek's (1988) *Le plus sublimes des hystériques – Hegel passe* (Paris: Point Hors Ligne).

59. See Rebecca Mead (2003) 'The Marx brother', *The New Yorker*, http://www.lacan.com/ziny/htm (accessed 6 May 2003).

60. We must beware, of course, the temptation to think that even this confession gets at what is really going on. This quote carries on 'I use Lacan to re-actualise Hegel in the same way that Lacan used Sade', which also raises some interesting issues about how Žižek views Lacan. Guy Mannes Abbott (1998) 'Never mind the bollocks', http://www.g-m-a.net/docs/c_zizek.html (accessed 15 May 2001).

61. During his 1964 seminar (XI), however, Lacan enthusiastically repeats Jacques-Alain Miller's phrase that it is rather a case of 'Lacan *against* Hegel', following which André Green backs up his observation that Lacan is a '*son of Hegel*' by shouting out '*The sons kill the fathers!*', Lacan, *Four Fundamental Concepts of Psycho-Analysis*, p. 215.

62. Mead, 'The Marx brother'.

63. See, for example, David Bakan (1990) *Sigmund Freud and the Jewish Mystical Tradition* (London: Free Association Books).

64. Nevertheless critics have already argued that 'Lacan rewrites Freud's psychoanalysis in a Christian key, a softening for which the intellectuals were extremely grateful'. André Green (1995–1996) 'Against Lacanism: A conversation of André Green with Sergio Benvenuto', *Journal of European Psychoanalysis*, 2, http://www.psychomedia.it/jep/number2/greenbenv.htm (accessed 5 August 2002). (Green, although a member of an IPA group in Paris, had been sympathetic to Lacan, attending his seminar for some years until 1967, well after Lacan's 'excommunication' from the IPA. This interview with Green was conducted in May 1994.)

65. The term 'excommunication' is Lacan's, and when he spoke of this he drew a parallel between the IPA demand that he should not be allowed to train analysts – an attempt to silence him which made his position in the IPA untenable – with the Rabbinical decree against Baruch Spinoza for heresy. See Lacan, *Four Fundamental Concepts of Psycho-Analysis*, p. 3. Spinoza is still a potent signifier of secularism, recently so in Israel for example, with one reviewer of a book on his work commenting that although he 'offers much to be esteemed', 'he also offers much to be deplored, advocating in somewhat encrypted fashion the dismantling of revealed religion and its replacement by a positive, secular civil religion'. Alan Mittleman (1998) 'Spinoza, liberalism and the question of Jewish identity', *First Things*, 79, http://www.firstthings.com/ftissues/ft9801/reviews/mittleman.html (accessed 29 April 2003). Žižek has commented that the Spinozist take on rationalism is quite compatible with late capitalism and (it would also seem from the way he characterises Spinoza) with 'post-politics'. See, for example, the interview in Josefina Ayerza (1994) '"It doesn't have to be a Jew"', *Lusitania*, 1 (4), http://www.lacan.com/perfume/Zizekinter.htm (accessed 14 June 2002). Žižek does not at all, therefore, want to be part of the fashionable return to Spinoza – instead, he sees the debate opened up around Spinoza as another

opportunity to return to Hegel: 'what both Spinozans and Levinasians share is a radical anti-Hegelianism'. PD, p. 33.

66. See Susan Handelman (1983) 'Jacques Derrida and the heretic hermeneutic', in M. Krupnick (ed.) *Displacement: Derrida and After* (Bloomington: Indiana University Press). Žižek's critique of Derrida from a quasi-Schmittian position also includes an attack on Emmanuel Levinas, Derrida's mentor and theorist of an ethics explicitly rooted in his experience in a special POW camp. The issue here is not the critique of Derrida and Levinas – whose liberal ethical and political positions are problematic – but the vantage point from which they are being opposed, from the point of enunciation of the critique. See Erik Vogt (2002) 'Derrida, Schmitt, Žižek', paper at the 'Globalization ... and beyond' conference, Rotterdam, June.

67. See, for example, his reflections on the September 11 attacks in Jacques-Alain Miller (2001) *The Tenderness of Terrorists* (New York: Wooster Press). This intervention, touted by the World Association of Psychoanalysis as Miller's return to politics (see www.wapol.org), offers no actual political programme, and Millerians in different countries seem to be rather bemused by what they should do with it. The book is one of three 'letters to the enlightened opinion' published by Wooster Press, the publishing arm of www.lacan.com, which is loyally Millerian but also open to publishing on its website and journal *Lacanian Ink* contributions by Žižek and Badiou, as well as Hardt and Negri.

68. Brecht's radical 'over-orthodoxy', Žižek claims, is in contrast to Georg Lukács – 'the "soft" European humanist' who 'played the role of the "closet dissident"', became part of the Hungarian regime in 1956 and was thus really the *'ultimate Stalinist'*. RG, p. 196. This scathing assessment of poor Lukács, who did indeed serve a convenient function as the humanist left flank of Hungarian Stalinism and then as a rallying point for the Belgrade *Praxis* group, is very different from Žižek's (just as revealing) praise for him elsewhere: 'if there ever was a philosopher of Leninism, of the Leninist party, it is the early Marxist Lukács who went to the very limit in this direction, up to defending the "undemocratic" features of the first year of the Soviet power against Rosa Luxemburg's famous criticism, accusing her of "fetishising" formal democracy' (p.153). Slavoj Žižek (2000) 'Postface: Georg Lukács as the philosopher of Leninism', in G. Lukác, *A Defence of* History and Class Consciousness: *Tailism and the Dialectic* (London: Verso), p. 153. For a Marxist assessment of Lukács which does not slide into admiration for such quasi-Stalinist errors, see Michael Löwy (1979) *Georg Lukács: From Romanticism to Bolshevism* (London: New Left Books).

69. Rebecca Mead, 'The Marx brother'.

70. RG, p. 318.

71. One example of this is the presentation with Jacques-Alain Miller (1996) A discussion of Lacan's 'Kant with Sade'. In R. Feldstein, B. Fink and M. Jaanus (eds) *Reading Seminars I and II: Lacan's Return to Freud* (New York: State University of New York Press). Žižek's contributions to other Lacanian English-language journals have been for groups that keep Miller at arm's length.

72. Žižek's phrase to describe where Alenka Zupančič stands, in ME, p. 213.

73. Slavoj Žižek (2002) 'The interpassive subject', http://www.lacan.com/interpass.htm (accessed 2 December 2002).'Interpassivity' designates practices like having something laugh for you in the form of canned laughter on television, so that you really do feel that you enjoyed yourself, having a video record your television so you can accumulate a collection of films that you sense you have watched yourself and having someone believe for you in the domain of party politics so that you imagine that there are others who keep a belief system in place. The position adopted in such an interpassive

relation is not really passive at all but – as 'the primordial form of the subject's *defense* against *jouissance*' – requires active maintenance of enjoyment or belief in the Other, and something that approximates to the defensive procedures of obsessional neurosis. Žižek has borrowed this term from Robert Pfaller's work on avant-garde art practices in Vienna. For one review see Pfaller's (2002) 'The work of art that observes itself: Interpassivity and social ontology', paper at the 'Globalization … and beyond?' conference, Rotterdam, June.

74. Žižek, 'The interpassive subject'. The analyst as 'subject supposed to know' is an exception through which there is an attribution of something beyond symbolic belief to an 'absolutely infallible certainty' on the part of the analyst as something in the real.

75. Blaise Pascal (1670) *Pensées: Notes on Religion and Other Subjects*, translated by John Warrington, 1973 (London: Dent).

76. See, for example, Bill Ashcroft, Gareth Griffiths and Helen Tiffin (eds) (1995) *The Post-Colonial Studies Reader* (London: Routledge).

77. The juggling of Hitchcock's films into different categories to trace binary oppositions and transformations of themes is one example, and the analysis of films he has never seen is another; but we also need to be aware that his mocking admission that he has not seen the films is also part of the performance. See 'Alfred Hitchcock, or, The form and its historical mediation' in EYW.

78. Žižek, 'The interpassive subject'.

79. Ibid.

80. Ibid.

81. SOI, p. 181.

82. EYW.

83. PF.

84. EYW, p. 222.

85. PF, pp. 163–4.

86. Ibid., p. 164.

87. EYW, p. 224.

88. This notion treats the knotting of the symbolic, imaginary and real as a symptomatic operation for every subject, and it thus refocuses readings of so-called 'psychotic structure' in Lacan. 'With the concept of the "*Sinthome*" [Lacan] adds a crucial fourth circle – the "symptom" to his triple knot [of Real, Imaginary and Symbolic]. This has the important effect of both untying the earlier knot and suggesting a more dynamic process of naming as writing, or writing as naming.' Jean-Michel Rabaté (2001) *Jacques Lacan: Psychoanalysis and the Subject of Literature* (London: Palgrave), p. 158.

89. SOI, p. 75.

90. SOI, p. 75.

91. Ibid., p. 74.

92. Žižek argues that 'The whole point of Lacan is that the subject of psychoanalysis is a hysterical subject, a hysterical subject in reaction to the scientific discourse which was founded through Cartesian Science.' In Josefina Ayerza (1992) 'Hidden prohibitions and the pleasure principle [interview with Žižek]', http://www.lacan.com/ perfume/zizek.htm (accessed 25 February 2003). Lacan follows Freud in seeing obsessional neurosis as a 'dialect' of hysteria. In Hegelian terms, then, we could see hysteria as a genus in which there are two species – hysteria and obsessional neurosis – with hysteria as a species of itself. This Hegelian motif, of the division of a genus and reflexive inclusion of species in it, is often used by Žižek to conceptualise the way a category is included in itself. For example, the Manchester-based brand of tea 'PG

Tips' is not really a specific kind of tea at all, but a blend of teas. PG Tips is a genus in which there are two species – the blend and PG Tips – with PG Tips as a species of itself (and the 'PG' actually stands for 'Poor Grade', a meaning washed away by the teas of time). Žižek himself is a blend of theories, and when he is included in texts about other theorists – Hegel, Lacan, Marx – he becomes a blend of himself. He does not actually add any specific concepts to those of the other theorists but articulates and blends the concepts of others, which is one reason why it does not make sense to include in this book a glossary that pretends to be distinctively 'Žižekian'.

Bibliography

BOOKS BY SLAVOJ ŽIŽEK

Butler, J., Laclau, E. and Žižek, S. (2000) *Contingency, Hegemony, Universality: Contemporary Dialogues on the Left* (London: Verso).

Žižek, S. (1989) *The Sublime Object of Ideology* (London: Verso).

—— (1991) *For They Know Not What They Do: Enjoyment as a Political Factor* (London: Verso).

—— (1991) *Looking Awry: An Introduction to Jacques Lacan through Popular Culture* (Cambridge, MA: MIT Press).

—— (1992) *Enjoy Your Symptom: Jacques Lacan In Hollywood and Out* (London: Routledge).

—— (ed.) (1992) *Everything You Always Wanted to Know about Lacan (But Were Afraid to Ask Hitchcock)* (London: Verso).

—— (1993) *Tarrying with the Negative: Kant, Hegel, and the Critique of Ideology* (Durham: Duke University Press).

—— (1994) *The Metastases of Enjoyment: Six Essays on Woman and Causality* (London: Verso).

—— (ed.) (1995) *Mapping Ideology* (London: Verso).

—— (1996) *The Indivisible Remainder: An Essay on Schelling and Related Matters* (London: Verso).

—— (1997) *The Plague of Fantasies* (London: Verso).

—— (1999) *The Ticklish Subject: The Absent Centre of Political Ontology* (London: Verso).

—— (2000) *The Art of the Ridiculous Sublime: On David Lynch's* Lost Highway (Seattle: University of Washington Press).

—— (2000) *Did Somebody Say Totalitarianism? Five Interventions in the (Mis)use of a Notion* (London: Verso).

—— (2000) *The Fragile Absolute – Or, Why Is the Christian Legacy Worth Fighting For?* (London: Verso).

—— (2001) *The Fright of Real Tears: Kieslowski and the Future* (Bloomington: Indiana University Press).

—— (2001) *On Belief* (London: Routledge).

—— (ed.) (2002) *Revolution at the Gates: A Selection of Writings from February to October 1917: V. I. Lenin,* edited with an Introduction and Afterword by Slavoj Žižek (London: Verso).

—— (2002) *Welcome to the Desert of the Real! Five Essays on September 11 and Related Dates* (London: Verso).

—— (2003) *The Puppet and the Dwarf: The Perverse Core of Christianity* (Cambridge, MA: MIT Press).

—— (2004) *Organs without Bodies: Deleuze and Consequences* (New York: Routledge).

SELECTED ARTICLES, INTERVIEWS AND REVIEWS BY SLAVOJ ŽIŽEK

Žižek, S. (1990) 'Beyond Discourse-Analysis', appendix in E. Laclau. (1990) *New Reflections on The Revolution of Our Time* (London: Verso).

——— (1990) 'Eastern Europe's Republics of Gilead', *New Left Review*, 183, pp. 50–62.

——— (1996) 'Hegel with Lacan, or the subject and its cause', in Feldstein, R., Fink, B. and Jaanus, M. (eds) *Reading Seminars I and II: Lacan's Return to Freud* (New York: State University of New York Press).

——— (1996) 'Re-visioning "Lacanian" social criticism: The Law and its obscene double', *Journal for the Psychoanalysis of Culture and Society*, 1 (1), pp. 15–25.

——— (1997) 'Multiculturalism, or, the cultural logic of multinational capitalism', *New Left Review*, 225, pp. 28–51.

——— (1998) 'A leftist plea for "Eurocentrism"', *Critical Inquiry*, 24 (2), pp. 988–1,009.

——— (1998) 'Psychoanalysis in post-Marxism: The case of Alain Badiou', *The South Atlantic Quarterly*, 2, pp. 235–63.

——— (1998) 'Risk society and its discontents. *Historical Materialism*, 2, pp. 143–64.

——— (1999) 'Against the double blackmail (circulated via email).

——— (1999) 'Against the double blackmail', *New Left Review*, 234, pp. 76–82.

——— (1999) 'Against the double blackmail', http://www.lacan.com/kosovo.htm (accessed 23 September 2000).

——— (1999) 'Carl Schmitt in the age of post-politics', in Mouffe, C. (ed.) *The Challenge of Carl Schmitt* (London: Verso).

——— (1999) 'Human rights and its discontents', http://www.bard.edu/hrp/zizektranscript. htm (accessed 7 June 2002).

——— (1999) 'When the party commits suicide', *New Left Review*, 238, pp. 26–47.

——— (2000) 'Postface: Georg Lukács as the philosopher of Leninism', in Lukács, G. *A Defence of* History and Class Consciousness: *Tailism and the Dialectic* (London: Verso).

——— (2000) 'Why we all love to hate Haider', *New Left Review (II)*, 2, pp. 37–45.

——— (2001) 'Repeating Lenin', http://www.lacan.com/replenin.htm (accessed 27 March 2001).

——— (2002) 'Are we in a war? Do we have an enemy?', *London Review of Books*, 24, (10), http://www.lrb.co.uk/v24/n10/zize2410.htm (accessed 30 May 2002).

——— (2002) 'The interpassive subject', http://www.lacan.com/interpass.htm (accessed 2 December 2002).

——— (2002) 'The Real of sexual difference', in Barnard S. and Fink S. (eds) (2002) *Reading Seminar XX: Lacan's Major Work on Love, Knowledge, and Feminine Sexuality* (New York: State University of New York Press).

——— (2002) 'To know or not to know', *New Scientist, 20 April*, p. 45.

——— (2003) 'The Iraq war: Where is the true danger?', www.lacan.com/iraq.htm (accessed 24 March 2003).

——— (2003) 'Today, Iraq. Tomorrow … democracy?', *In These Times*, http:// inthesetimes.com/comments.php?id=119_0_1_0_C (accessed 26 March 2003).

——— (2003) 'Too much democracy?', http://www.lacan.com/toomuch.htm (accessed 22 April 2003).

——— (2003) '"What some would call …": A response to Yannis Stavrakakis', *Umbr(a)*, pp. 131–5.

SELECTED JOURNALIST PROFILES AND
INTERVIEWS WITH SLAVOJ ŽIŽEK

Ayerza, J. (1992) 'Hidden prohibitions and the pleasure principle [interview with Žižek]', http://www.lacan.com/perfume/zizek.htm (accessed 25 February 2003).

—— (1994) '"It doesn't have to be a Jew"', *Lusitania*, 1 (4), http://www.lacan.com/ perfume/Zizekinter.htm (accessed 14 June 2002).

Beaumont, M. and Jenkins, M. (2000) 'An interview with Slavoj Zizek', *Historical Materialism*, 7, pp. 181–97.

Boynton, R. S. (1998) 'Enjoy your Žižek!: An excitable Slovenian philosopher examines the obscene practices of everyday life – including his own', *Linguafranca: The Review of Academic Life*, 7 (7), http://www.linguafranca.com/9810/zizek.html (accessed 15 May 2001).

Dews, P. and Osborne, P. (1991) 'Lacan in Slovenia: An interview with Slavoj Žižek and Renata Salecl', *Radical Philosophy*, 58, pp. 25–31.

Henwood, D. (2002) 'I am a fighting atheist: Interview with Slavoj Žižek', *Bad Subjects*, 59, http://eserver.org/bs/59/zizek.html (accessed 3 June 2002).

Long, A. and McGunn, T. (1997) 'Slavoj Žižek interview', *Journal for the Psychoanalysis of Culture and Society*, 2 (2), pp. 133–7.

Lovink, G. (1995) 'Civil society, fanaticism, and digital reality: A conversation with Slavoj Zizek', http://www.ctheory.com/article/1037.html (accessed 8 May 2001).

Mannes Abbott, G. (1998) 'Never mind the bollocks', http://www.g-m-a.net/docs/c_zizek.html (accessed 15 May 2001).

Mead, R. (2003) 'The Marx brother', *The New Yorker*, http://www.lacan.com/ziny/htm (accessed 6 May 2003).

Reul, S. and Deichmann, T. (2001) 'The one measure of true love is: You can insult the other', http://www.spiked-online.com/Articles/00000002d2C4.htm (accessed 19 November 2001).

OTHER BOOKS AND ARTICLES

(**indicates secondary descriptive and critical material on Žižek)

Agamben, G. (1998) *Homo Sacer: Sovereign Power and Bare Life* (Stanford: Stanford University Press).

Althusser, L. (1971) *Lenin and Philosophy, and Other Essays* (London: New Left Books).

Ashcroft, B., Griffiths, G. and Tiffin, H. (eds) (1995) *The Post-Colonial Studies Reader* (London: Routledge).

Bakan, D. (1990) *Sigmund Freud and the Jewish Mystical Tradition* (London: Free Association Books).

Barker, J. (2002) *Alain Badiou: A Critical Introduction* (London: Pluto Press).

Barnard, S. and Fink, B. (eds) (2002) *Reading Seminar XX: Lacan's Major Work on Love, Knowledge, and Feminine Sexuality* (New York: State University of New York Press).

Beauvoir, S. de (1949) *The Second Sex*, 1968 (London: Jonathan Cape).

Bentley, J. (1982) *Between Marx and Christ: The Dialogue in German-Speaking Europe 1870–1970* (London: Verso).

Bernstein, R. and Marković, M. (1981) 'Why *Praxis International?*', 1 (1), pp. 1–5.

Bettelheim, B. (1985) *Freud and Man's Soul* (London: Flamingo).

Black, R. (1970) *Stalinism in Britain: A Trotskyist Analysis* (London: New Park Publications).

Blackburn, R. (1993) 'The break-up of Yugoslavia and the fate of Bosnia', *New Left Review*, 199, pp. 100–19.

Bohak, J. and Možina, M. (2002) 'Psychotherapy in Slovenia', http://marela.uni-mb.si/skzp/Srecanja/SloScena/StudDneviSKZP/Zborniki/Rogla2001 (accessed 3 January 2003).

Bracher, M., Alcorn, M. W., Corthell, R. J. and Massardier-Kenney, F. (eds) (1994) *Lacanian Theory of Discourse: Subject, Structure and Society* (New York: New York University Press).

Brah, A. (1993) 'Re-framing Europe: En-gendered racisms, ethnicities and nationalisms in contemporary Western Europe', *Feminist Review*, 45, pp. 9–28.

**Braidotti, R. (2002) *Metamorphoses: Towards a Materialist Theory of Becoming* (Cambridge: Polity Press).

Burgoyne, B. and Sullivan, M. (eds) (1997) *The Klein-Lacan Dialogues* (London: Rebus Press).

Butler, J. (1990) *Gender Trouble: Feminism and the Subversion of Identity* (London: Routledge).

——— (1993) *Bodies that Matter: On the Discursive Limits of 'Sex'* (London: Routledge).

——— (2000) *Antigone's Claim: Kinship Between Life and Death* (New York: Columbia University Press).

**Callinicos, A. (2001) 'Review of *The Ticklish Subject* and *Contingency, Hegemony, Universality*', *Historical Materialism*, 8, pp. 373–403.

**Chapman, L. (2002) 'Ideology and psychoanalysis: Žižek in the clinic?', presented at Centre for Freudian Analysis and Research, London, October, unpublished ms.

**Chisolm, D. (2001) 'Žižek's exemplary culture', *Journal for the Psychoanalysis of Culture and Society*, 6 (2), pp. 242–52.

Colletti, L. (1970) 'The question of Stalin', *New Left Review*, 61, pp. 61–81.

Collier, A. (2001) *Christianity and Marxism: A Philosophical Contribution to Their Reconciliation* (London: Routledge).

Copjec, J. (1993) *Read My Desire: Lacan Against the Historicists* (Cambridge, MA: MIT Press).

——— (ed.) (1996) *Radical Evil* (London: Verso).

Coulson, M. (1993) 'Looking behind the violent break-up of Yugoslavia', *Feminist Review*, 45, pp. 86–101.

Deleuze, G. (1994) *Masochism: Coldness and Cruelty* (New York: Zone Books).

——— (1995) *Negotiations.* (New York: Columbia University Press).

Derrida, J. (1994) *Spectres of Marx: The State of the Debt, the Work of Mourning, and the New International* (London: Routledge).

Descartes, R. (1641) *Meditations on First Philosophy with Selections from the Objections and Replies*, translated by John Cottingham, 1996 (Cambridge: Cambridge University Press).

Descombes, V. (1980) *Modern French Philosophy* (Cambridge: Cambridge University Press).

**Dews, P. (1995) *The Limits of Disenchantment: Essays on Contemporary European Philosophy* (London: Verso).

Djilas, M. (1966) *The New Class: An Analysis of the Communist System* (London: Allen and Unwin).

Dreyfus, H. and Rabinow, P. (1982) *Michel Foucault: Beyond Structuralism and Hermeneutics* (Brighton: Harvester Press).

Dunand, A. (1995) 'The end of analysis (II)'. In Feldstein, R., Fink, B. and Jaanus, M. (eds) *Reading Seminar XI: Lacan's Four Fundamental Concepts of Psychoanalysis* (New York: SUNY Press).

Easthope, A. and McGowan, K. (1992) *A Critical and Cultural Theory Reader* (Buckingham: Open University Press).

**Ebert, T. (1996) *Ludic Feminism and After: Postmodernism, Desire, and Labor in Late Capitalism* (Ann Arbor: The University of Michigan Press).

**——— (1999) 'Globalization, internationalism, and the class politics of cynical reason', *Nature, Society and Thought*, 12 (4), pp. 389–410.

Fink, B. (1997) *A Clinical Introduction to Lacanian Psychoanalysis: Theory and Technique* (Cambridge, MA: Harvard University Press).

Foucault, M. (1975) *Discipline and Punish: The Birth of the Prison*, translated by Alan Sheridan, 1979 (Harmondsworth: Penguin).

——— (1976) *The History of Sexuality, Volume 1: An Introduction*, translated by Robert Hurley, 1981 (Harmondsworth: Pelican).

——— (1984) *The Care of the Self: The History of Sexuality Volume 3*, translated by Robert Hurley, 1990 (Harmondsworth: Penguin).

Freud, S. (1953) *The Standard Edition of the Complete Psychological Works of Sigmund Freud, Volume V* (1900–1901) (London: Hogarth Press).

——— (1953) *The Standard Edition of the Complete Psychological Works of Sigmund Freud, Volume VII (1901–1905)* (London: Hogarth Press).

——— (1955) *The Standard Edition of the Complete Psychological Works of Sigmund Freud, Volume VII (1909)* (London: Hogarth Press).

——— (1964) *The Standard Edition of the Complete Psychological Works of Sigmund Freud, Volume XXI (1927–1931)* (London: Hogarth Press).

——— (1964) *The Standard Edition of the Complete Psychological Works of Sigmund Freud, Volume XXII (1932–1936)* (London: Hogarth Press).

——— (1964) *The Standard Edition of the Complete Psychological Works of Sigmund Freud, Volume XXIII (1937–1939)* (London: Hogarth Press).

Fyson, G., Malapanis, A. and Silberman, J. (1993) *The Truth about Yugoslavia: Why Working People Should Oppose Intervention* (New York: Pathfinder Press).

Giddens, A. (1998) *The Third Way: The Renewal of Social Democracy* (Cambridge: Polity Press).

**Gigante, D. (1998) 'Toward a notion of critical self-creation: Slavoj Žižek and the "vortex of madness"', *New Literary History*, 29 (1), pp. 153–68.

Glenny, M. (1993) *The Rebirth of History: Eastern Europe in the Age of Democracy*, second edition (Harmondsworth: Penguin).

Green, A. (1995–1996) 'Against Lacanism: A conversation of André Green with Sergio Benvenuto', *Journal of European Psychoanalysis*, 2, http://www.psychomedia.it/jep/number2/greenbenv.htm (accessed 5 August 2002).

**Grigg, R. (2001) 'Absolute freedom and major structural change', *Paragraph*, 24 (2), pp. 111–24.

Handelman, S. (1983) 'Jacques Derrida and the heretic hermeneutic', in Krupnick, M. (ed.) *Displacement: Derrida and After* (Bloomington: Indiana University Press).

Hardt, M. and Negri, A. (2000) *Empire*. (Cambridge, MA: Harvard University Press).

**Harpham, G. G. (2003) 'Doing the impossible: Slavoj Žižek and the end of knowledge', *Critical Enquiry*, 29 (3), pp. 453–85.

Hegel, G. W. F. (1807) *Phenomenology of Spirit*, translated by A. V. Miller, 1977 (Oxford: Oxford University Press).

Hobsbawm, E. and Ranger, T. (eds) (1983) *The Invention of Tradition* (Cambridge: Cambridge University Press).

Homer, S. (1996) 'Psychoanalysis, representation, politics: on the (im)possibility of a psychoanalytic theory of ideology?', *The Letter: Lacanian Perspectives on Psychoanalysis*, 7, pp. 97–109.

**——— (2001) 'It's the political economy stupid!' On Žižek's Marxism', *Radical Philosophy*, 108, pp. 7–16.

Jacoby, R. (1983) *The Repression of Psychoanalysis* (New York: Basic Books).

Jameson, F. (1972) *The Prison-House of Language: A Critical Account of Structuralism and Russian Formalism* (New Jersey: Princeton University Press).

Jeffs, N. (1995) 'Transnational dialogue in times of war: The peace movement in ex-Yugoslavia', *Radical Philosophy*, 73, pp. 2–4.

Kalaianov, R. (2001) 'Hegel, Kojève and Lacan – The metamorphoses of dialectics – Part II: Hegel and Lacan', www.academyanalyticarts.org/Kalo2.html (accessed 9 October 2001).

Kant, I. (1784) 'An answer to the question: What is enlightenment?', htttp://www.english.upenn.edu/~mgamer/Etexts/kant.html (accessed 24 February 2003).

Kardelj, E. (1978) *Democracy and Socialism* (London: Summerfield).

**Kay, S. (2003) *Žižek: A Critical Introduction* (Cambridge: Polity Press).

**Kesel, M. de (2002) 'Is not Antigone a proto-totalitarian figure? On Slavoj Žižek's interpretation of Antigone', Globalization ... and beyond, Erasmus Summer Seminar, Rotterdam, June, unpublished ms.

Kojève, A. (1969) *Introduction to the Reading of Hegel* (New York: Basic Books).

Kovač, M. (1988) 'The Slovene spring', *New Left Review*, 171, pp. 115–28.

Krstic, I. (2002) 'Re-thinking Serbia: A psychoanalytic reading of modern Serbian history and identity through popular culture', *Other Voices*, 2 (2), http://www.othervoices.org/2.2/krstic/ (accessed 14 June 2002).

Lacan, J. (1966) 'Position of the unconscious: remarks made at the 1960 Bonneval colloquium rewritten in 1964', translated by Bruce Fink, 1995, in Feldstein, R., Fink, B. and Jaanus, M. (eds) (1995) *Reading Seminar XI: Lacan's Four Fundamental Concepts of Psychoanalysis* (New York: State University of New York Press).

——— (1967–1968) *The Seminar of Jacques Lacan, Book XV, The Psychoanalytic Act*, translated by Cormac Gallagher from unedited French manuscripts, Annex 3.

——— (1971) *The Seminar of Jacques Lacan, Book XVIII, On a Discourse That Might Not Be a Semblance*, translated by Cormac Gallagher from unedited French manuscripts.

——— (1973) *Four Fundamental Concepts of Psycho-Analysis*, translated by Alan Sheridan, 1979 (Harmondsworth: Penguin).

——— (1975) *On Feminine Sexuality, The Limits of Love and Knowledge, 1972–1973: Encore, The Seminar of Jacques Lacan, Book XX*, translated with notes by Bruce Fink, 1998 (New York: Norton).

——— (1977) *Écrits: A Selection*, translated by Alan Sheridan (London: Tavistock).

——— (1981) *The Psychoses: The Seminar of Jacques Lacan, Book III 1955–1956*, translated with notes by Russell Grigg, 1993 (London: Routledge).

——— (1986) *The Ethics of Psychoanalysis 1959–1960: The Seminar of Jacques Lacan Book VII*, translated with notes by Dennis Porter, 1992 (London: Routledge).

——— (1987) '*Television*', *October*, 40, pp. 7–50.

——— (1989) 'Kant with Sade', *October*, 51, pp. 55–104.

——— (1991) *The Other Side of Psychoanalysis: The Seminar of Jacques Lacan, Book XVII 1969–1970*, translated with notes by Russell Grigg. unpublished ms.

——— (2002) *Écrits: A Selection*, translated by Bruce Fink (New York: W. W. Norton and Company).

Laclau, E. (1990) *New Reflections on The Revolution of Our Time* (London: Verso).

Laclau, E. and Mouffe, C. (1985) *Hegemony and Socialist Strategy* (London: Verso).

Lévi-Strauss, C. (1963) *Structural Anthropology* (New York: Basic Books).

Löwy, M. (1979) *Georg Lukács: From Romanticism to Bolshevism* (London: New Left Books).

MacCannell, J. F. (1986) *Figuring Lacan: Criticism and the Cultural Unconscious* (Beckenham, Kent: Croom Helm).

Macey, D. (1988) *Lacan in Contexts* (London: Verso).

MacGregor, D. (1984) *The Communist Ideal in Hegel and Marx* (Toronto: University of Toronto Press).

**Mackendrick, K. (2001) 'Slovene Lacanian school', in Winquist, C. and Taylor. V. (eds) *Encyclopaedia of Postmodernism*. (London: Routledge).

Magaš, B. (1993) *The Destruction of Yugoslavia: Tracking the Break-up 1980–92* (London: Verso).

Mandel, E. (1978) *From Stalinism to Eurocommunism: The Bitter Fruits of 'Socialism in One Country'* (London: New Left Books).

Mariage, V. (2003) 'The Psychoanalyst: An effect of the act', *Psychoanalytical Notebooks: A Review of the London Society of the New Lacanian School*, 10, pp. 78–86.

Marković, M. (1974) *The Contemporary Marx: Essays on Humanist Communism* (Nottingham: Spokesman Books).

Marković, M. and Cohen, R. S. (1975) *The Rise and Fall of Socialist Humanism: A History of the Praxis Group* (Nottingham: Spokesman Books).

Marx, K. (1869) *The Eighteenth Brumaire of Louis Bonaparte*, http://www.e-bookshop.gr/gutenberg/files/mar1810.pdf (accessed 17 June 2003).

―――― (1975) *Early Writings*, translated by Rodney Livingstone and Gregor Benton (Harmondsworth: Pelican).

Marx, K. and Engels, F. (1971) *Ireland and the Irish Question* (Moscow: Progress Publishers).

Mastnak, T. (1991) 'From the new social movements to political parties', in Simmie, J. and Dekleva, J (eds) *Yugoslavia in Turmoil: After Self-Management?* (London: Pinter Publishers).

**McLaren, P. (2002) 'Slavoj Žižek's naked politics: Opting for the impossible, a secondary elaboration', *Journal of Advanced Composition Quarterly*, 21 (3), pp. 614–37.

**Miklitsch, R. (1998) 'Going through the fantasy': Screening Slavoj Žižek', *The South Atlantic Quarterly*, 91 (2), pp. 475–507.

Miller, J.-A. (1986) '*Extimité*', in Bracher, M., Alcorn, M. W., Corthell, R. J. and Massardier-Kenney, F. (eds) (1994) *Lacanian Theory of Discourse: Subject, Structure and Society* (New York: New York University Press).

―――― (1989) 'Michel Foucault and psychoanalysis', in Armstrong, T. J. (ed.) (1992) *Michel Foucault: Philosopher* (New York: Harvester Wheatsheaf).

―――― (1996) 'A discussion of Lacan's "Kant with Sade"'. In Feldstein, R., Fink, B. and Jaanus, M. (eds) *Reading Seminars I and II: Lacan's Return to Freud* (New York: State University of New York Press).

―――― (1998) 'Report for the General Assembly in Barcelona – 23 July 1998', *Psychoanalytical Notebooks of the London Circle*, 1, pp. 117–52.

―――― (2001) *The Tenderness of Terrorists* (New York: Wooster Press).

Mittleman, A. (1998) 'Spinoza, liberalism and the question of Jewish identity', *First Things*, 79, http://www.firstthings.com/ftissues/ft9801/reviews/mittleman.html (accessed 29 April 2003).

Mladjenovic, L. and Litricin, V. (1993) 'Belgrade feminists 1992: Separation, guilt and identity crisis', *Feminist Review*, 45, pp. 113–19.

Monk, R. (1990) *Ludwig Wittgenstein: The Duty of Genius* (New York: The Free Press).

Mouffe, C. (ed.) (1999) *The Challenge of Carl Schmitt* (London: Verso).

Mowitt, J. (2000) 'Trauma envy', *Cultural Critique*, 46, pp. 272–97.

**Myers, T. (2003) *Slavoj Žižek* (London: Routledge).

Nasio, J.-D. (1992) *Five Lessons on the Psychoanalytic Theory of Jacques Lacan*, translated by David Pettigrew and François Raffoul, 1998 (New York: State University of New York Press).

New Albania Society (1970s, nd.) *Albania, The Most Successful Country in Europe* (London: New Albania Society).

**Nicol, B. (2000) 'Normality and other kinds of madness: Žižek and the traumatic core of the subject', *Psychoanalytic Studies*, 2, (1), pp. 7–19.

Nierenberg, O. (1998) 'A hunger for science: Psychoanalysis and the "Gay Gene"', http://www.apres-coup.org/Papers/ONierenberg-GayGene.htm (accessed 11 February 2003).

O'Connor, N. and Ryan, J. (1993) *Wild Desires and Mistaken Identities: Lesbianism and Psychoanalysis* (London: Virago).

Osborne, P. (ed.) (1996) *A Critical Sense: Interviews with Intellectuals* (London: Routledge).

**—— (2003) 'Interpreting the world: September 11, cultural criticism and the intellectual Left', *Radical Philosophy*, 117, pp. 2–12.

Osborne, P. and Segal, L. (1993) 'Gender as performance: An interview with Judith Butler', *Radical Philosophy*, 67, pp. 32–9.

Parker, I. (1997) *Psychoanalytic Culture: Psychoanalytic Discourse in Western Society* (London: Sage).

—— (1999) 'Clinical Lacan: Review essay on Bruce Fink's *A Clinical Introduction to Lacanian Psychoanalysis: Theory and Technique*', *PS: Journal of the Universities Association for Psychoanalytic Studies*, (2), pp. 69–74.

—— (2001) 'What is wrong with the discourse of the university in psychotherapy training?', *European Journal of Psychotherapy, Counselling and Health*, 4 (1), pp. 1–17.

**—— (2003) 'Lacanian social theory and clinical practice', *Psychoanalysis and Contemporary Thought*, 26 (2), pp. 51–77.

Pascal, B. (1670) *Pensées: Notes on Religion and Other Subjects*, translated by John Warrington, 1973 (London: Dent).

Petras, J. and Vieux, S. (1996) 'Bosnia and the revival of US hegemony', *New Left Review*, 218, pp. 3–25.

Pfaller, R. (1997) 'Philosophie und spontane philosophie der kunst-schaffenden / Philosophy and the spontaneous philosophy of the artists', *95/97 Projekte, Archimedia*, pp. 171–82.

—— (1998) 'The work of art that observes itself: Eleven steps towards an aesthetics of interpassivity', *Presencias en el Espacio Publico Contentemporaneo, Universitat de Barcelona*, pp. 229–40.

**—— (2002) 'The work of art that observes itself: Interpassivity and social ontology', paper at 'Globalization … and beyond' conference, Rotterdam, June.

Pinkard, T. (1994) *Hegel's Phenomenology: The Sociality of Reason* (Cambridge: Cambridge University Press).

—— (2000) *Hegel: A Biography* (Cambridge: Cambridge University Press).

Quinet, A. (1999) 'The functions of the preliminary interviews', *Journal of European Psychoanalysis*, 8–9, http://www.psychomedia.it/jep/number8–9/quinet.htm (accessed 5 August 2002).

Rabaté, J.-M. (2001) *Jacques Lacan: Psychoanalysis and the Subject of Literature* (London: Palgrave).

Richardson, J. (2000) 'NSK 2000? Irwin and Eda Cufer interviewed by Joanne Richardson', http://subsol.c3.hu/subsol_2/contributors/nsktext.html (accessed 3 January 2003).

Rotenstreich, N. (1963) *The Recurring Pattern: Studies in Anti-Judaism in Modern Thought* (London: Weidenfeld and Nicolson).

Roth, M. (ed.) (1988) *Knowing and History: Appropriations of Hegel in Twentieth Century France* (Ithaca: Cornell University Press).

Roudinesco, E. (1990) *Jacques Lacan & Co.: A History of Psychoanalysis in France, 1925–1985* (London: Free Association Books).

Ryan, G. (1994) *Bosnia 1994: Armageddon in Europe* (London: Socialist Outlook).

Salecl, R. (1994) *The Spoils of Freedom: Psychoanalysis and Feminism After the Fall of Socialism* (London: Routledge).

——— (1996) 'See no evil, speak no evil: Hate speech and human rights', in Copjec, J. (ed.) (1996) *Radical Evil* (London: Verso)

——— (ed.) (2000) *Sexuation* (Durham, NC: Duke University Press).

Santner, E. (1999) 'Freud's *Moses* and the ethics of nomotropic desire', in Salecl, R. (ed.) (2000) *Sexuation* (Durham, NC: Duke University Press).

Sartre, J.-P. (1943) *Being and Nothingness: An Essay on Phenomenological Ontology*, translated by Hazel Barnes, 1969 (London: Methuen).

Saussure, F. de (1915) *Course in General Linguistics*, translated by Wade Baskin, 1974 (Glasgow: Fontana/Collins).

Simmie, J. and Dekleva, J. (eds) (1991) *Yugoslavia in Turmoil: After Self-Management* (London and New York: Pinter Publishers).

Sloterdijk, P. (1988) *Critique of Cynical Reason* (London: Verso).

Spivak, G. C. (1988) Can the subaltern speak?', in Nelson, C. and Grossberg, L. (eds) *Marxism and the Interpretation of Culture* (Urbana: University of Illinois Press).

Stafford-Clark, D. (1967) *What Freud Really Said* (Harmondsworth: Penguin).

**Stavrakakis, Y. (1999) *Lacan and the Political* (London: Routledge).

**——— (2003) 'The lure of Antigone: Aporias of an ethics of the political', *Umbr(a)*, pp. 117–29.

Symington, N. (1986) *The Analytic Experience: Lectures from the Tavistock* (London: Free Association Books).

Trotsky, L. (1969) *The Permanent Revolution and Results and Prospects* (New York: Pathfinder Press).

——— (1973) *The Revolution Betrayed: What is the Soviet Union, and Where is it Going?* (London: New Park Publications).

**Vogt, E. (2002) 'Derrida, Schmitt, Žižek', paper at 'Globalization ... and beyond' conference, Rotterdam, June.

Volkan, V. (2001) 'Transgenerational transmissions and chosen traumas: An aspect of large-group identity', *Group Analysis*, 34 (1), pp. 79–97.

Whitebook, J. (1994) 'Hypostatizing Thanatos: Lacan's analysis of the ego', *Constellations*, 1 (2), pp. 214–30.

Wohlforth, T. and Westoby, A. (1978) *'Communists' Against Revolution: Two Essays on Post-War Stalinism* (London: Folrose Books).

Wood, D. and Bernasconi, R. (eds) (1988) *Derrida and* Différance (Evanston Il: Northwestern University Press).

Zupančič, A. (2000) *Ethics of the Real: Kant, Lacan* (London: Verso).

Index

Compiled by Sue Carlton